D1482853

RECONCILIATION AND REPAIR

NOMOS

LXV

NOMOS

Harvard University Press
I *Authority* 1958, reissued in 1982 by Greenwood Press

The Liberal Arts Press
II *Community* 1959
III *Responsibility* 1960

Atherton Press
IV *Liberty* 1962
V *The Public Interest* 1962
VI *Justice* 1963, reissued in 1974
VII *Rational Decision* 1964
VIII *Revolution* 1966
IX *Equality* 1967
X *Representation* 1968
XI *Voluntary Associations* 1969
XII *Political and Legal Obligation* 1970
XIII *Privacy* 1971

Aldine-Atherton Press
XIV *Coercion* 1972

Lieber-Atherton Press
XV *The Limits of Law* 1974
XVI *Participation in Politics* 1975

New York University Press
XVII *Human Nature in Politics* 1977
XVIII *Due Process* 1977
XIX *Anarchism* 1978
XX *Constitutionalism* 1979
XXI *Compromise in Ethics, Law, and Politics* 1979
XXII *Property* 1980
XXIII *Human Rights* 1981
XXIV *Ethics, Economics, and the Law* 1982
XXV *Liberal Democracy* 1983
XXVI *Marxism* 1983

NOMOS LXV

Yearbook of the American Society for Political and Legal Philosophy

RECONCILIATION AND REPAIR

Edited by

Melissa Schwartzberg and Eric Beerbohm

NEW YORK UNIVERSITY PRESS • *New York*

NEW YORK UNIVERSITY PRESS
New York
www.nyupress.org

© 2023 by New York University
All rights reserved

References to Internet websites (URLs) were accurate at the time of writing. Neither the author nor New York University Press is responsible for URLs that may have expired or changed since the manuscript was prepared.

Please contact the Library of Congress for Cataloging-in-Publication data.
ISBN: 9781479822553 (hardback)
ISBN: 9781479822591 (library ebook)
ISBN: 9781479822560 (consumer ebook)

New York University Press books are printed on acid-free paper, and their binding materials are chosen for strength and durability. We strive to use environmentally responsible suppliers and materials to the greatest extent possible in publishing our books.

Manufactured in the United States of America

10 9 8 7 6 5 4 3 2 1

Also available as an ebook

CONTENTS

PART III: PUBLIC APOLOGIES AS
MORAL REPAIR

PREFACE

MELISSA SCHWARTZBERG

This volume of NOMOS—the sixty-fifth in the series—emerged from papers and commentaries given at the 2020 annual meeting of the American Society for Political and Legal Philosophy (ASPLP). Though the conference was scheduled to take place at Cardozo Law School in New York City, because of the COVID-19 pandemic, it instead became a Zoom webinar hosted by the Princeton University Center for Human Values on September 25, 2020. Our topic, "Reconciliation and Repair: Mending Frayed Civic Bonds," was selected by the Society's membership.

The ASPLP conference consisted of three panels, representing the traditional three contributing disciplines: political science, philosophy, and law. The first panel featured Linda Radzik, who presented the paper from the field of philosophy, "The Role of the Public in Public Apologies." Martha Minow (law) and Burke Hendrix (political science) provided commentaries. The second panel, from the field of law, featured Roy Brooks's paper, "Framing Redress Discourse." Desmond Jagmohan (politics) and Colleen Murphy (philosophy) served as commentators. The final panel featured Catherine Lu's from the field of political science, "Reconciliation as Non-Alienation," with commentaries from Saira Mohamed (law) and Ryan Preston-Roedder (philosophy). This volume includes revised papers and commentaries from all the participants. Eric Beerbohm and I are grateful to all the authors and to Sam Boren Reast for his editorial assistance and his excellent work on the index.

I would like to thank the editors and production team at New York University Press, particularly Ilene Kalish, Alexia Traganas, and Sonia Tsuruoka, for their help throughout the production of this volume. On behalf of the ASPLP, I would also like to express our gratitude to the Press for its ongoing support both for the NOMOS series and for the tradition of interdisciplinary scholarship that it represents. The ASPLP is also grateful for subventions from Brown University, Duke University, New York University, Princeton University, and Stanford University in support of this and future NOMOS volumes.

Finally, I would like to thank the members of the ASPLP council who shepherded this volume—President Stephen Macedo, Vice Presidents Derrick Darby and Yasmin Dawood, at-large members Michael Blake, Ekow Yankah, Tommie Shelby, Sarah Song, and Immediate Past President and Secretary-Treasurer James Fleming—for their support and guidance.

Reconciliation and Repair is my seventh and final volume as editor or co-editor of NOMOS. It has been a pleasure and an honor to serve in this role. From my experience co-editing this volume with Eric Beerbohm, I know NOMOS will be in excellent hands.

CONTRIBUTORS

Eric Beerbohm
Professor of Government, Harvard University

Roy L. Brooks
Warren Distinguished Professor of Law, University of San Diego

Burke A. Hendrix
Professor of Political Science, University of Oregon

Desmond Jagmohan
Assistant Professor of Political Science, University of California, Berkeley

Catherine Lu
Professor of Political Science, McGill University

Martha Minow
300th Anniversary University Professor, Harvard Law School

Saira Mohamed
Professor of Law, University of California, Berkeley, School of Law

Colleen Murphy
Roger and Stephany Joslin Professor of Law, University of Illinois at Urbana-Champaign

Ryan Preston-Roedder
Associate Professor of Philosophy, Occidental College

Linda Radzik
Professor of Philosophy, Texas A&M University

Melissa Schwartzberg
Silver Professor of Politics, New York University

INTRODUCTION

MELISSA SCHWARTZBERG AND ERIC BEERBOHM

The full title of this volume is *Reconciliation and Repair (Following the Fraying of Civic Bonds)*. Chosen in 2018 for the 2020 conference, the topic sought to respond to deep challenges to social cohesion, such as those presented by the Unite the Right rally in Charlottesville. Yet civic bonds have not merely frayed in the intervening years but torn, as the COVID-19 pandemic and searing disagreement about appropriate remedies have riven societies. The challenge of mustering a global response to the pandemic, exacerbated by the rise of authoritarianism, has further strained the fragile connections among the world community, sharpening disparities in terms of coronavirus outcomes as well as other forms of basic well-being and political rights. Can we possibly repair our communities, whether local or global? The chapters of this volume grapple with the demands of reconciliation.

The first section of the volume, "Reconciliation After Alienation," analyzes the concept of reconciliation by closely studying the contexts of historical wrongs of colonialism and of ongoing state and structural oppression. In "Reconciliation as Non-Alienation: The Politics of Being at Home in the World," Catherine Lu argues that we should understand reconciliation as a response to the alienation generated by unjust or oppressive contexts. For Lu, alienation in politics constitutes the loss of the ability to see oneself as a self-realizing agent who is able to create a home in the world. Although Lu is sensitive to critiques of reconciliation as illusory or domesticating responses to profound historical injustices, she argues that if reconciliation is instead understood as a means of

1

transforming the social and political structures that inhibit flourishing, it can be emancipatory.

In her chapter, "Reconciliation and the Military," Saira Mohamed draws on Lu's concept of non-alienation and structural reconciliation as a potential framework to address American service members' experience of betrayal on the part of their leadership. Mohamed argues that service members are too often represented as mere instruments of the state, denying their status as human agents and as subject to exploitation and oppression by their government. Mohamed highlights in particular the stationing of the military at protests in Lafayette Square and the orders to participate in the US torture program under the war on terror as sources of moral injury for service members. These harms call for reconciliation, insofar as they enable members of the armed services an opportunity to recognize soldiers as persons with agency apart from the state, and because of the threat alienation poses to military discipline and cohesion.

In "Sources of Shame, Images of Home," a response to Lu's chapter, Ryan Preston-Roedder cautions that the project of reconciliation can threaten privileged agents' self-understanding, their own sense of being home in the world. As such, marginalized agents may find that their efforts at reconciliation, through reparatory dialogue, are hampered by the privileged. Preston-Roedder argues that Black American communities mitigated their alienation from the social world from within, through transformation in their own narratives and conceptions of home, without engagement with White Americans, though the persistence of injustice inhibited their ability to truly flourish. Drawing on James Baldwin, who called upon Black Americans to exhibit love for White Americans even when they respond with shame and fear to confrontation with their society's racism, Preston-Roedder notes the exceptionally demanding quality of the conception of reconciliation, even if justified.

The second section of the book, "Reparations for Racial Injustice," focuses specifically on Black reparations for slavery and Jim Crow. Roy L. Brooks's chapter, "Framing Redress Discourse," begins by distinguishing two models of redress for atrocities: a tort model and an atonement model. He defends the atonement model against the tort model as appropriately aiming at forward-looking reconciliation, which he argues requires both apology and reparation. Brooks then distinguishes among four theories of racial progress: traditionalism (racial neutrality); reformism (racial integration); critical race theory (social transformation); and limited solidarity (Black solidarity). He argues that the choice among these theories should drive the approach to redress for slavery, and that ultimately the country itself will need to debate the merits of these approaches.

Desmond Jagmohan draws on Brooks's framework to raise concerns about the reconciliation view in his chapter, "Reparations without Reconciliation." Like Brooks, he defends reparations, but argues that the framework of atonement and forgiveness may demand too much of victims and be incompatible with the angry responses of many Whites to racial progress. To support these arguments, Jagmohan turns to nineteenth-century liberal egalitarians, who sought to provide freedpeople with land and a home for compensation and as a safeguard against domination, and to Black nationalists, who sought property and the development of a Black economy as a means of security against White anger and vengeance. Restitution for slavery and Jim Crow must ultimately aim at increasing the power and dignity of African Americans. At its core, reparation entails compensation for wrongs, and should not be tied to the broader aim of societal reconciliation or redemption.

In "Transitional Justice and Redress for Racial Injustice," Colleen Murphy argues that a third model, "transitional justice," should be added to the tort and atonement models. In cases in which societal transformation is required—because wrongdoing has been normalized, and pervasive structural inequality obtains—transitional justice is required. The conditions are ripe, Murphy suggests, because the United States faces a moment of serious existential uncertainty, in which efforts at structural reform and accountability for perpetrators of normalized violence against Black people confront predictable backlash. Transitional justice also adds to reparations and apology three additional parameters for redress: truth, institutional reform, and memorializations.

The specific dynamics of public apologies constitute the third section of the book, "Public Apologies as Moral Repair." In "The Role of the Public in Public Apologies," Linda Radzik characterizes reconciliation as the normalization of relationships harmed or threatened by wrongdoing. Reconciliation is a form of moral repair, and apologies, including public apologies, can be valuable means to that end. Radzik is especially interested in cases in which public apologies are intentionally performed in front of third parties, people who are neither victims nor wrongdoers. Although there are some permissible roles for third parties—such as in cases in which third parties may have standing to serve as proxies for victims—other cases, notably those of passive witnesses, may pose significant issues of desert, proportionality, and authority to punish. The instability in third-party roles may produce "mission creep," in which the public plays active roles that may not be appropriate.

In "The Public Chorus and Public Apologies," a comment on Radzik's chapter, Martha Minow characterizes the role of the public in such apologies as akin to the Greek chorus, providing both possibilities for advice, consolation, and judgment, as well as theatrical spectacle. Public audiences may also play a key role in restorative justice efforts, insofar as such efforts tend to implicate larger communities beyond wrongdoers and victims, enabling deeper, structural issues to come to the fore. They can turn what might be dismissed as mere media spectacles into transformative moments of public meaning-making.

Finally, in his chapter, "Apology, Accusation, and Punishment/ Harm: Audiences as Multipliers," Burke A. Hendrix examines how social media audiences in particular might inflict undue suffering, and disproportionate punishment, on apologizers. Hendrix defends cases in which audiences seek to generate feelings of guilt and productive shame in their targets, while resisting attempts to nonproductively humiliate except in cases in which there are reasons to believe the wrongdoer will evade consequences for wrongdoing. Yet even in those cases where retributive justice against wrongdoers who are unlikely to be punished may seem appropriate, reasonable questions about the merits of the accusation, flawed heuristics, and clamorous audiences may lead to punitive humiliation. This in turn may lead to cycles of counter-punishment and counter-humiliation. As such, Hendrix argues that encouraging audiences online to distinguish between productive shame and humiliation, potentially through markers and hashtags, might prove a beneficial strategy.

PART I

RECONCILIATION AFTER ALIENATION

1

RECONCILIATION AS NON-ALIENATION

THE POLITICS OF BEING AT HOME IN THE WORLD

CATHERINE LU

How could you explain that four hundred years in a place didn't make it a home?

> —Saidiya Hartman, *Lose Your Mother*

We feel that one of the things taken from many Indigenous Peoples through colonization, perhaps even, I would argue, the most important thing was our ability to dream for ourselves.

> —Cindy Blackstock, quoted in *Reclaiming Power and Place*

[I]t is the colonized man who wants to move forward, and the colonizer who holds things back.

> —Aimé Césaire, *Discourse on Colonialism*

The killing of George Floyd on May 25, 2020, sparked hundreds of protests in America, and across the world, against structural anti-Black racism and police violence.[1] Demands for justice for Floyd, as well as for hundreds of other victims of racist and state-sponsored violence, have come from human rights organizations such as Amnesty International,[2] as well as many other grassroots initiatives, from online petitions to street murals to mass protests.[3] In conjunction with demands for individual accountability of the police officers involved, there have been calls for police forces as well as various levels of government in the United States to address systemic or structural racism.[4] Such demands for corrective inter-actional, institutional, and structural justice have been part of the Black Lives Matter Movement, now a global social force dedicated to countering state-sanctioned violence and anti-Black racism, in order to promote "freedom and justice for Black people and, by extension, all people."[5]

A steady companion to such calls for justice are pleas for reconciliation.[6] Pope Francis implored "the national reconciliation and peace for which we yearn."[7] Scholars and journalists have also advocated the creation of truth and reconciliation commissions.[8] The district attorneys of San Francisco, Philadelphia, and Boston announced in July 2020 the launch of "Truth, Justice, and Reconciliation" commissions to address structural racism and police brutality in the criminal justice system, although there have been no news reports of progress toward their establishment in the two years following the announcement.[9] While the US House Judiciary Committee held a historic vote on H.R. 40 in April 2021, approving a bill to create a commission to examine appropriate remedies for the "lingering negative effects of the institution of slavery" in the United States, some American cities are embarking on reparations commissions that aim to address a wide range of race-based structural inequities in the areas of property and commerce, health care, education, and employment, as well as criminal justice.[10]

The political discourse of reconciliation has been salient in Canada since the mid-2000s. A 2006 court-mandated settlement of one of the largest class action suits in Canadian history included compensation to Indian Residential School survivors, as well as funds to assist their psychological healing, and for various commemorative activities.[11] The settlement also instituted the Truth and Reconciliation Commission (TRC) of Canada to hear survivor testimonies and to provide a comprehensive accounting of the historic wrongs of the residential school system. In addition to its final report in 2015, the TRC of Canada issued 94 Calls to Action, calling on state agencies and civil society organizations to address a variety of social, political, and economic injustices and inequities in contemporary state policies, practices, as well as social structures.[12] The 2019 Final Report of the National Inquiry into Missing and Murdered Indigenous Women and Girls established that the heightened vulnerability of Indigenous women and girls, as well as of 2SLGBTQQIA people,[13] to violence amounts to race-, identity-, and gender-based genocide. The report also called on police services to establish "an independent, special investigation unit for the investigation of incidents of failures to investigate, police misconduct, and all forms of discriminatory practices and mistreatment of Indigenous peoples within their police service."[14]

In the summer of 2021, the unfinished work of the TRC became apparent upon the discovery of more than 1,300 unmarked potential burial sites of children in plots next to residential schools.[15] The 2015 TRC report had estimated 4,000–6,000 deaths of children from the Indian Residential School system, and its Calls to Action (numbers 71–76) included calls to federal, provincial, and municipal governments to work with churches and Indigenous groups to locate and identify missing and deceased residential schoolchildren, inform families, provide appropriate commemoration, and protect sites where residential schoolchildren are buried. According to the former Chair of the TRC, and Senator, Murray Sinclair, the number of dead children may be close to 15,000–25,000; the higher number would represent one out of six children who attended the Indian Residential School system.[16] The grim revelations from a long century of a genocidal assimilationist education system have forced deeper public grappling with how far Canadians are from a true acknowledgment of the toll of settler colonialism. They have also led to renewed demands for greater accountability of governments, and of the Catholic Church, to allow public access to their residential school records, as well as to increase other reparative measures, including reforming contemporary child welfare policies.[17]

According to Sheryl Lightfoot, Indigenous peoples have embarked on the process of reconciliation because it requires from states "a credible commitment to change its future power relations and give up a certain degree of real, material, and political power in exchange for a new, renegotiated, more just and legitimate relationship with Indigenous peoples."[18] In addition, police forces,[19] churches, universities, the arts, and many other professional and civic communities have engaged in various projects of reconciliation aimed at improving relations between Indigenous and non-Indigenous peoples.

While those who have been or are oppressed have engaged with the politics of reconciliation with structural transformation in view, others, including states and dominant groups, have also engaged with discourses of reconciliation, but often in ways that aim to dampen exposed social divides, blunt accountability, and/or forestall structural change. For example, in response to the assault on the US Capitol on January 6, 2021, by far-right groups and supporters of former US President Donald Trump who refused to acknowledge his electoral defeat, both Trump and then President-elect Joe Biden called for "healing" and "reconciliation."[20]

Many are, understandably, skeptical about reconciliation as a political project, or uncertain what value it can have. Why should anyone, especially those who are victimized and oppressed, as well as their allies, care about reconciliation? What value does reconciliation have that is distinct from justice? Especially in cases of clear wrongdoing, why not just focus on justice as accountability of the wrongdoers?

In my work, I have argued that whereas justice refers to tasks related to remedying various kinds of injustices, reconciliation should be understood as responding to various kinds of alienation implicated in or produced by unjust or dominating contexts.[21] I draw on German critical theorist Rahel Jaeggi's conception of alienation, which refers to experiences of disconnection, disruption, or distortion in "the structure of human relations to self and world" and "the relations agents have to themselves, to their own actions, and to the social and natural worlds." Alienation is a "particular form of the loss of freedom" that involves "a relation of disturbed or inhibited appropriation of world and self." Successful appropriation by an agent "can be explicated as the capacity to make the life one leads, or what one wills and does, one's own; as the capacity to identify with oneself and with what one does; in other words, as the ability to realize oneself in what one does."[22] Alienation can thus be understood as an undermining or inhibition of an agent's appropriative agency that renders them incapable of seeing themselves as a self-realizing agent in the social world.[23] Alienated agents cannot be at home in the world.

When understood as a response to alienation so understood, the work of reconciliation is not the same as fulfilling the demands of justice. Reconciliation work is normatively important, however, because addressing alienation may provide or strengthen the motivational bases for agents to do justice, or redress injustice, at all, as well as shape the ways they pursue justice, and even how they conceive of the subjects and demands of justice. The work of reconciliation is fundamental to addressing agents' motivations to realize the transformation of social/political identities, practices, and conditions in ways that support collective efforts to create mutually affirmable and affirmed social/political orders and relations for the flourishing of non-alienated agents. I aim in this contribution to elaborate on how we should understand this call for reconciliation as non-alienation, and on that basis, show why reconciliation as a moral/political project cannot and should not be so easily relinquished.

In the following section, I provide an account of the historical context of contemporary reconciliation politics in order to explain the roots of skepticism. In contexts of political transition prompted by the end of civil wars, authoritarian regimes, or regimes of racial oppression, new regimes engaged in reconciliation processes to account for the crimes of past regimes as a way to mark or establish major political and ideological shifts. Commissions focused on past or historic injustice came to be adopted in established democracies not undergoing regime change, as a way to acknowledge past injustices and address their contemporary legacies. This focus on historic wrongs, however, has been inadequate in many contemporary democratic contexts. Highlighting the continuity between historic wrongs and contemporary structural injustice leads to different ways to think about the project of reconciliation. I then provide my account of reconciliation that is grounded in a regulative political ideal of non-alienation, and explain how it can aid our understanding and assessment of the politics of reconciliation as focused on "being at home in the world." I assert that this view of reconciliation should lead to a more critical acknowledgment and examination of the modern state as constituting a source of structural alienation for a variety of groups that have experienced or continue to experience statist and (settler) colonial subjugation. In combination with racial hierarchy, I argue that statist structural alienation has precipitated existential alienation for those in positions of structural indignity.

I move on to explore the challenge of disalienation as a struggle to resist and dismantle alienating subjectivities produced in dominating and oppressive social conditions. Disalienation politics, evident in contemporary social and political conflicts over public memory, statues, institutions, cultural practices, and public spaces, have the potential to provoke painful self-reflection as a way to stimulate the motivational resources of agents to pursue or support social and structural change. Conservative reactions to such politics, however, buttress more extreme right-wing ideologies and movements that aim to forestall this transformative potential and perpetuate structural injustice and domination. At the same time, I argue that the cultivation of non-alienated agency requires reconciliation to be an open-ended ongoing process, rather than one characterized by "closure" or a predetermined endpoint or end-state. There is not one path, but there are plural paths to non-alienation; reconciliation as non-alienation cannot presume or produce a final endpoint or closure, but points to ongoing, transformative projects of self-realization in changing structural contexts.

In the conclusion, I address the concern that reconciliation as non-alienation is an illusory or infeasible political ideal, given that contemporary conditions of structural injustice and alienation do not afford room for non-alienated agency. I also explore whether in some conditions, pursuing non-alienation as a regulative political ideal can precipitate irreconciliation. While it is true that the regulative ideal of non-alienation may close off possibilities for some forms of interactional reconciliation, I conclude that the struggle for non-alienation can open space for alternative, transformed, and more emancipated dreams of reconciliation.

HISTORICAL CONTEXT

The contemporary politics of reconciliation emerged in the 1990s as structural changes in regional and international orders precipitated significant regime transitions in Latin America, Africa, Asia, and central and eastern Europe. In the aftermath of violent conflict, authoritarianism, and oppression that ended with peace settlements or regime changes, societies struggled to build new institutions and transform political practices in ways that would avoid a repetition or return to a problematic past. In the "transitional justice"[24] literature that developed to study and assess these struggles, reconciliation came to enjoy as much prominence as justice as

an organizing normative purpose and framework for these efforts.
While its relationship with justice was contested, reconciliation took
on the normative task of repairing damaged relationships in order
to achieve a morally acceptable transition of power, despite not
applying the standard mechanisms of justice for wrongdoing, such
as criminal trials that yield punishment of wrongdoers. The ideal of
political reconciliation thus signified "moral ambition within political constraints."[25] The 1994 Truth and Reconciliation Commission
of South Africa became the model for reconciliation processes that
aimed to respond to political injustices and wrongdoing as part of
a political transition from a racially oppressive state and divided
society to a democratic human rights–respecting regime of multiracial equality.[26]

From a historical perspective, one could understand the global-
ization of the political discourse of reconciliation and transitional
justice—their embeddedness in the United Nations as well as their
promotion by powerful states and global civil society organizations—as a completion of a centrist-liberal narrative arc of the history of the twentieth century. That narrative concentrates on World
War II, the war against Nazi Germany, and the judgment at Nurem-
berg, as effecting the repudiation of White supremacy, right-wing
nationalism, and authoritarian militarism, and their replacement
by human rights–respecting, liberal democratic nation-states with
sovereign equality as the defining markers of the progressive endpoint of postwar reconciliation and transitional justice. In the postwar liberal international order, especially during the Cold War, the
fact that defeating Nazi Germany required an alliance of capitalist
(United States), communist (Soviet Union), and imperial (Great
Britain) powers, none of which were stalwart promoters of racial
equality, social justice, or disarmament, was relatively obscured.
According to historian Nikolai Koposov, the memory of the Holocaust was central to the reconstruction of Western Europe, and
later, the European Union, as a unifying symbol of a shared history of moral transgression and repentance. Creating a "common
European memory centered on the memory of the Holocaust" was
"a means of integrating Europe, combating racism, and averting
national and ethnic conflicts."[27] In this historical narrative, the col-
lapse of the Soviet empire in the 1990s, involving the fall of authoritarian communist regimes in eastern and central Europe, and the

end of apartheid in South Africa—the last remaining formal system of racial oppression at the international level—demonstrated the steady progress of a liberal international order and implied the inexorable global triumph of capitalist liberal democracy that could promise freedom and justice for all.

As Barry Buzan and George Lawson have noted, however, this progressive narrative obscured the racism, authoritarianism, and militarism that were integral to the development of Western-colonial international society.[28] Perhaps not surprisingly, then, the idea of reconciliation as a political project in transitional contexts of postconflict or regime change came to motivate activists seeking recognition, reparations, and structural transformation within contemporary Western and liberal democratic states. In the United States, the Greensboro Truth and Reconciliation Commission (1999–2006), examining events that led to the death of five people during an anti–Ku Klux Klan protest in 1979, was the first application of the South African model to racial injustice in that country, "designed to examine and learn from a divisive event in Greensboro's past in order to build the foundation for a more unified future."[29] Ronald W. Walters compared the cases of the United States and South Africa in his book, *The Price of Racial Reconciliation*, arguing for the applicability of the framework of reconciliation for racial oppression, a political project that is imperative for "the survival of the democratic idea" in America.[30]

Initially, the rationale for embarking on reconciliation projects was to acknowledge historic injustices, such as the Indian Residential school system in Canada, or the 1979 incident in Greensboro, to compensate survivors, and to close the books on past injustice. In contexts of regime transitions, truth and reconciliation commissions operated to expose the truth of past injustice as a way to forge a new regime's identity as no longer continuous with that unjust past. Such an approach typically also involves implicitly a claim that an injustice is past or has passed, and is no longer present, continuing, or being reproduced. There was another truth, however, that commissions so mandated potentially displaced, which is the ongoing reproduction of oppressive and dominating practices, conditions, and relations in contemporary social structures.

The temporal limitation of reconciliation processes, understood as a form of achieving closure for past injustices, without much scrutiny of the present ongoing reproduction of injustice, was a defect even in contexts of regime change such as post-apartheid South Africa. Indeed, protests against police brutality sparked by the killing of George Floyd extended to South Africa.[31] In settler colonial contexts, such reconciliation processes can distort or obscure contemporary social realities by historicizing injustices, and run into the danger of serving to maintain the status quo of "neocolonial affirmation."[32] According to Rauna Kuokkanen, discussing the recent contemporary efforts of Nordic states to embark on reconciliation processes with the Sámi people, "The process in the past 3 years leading toward establishing a truth and reconciliation commission shows no sign of a departure from the assimilationist policies. Therefore, the Sámi may well be reconciled into a contemporary injustice as the consequence of the TRC in Finland. As settler colonial policy making, reconciliation then represents a continuation and extension of the colonial order, subtly entrenching existing injustice and reaffirming and legitimating state control."[33]

Indeed, Glen Coulthard has criticized the project of reconciliation as an "individual and collective process of overcoming the subsequent *legacy* of past abuse, not the abusive colonial structure itself."[34] Instead of ushering in major social and political transformations, reconciliation seemed to mirror historical colonial practices, in which Indigenous peoples were forced or defrauded into signing treaties of friendship and protection with European colonizers. While reconciliation in interpersonal relations is often characterized as transformative of the social relations between agents, the critique of the discourse and politics of reconciliation is that they are employed or engaged in by states and dominant groups precisely to deny or forestall a transformative politics of redress.

There is, thus, much skepticism and criticism about reconciliation as a moral/political project.[35] Skeptics wonder whether the ideal of social harmony or unity underlying the concept of reconciliation is not just myth and illusion, whether major historic political or social injustices can ever be repaired, and whether reconciliation processes can ever transform, rather than merely reflect, the structure of power relations in which its agents are embedded. Critics of the politics of reconciliation reveal its tendency to yield reactionary political programs, especially when reconciliation strategies focus on a depoliticized, medicalized notion of individual psychological healing from traumatic experiences, or function to pressure the politically weak to accommodate evil and injustice in the name of national or civic unity, or focus too narrowly or superficially on repairing relations between victims and perpetrators, while leaving unexamined the structural sources of their alienating interactions.[36] Given these defects, reconciliation hardly seems to be a moral/political ideal.

If we take these challenges seriously, we may conclude that it would be better to forgo reconciliation as a necessary or constructive demand in moral and political life. The struggle against the pervasive injustices in our world would be more successful if reconciliation were no longer a part of the normative and political discourse. In my work, I have been sympathetic with these criticisms, and I acknowledge that there is great value in exposing the neocolonial, domestication, or legitimation functions of reconciliation discourse and practice in contemporary politics. Those involved in contemporary political struggles are wise to be cautious when engaging in reconciliation projects devised by states or their various agencies, from parliaments to police forces.

At the same time, I think there are compelling reasons to engage with this common discourse in a critical but constructive fashion. First, it is important to reveal what has been normatively deficient in contemporary ideas, discourses, and practices of reconciliation, and second, it is constructive to provide an alternative, more normatively and politically cogent reconstruction of the ideal, so that agents can reorient their understanding of the normative and political purpose of reconciliation practices, and hopefully transform them in more emancipatory directions.[37] This task is predicated on the assumption that there is nothing intrinsic to the concept of reconciliation (just as there is nothing intrinsic to the concept of justice or freedom) that renders it inevitably regressive, rather than emancipatory.

In my work, I have argued that we should think about both justice and reconciliation in structural terms, and not only as qualities of interactional relationships. We should be more concerned about the structures that mediate identities, institutions, social positions, interactions, and conditions, making some more vulnerable to victimization or harms and burdens, while enabling others to have more advantages or privileges, and even to commit wrongdoing with impunity. Social structures, when unjust, define in morally objectionable ways the social positions, identities, agency, roles, aspirations, and potential and actual achievements of persons and groups. Structural injustices can inform laws, norms, and discourse; shape the design and purposes of institutions and social practices; and produce material effects. They enable, legitimize, normalize, and entrench conditions under which structural and interactional injustice may persist on a regular and predictable basis. Structural injustices may produce "unintended, generalized, or impersonal harms or wrongs that result from social structural processes in which many may participate."[38]

For example, it would be difficult to account for persistently disparate outcomes with respect to health care, education, housing, income, and wealth, between Indigenous and non-Indigenous persons without reference to structural usurpation of Indigenous governance and dissociation from Indigenous interests, generated by policies of genocide and forcible incorporation of Indigenous peoples in settler colonial states, predicated on the ideologies of civilization and progress that posited a fundamental incompatibility between Indigeneity and modernity. Social hierarchies—often based on race, class, and gender categories that transcend nationalist and statist divides—expose large categories of persons or peoples to social positions of inferiority or structural indignity that heighten their historic and contemporary vulnerability to various forms of injustice, oppression, and domination.

Focusing on the structural continuities between contexts of historic colonialism and contemporary social structures at domestic, international, and transnational levels reveals that *debates about justice and reconciliation in response to colonial injustice need to move beyond a historic injustice framework.* Since structural injustices are contemporary, calls for reconciliation in contemporary politics are not about getting over the past, but about addressing the alienation of contemporary agents from contemporary social structures, including contemporary narrative structures about the past. Reconciliation, in this frame, is not only or mainly about closing the books on past injustice. It's not primarily about victims or survivors letting go of resentment about a past injustice. It's about how those whose social positions are produced by a structurally unjust order today can dismantle unjust and alienating social identities, positions, and structures, and build a world in which all agents can cultivate non-alienated forms of agency and self-realization.

Reconciliation should be understood as part of a regulative political ideal of non-alienation, aimed toward the creation of a mutually affirmable and affirmed social/political order that can support the flourishing of non-alienated agents.[39] Rather than addressing an abstract philosophical question about how rational individuals may feel at home in the modern world, reconciliation as a moral/political project can be formulated as addressing a more practical question: How can agents come to affirm the social/political structures that enabled or produced (and still may be enabling and producing) social and political injustices, and which still may constitute so many of the options and limits of their lives?

The politics of reconciliation ultimately is a struggle about the shape of the social world that defines, organizes, and mediates agents' social identities, positions, agency, well-being, and even their dreams. Such politics involves contestations over narratives of that order in historic terms, as well as over representations of the current social/political order, and reveal conflicting images of home, including who can be at home in the world, and what kinds of identities, positions, and roles are possible and available to agents in different social positions to enact, practice, as well as imagine, in this home. In struggling to be at home in the world, agents in different social positions reveal different images of that home from their standpoints, presenting others with sometimes discordant, jarring, and unsettling images of the social/political order. When revealing disparate images of the social/political order, the politics of reconciliation generates sources of immanent critique through unsettling socially dominant images of home, as well as the images of oneself that are attached to or associated with those images, thereby destabilizing the dominant schematic orderings of the social/political order, on which agents' ontological security and sense of home depend. Through responding to such confrontations, agents who participate in the project of reconciliation embark on remaking, and potentially transforming, themselves, and thereby their social world. Seen in this light, the political project of reconciliation, given the histories and continuities of human iniquity, has the potential to make radical demands on us all.

IMAGES OF HOME

In politics, agents engage in the quest for reconciliation by struggling to create a mutually affirmable and affirmed social/political order, a regulative ideal that we can characterize as being at home in the world.[40] Understanding reconciliation in this way entails an examination of what images of home are available in the social and political schemas and imaginaries[41] that provide the ground or structure for developing and mediating agents' social identities, aspirations, and appropriative agency. "Home" is the definer of personal and collective identity, and fulfillment or self-realization. Just as the domestic familial home is conceived by its defenders as "the only setting where intimacy can flourish, providing meaning, coherence, and stability in personal life,"[42] the social/political home can be viewed as the setting that organizes meaning, coherence, and stability in individuals' social existence, and the basis from which they flourish or flounder as social and political beings. We can understand contemporary struggles over public discourse, museum exhibits, monuments and statues, public space, and other social practices as windows into deeper contestations about the politics of being at home in the social world. Home is a social imaginary with which individual and group social identities are inextricably bound, and by which their social agency and activities are unavoidably mediated.

The politics of reconciliation is thus a politics of homemaking. But what does it mean to be at home in the world? Psychology studies have shown that "among adults, and on the level of countries and ethnic groups, collective psychological ownership serves as a strong justification for territorial and nationalist sovereignty claims, and disputes about ownership of objects, cultural artifacts, and territories are frequent and tend to escalate to violent intergroup conflicts."[43] Reconciliation as the politics of homemaking thus involves interrogating the fusion of collective psychologies of ownership with ideas of home and belonging. This way of understanding the politics of reconciliation, as one based on competing claims of home ownership, also helps to explain why such conflicts are so emotionally charged, such as when communities are divided over the maintenance or removal of monuments of historic figures in public squares, or the renaming of sports teams, schools, and universities; over the creation and direction of national museums of cultural heritage; over the revision of portrayals of past events in school history textbooks; over revisions to contemporary celebratory traditions; or over which figures should or should no longer be commemorated through national holidays, street names, or currencies.

However these struggles play out, a dominant conception of the structure of the home that is the site of such collective struggles is the modern nation-state. The territorial nation-state, and the international system of states, are the presumed institutional frameworks in which contemporary individuals or groups struggle to realize freedom, equality, justice, and community. Hilary Pilkington has observed that the persistence of the idea of "homeland" in contemporary political discourse suggests that "an important element of the modern world outlook is the linking of individual identity to a territorially bound collective identity."[44] While liberal conceptions of national belonging eschew primordial, ethnic, and organic notions of national or political community, they generally accept the modern territorial state as the given institutional framework of political life. As for the international level, proponents of liberal international order interpret decolonization as an extension of the value of national self-determination to previously colonized peoples, and the universalization of sovereign equality as a progressive repudiation of the unequal status of peoples that was a defining feature of colonial international order.[45]

The historical construction and expansion of modern international order, however, has been entangled with "scientific racism" and civilizational thought and discourse. According to Duncan Bell, in the nineteenth century and early twentieth century, "White supremacist visions of global governance circulated widely in the Anglo-American world."[46] While "civilized" populations were entitled to their own state, the logic of civilized nations "justified imperial and colonial rule over Africans and even genocide in accordance with racial hierarchies, as well as forced deportations in accordance with visions of sovereignty based on national or ethnic

homogeneity."[47] The construction of racial and civilizational hierarchies, backed by military domination, meant that the inclusion
of non-Europeans and non-Whites, whether in imperial projects,
colonial civilizing missions, or later, in a system of formally independent states embedded in a capitalist global economy, would be
marked by deep asymmetries and inequalities in standing, status,
rights, burdens, and powers.[48]

In my work, I have argued that state-centric institutions and
practices of global governance reflect deep structural injustices
that emanate from the colonial origins of modern international
order. While historical decolonization conferred the status of formal sovereignty to postcolonial states, precolonial peoples who
found themselves within a newly decolonized state or a settler state
were denied any international standing as peoples in the interstate
order and thus did not enjoy an internationally recognized right
to self-determination as peoples, or the freedom to determine
their political status or pursue their economic, social, and cultural
development. Decolonization thus did not allow for secession or
a reconfiguration of territory, or guarantee international standing, or moral and political reciprocity, to peoples and other organized social groups within settler colonial and postcolonial states.
Entrenchment of a state-centric international society has thus generated a structural legacy of injustice and alienation for those who
continue to experience subjection to the state and international
system as a colonizing project.

The Eurocentric narrative of civilizational progress that for-
warded the nation-state as a marker of civilization, also fated Indigenous peoples to extinction with the advent of modernity. In the
"civilized" home, Indigenous people are alienated from an epistemic, social, ethical, normative, and material order that is predicated on denying the very possibility of realizing Indigenous ways
of being—knowledge, philosophy, governance, or culture—in conditions of modernity.[49] Acknowledging that the forcible incorporation of Indigenous peoples as members of a largely "departed
race" is not only a historic injustice, but a contemporary or ongoing structural injustice in postcolonial and settler colonial contexts,
raises fundamental challenges to the legal and political authority
and legitimacy of postcolonial and settler colonial states as well
as of the international order of sovereign states.[50] Thus, Robert

Nichols has observed that the most important aspect of struggles of Indigenous peoples in contemporary politics—over development projects, pipelines, burial sites, or mountain ranges—is that they are "*interpretive struggles*, challenging and unsettling the very terms of global political order."[51] Given the lack of fit between Indigenous governance and settler state structures, redressing the existential and structural alienation of Indigenous peoples from the contemporary international order entails revolutionary structural transformations of world order. Decolonizing the global home will thus require fundamental modifications of the constitutive political and territorial rights of states, and the coercive architecture of the modern sovereign states system that enforces such rights.[52]

In the case of Black people, the construction of Black identity in civilizational discourse as having "no culture, no civilization, no 'long historical past',"[53] and the "thingification" of Black subjects under colonial rule[54] left an enduring legacy in postcolonial Africa,[55] as well as in the African and Black diaspora. Contemporary Black scholars emphasize that Black subjectivity is constrained not only by legacies of past injustice, but by "the ongoing problem of Black exclusion from social, political and cultural belonging; our abjection from the realm of the human."[56] Thus, for Christina Sharpe, anti-Black violence in the United States is not just a blemish on an otherwise well-functioning democracy, but "a predictable and constitutive aspect of this democracy." She asks, instead of calling for justice as accountability, what political and social spaces would be opened if Americans were to understand that, "The ongoing state-sanctioned legal and extralegal murders of Black people are normative and, for this so-called democracy, necessary; it is the ground we walk on. . . . What happens when we proceed as if we *know* this, antiblackness, to be the ground on which we stand."[57] Such existential alienation is pointedly captured by Saidiya Hartman's account of her attempt to explain to the chief of Salaga, Ghana, the impact of slavery on Blacks in America: "How could you explain that four hundred years in a place didn't make it a home?"[58]

The Pain and Promise of Disalienation Politics

Nishnaabeg writer and educator Leanne Simpson has expressed her concerns about the progressive potential of the project of reconciliation in Canada through the use of a domestic analogy to describe the relationship between Indigenous and non-Indigenous peoples: "It reminds me of an abusive relationship where one person is being abused physically, emotionally, spiritually and mentally. She wants out of the relationship, but instead of supporting her, we are all gathered around the abuser, because he wants to 'reconcile.' But he doesn't want to take responsibility. He doesn't want to change. In fact, all through the process he continues to physically, emotionally, spiritually and mentally abuse his partner. He just wants to say sorry so he can feel less guilty about his behaviour. He just wants to adjust the ways he is abusing; he doesn't want to stop the abuse."[59]

Despite recognition by a majority of Canadians that much work remains to build a racially just society,[60] the image of Canada as an abusive and even genocidal home would be disorienting and unsettling for a population that considers the injustices of genocide, dispossession, and forcible incorporation to belong to a distant and remote past. With a vague and general understanding of the country's history, many Canadians continue to hold a positive self-image of the nation and its "values" of "peace, freedom, democracy and human rights."[61] Such a positive self-image is difficult to reconcile with the image of Canada as an agent of past and ongoing Indigenous genocide, a controversy that has afflicted the Canadian Museum for Human Rights (CMHR) since its foundation. The museum's mission, until recently, included "celebrating Canadians' commitment to human rights."[62] Established in 2014, the CMHR took five years to acknowledge that the Indian Residential Schools system amounted to a genocidal policy directed at Indigenous peoples in Canada, an admission prompted by the National Inquiry into Missing and Murdered Indigenous Women and Girls (MMIWG).[63]

How can agents, whose social imaginaries and associated conceptions of the right and the good may be distorted by structural injustice, come to be motivated to pursue self- and political transformation? Frantz Fanon articulated this question as a challenge of "disalienation" as a response to colonial domination and oppression: "Before embarking on a positive voice, freedom needs to make an effort at disalienation."[64] According to Fanon, both the oppressed, as well as the oppressors, need to engage in processes of disalienation, for a new politics to be born. The project of reconciliation as non-alienation is intimately related to the disalienation of those who have developed their subjectivities (or sense of self and one's place in the world) in conditions of structural domination and oppression.

For those who are dominated, alienation makes it difficult to engage in struggles against injustice or domination. The alienated may suffer from lacking the requisite self-respect required to mount a radical critique, or the requisite bases of social respect to participate effectively in the space of "public reason" distorted by structural injustice. Nor may the public engagement of the alienated conform to the standards of sober social analysis.[65] Alienated agency may produce engagement with unjust structures that are limited by those structures. Disalienation is essential to meet the challenge of agents *becoming* free and equal authors of their social structures, which is not resolved by others, such as the state, conferring on them the status of persons or citizens. Glen Coulthard has thus argued that the politics of liberal multicultural recognition is not enough to redress the ongoing settler colonial domination and oppression of Indigenous peoples. Following Fanon, he argues that dominated agents need to struggle to create new decolonized terms of association that they can call their own, and not only seek equal justificatory status based on structures of colonial power, otherwise "the colonized will have failed to reestablish themselves as truly self-determining: as creators of the terms, values, and conditions by which they are to be recognized."[66] As Leanne Simpson has put it, "We [Indigenous peoples] need to be able to articulate in a clear manner our visions for the future, for living as Indigenous Peoples in contemporary times. . . . [This involves] articulating and living our legal systems; language learning; ceremonial and spiritual pursuits; creating and using our artistic and performance-based traditions."[67] Disalienation may thus involve a refusal[68] of the social position or identities one has been assigned in the dominating home, withdrawal from the social world, creative reappropriation, and strategies of self-development and self-affirmation.[69] While disalienation for the oppressed requires such acts of imaginative resistance to the dominant social identities and positions offered, the space for such imaginings may require state and international support for the revival of Indigenous languages, cultures, and governance, since their resurgence is a precondition for Indigenous and other subjugated peoples being able to engage in decolonized and non-alienated struggles to be at home in the modern world.

For others occupying dominant social positions, disalienation practices need to aim to provoke recognition of problematic identities, beliefs, and practices (or the occurrent experience of psychoaffective alienation), while also providing positive motivational resources for agents to do the hard work of self-reflection and transformation. The Canadian TRC, however, faced obstacles from government, churches, and other agencies or organizations to provide a full examination of the schools, including an accounting of the victims, whose unmarked graves are now being uncovered, as well as an accounting of the officials who were responsible for the assimilationist and eliminationist policies of successive Canadian governments over its 150-year history.[70]

Indeed, the pain that attends processes of disalienation has provoked reactionary politics that aim to re-entrench the terms of structural domination. In response to growing awareness of the Dutch nation's history of slavery and colonialism, for example, far-right nationalists have employed the language of self-hatred to resist collective engagement in painful reflections about Dutch national history. According to Thierry Baudet, leader of the far-right, White supremacist/nationalist Dutch Forum for Democracy Party (FvD), "The West is suffering from an autoimmune disorder . . . Part of our organism—an important part: our immune system, that which should protect us—has turned against us. We're being weakened, undermined, surrendered in every respect. Malevolent, aggressive elements are being smuggled into our social body in unprecedented numbers, while true causes and consequences are kept hidden."[71] Baudet employs the concept of *oikophobia*, or "fear of the home," which, he argues, feminist, Black, postcolonial, and other social movements have engendered by challenging the golden narrative of Dutch national history and "Western values" more generally, producing a citizenry that is ashamed of and alienated from its national identity.

The concept of *oikophobia* was developed by the conservative philosopher Roger Scruton.[72] In an essay on American education, he characterizes those who embrace multiculturalism as suffering from a "pathological *oikophobia*, a hatred of home, which has been a frequent disease among intellectuals since the Enlightenment. He sees that which is his 'own,' his inheritance, as alien; he has fallen out of communication with it and feels tainted by its claim on him." The picture of America that Scruton sees threatened by the liberal multicultural politics of recognition is one in which the democratic process and the rule of law function aptly to resolve social problems. Not "nationalist or xenophobic," his American citizen "assumed that it is right and normal to be proud of your country," a country with "a core of moral instinct, in which respect for freedom went hand in hand with an equal respect for public decency."[73] His account of American society, however, clearly is dominated by a White majority culture, such that "Harlem" represents a "cultural minority" that is equal to "a Shi'ite village in Iran."[74] In Scruton's image of America, the White majority is implicitly the great definer of who can call America their home, and Blacks and other minorities can only claim to belong if they accept their racial subordination.

In offering this image of the American home, Scruton seems to engage in what philosopher Simon Keller has called a "patriotism of bad faith."[75] The diagnosis of *oikophobia* also seems to misunderstand the motivation of the politics of disalienation; far from expressing a "hatred of home," those whom Scruton criticizes for contesting dominant images of home seek to make the home better for all those who must live in it. Politically, the instrumentalization of *oikophobia* in far-right ideologies serves to reinvigorate the resolve of dominant social groups to cling to their distorted subjectivities, and to aspire to continue determining without reciprocation whose image of home is realized in social and political life. The resonance of the concept of *oikophobia* with many ordinary people, and its instrumentality to the far-right political agenda, are indications of the serious pain engendered by the politics of disalienation. For to admit negative versions of the American home as "materialist, patriarchal, racist, imperialist and obsessed with property and power"[76] is to expose the bright self-image of Americans to a darker mirror image that provokes powerful emotions of inadequacy or shame, according to their own standards. It is the pain generated by the alienation or separation from a positive self-image, provoked by practices of disalienation, and the desire to avoid such pain, that motivates some to support the reactionary politics of the far right. My point is that the politics of *oikophobia* is not primarily about the existential alienation of dominant social groups to participate meaningfully in the social world, but about their attempt to dominate (or "determine without reciprocation"[77]) whose image of home will define and organize social and political life. By deflecting the painful and potentially transformative self-examination provoked by disalienation politics, conservative and far-right politics also close off possibilities for moving forward in struggles against structural domination and alienation.

RECONCILIATION AS AN OPEN-ENDED PROCESS OF SELF-REALIZATION

Lorraine Hansberry's play, *Les Blancs,* vividly and presciently portrays these challenges that attend the politics of reconciliation in a postcolonial world.[78] Set in a fictional African country on the verge of anticolonial insurrection, the action begins with Tshembe Matoseh, a young African man, returning home from a comfortable life in Europe for his father's funeral. The play makes trenchant critiques and poses difficult challenges about the ends and means of anticolonial struggle, challenges that apply to African Americans fighting for civil rights in America as well as to Africans fighting European colonial rule. Hansberry's play deftly and poignantly exposes the dilemmas encountered by racialized subjects attempting to fashion a home in a world built on racial oppression and domination. While Tshembe's brother Abioseh, a Roman Catholic about to enter the priesthood, takes an assimilationist route that threatens the anticolonial struggle, the most poignant character in the play is Tshembe's half-brother, Eric, an African European child of rape, who is eager to join the revolution, but becomes its casualty.

The colonial administration is represented by Major Rice, who is in charge of security in the shadow of an imminent insurrection. In explaining his attachment to the colonial project, Major Rice explains to the American journalist, Mr. Morris: "This is my country, you see. I came here when I was a boy. I worked hard. I married here. . . . This is our home, Mr. Morris. Men like myself had the ambition, the energy and the ability to come here and make this country into something . . . (He turns ever so slightly from time to time to catch Tshembe's expression.) They had it for centuries and did nothing with it. It isn't a question of empire, you see. It is our home . . . We wish the blacks no ill. But—(Simply, matter-of-factly, a man confirmed)—*it is our home*, Mr. Morris."[79] The thorough sense of entitlement to ownership expressed by Major Rice is buttressed by the play's revelation that he is also Eric's father, and the rapist of Tshembe's mother.

Hansberry's play shows vividly what is at stake in the struggle for home, even as she also sharply portrays the challenges confronting those who aim to forge a new politics of homemaking. One route she dismisses is the one taken by the American journalist, Charlie Morris, who views himself as far removed from the colonial projects of Europe and offers new terms of association on equal terms. Tshembe criticizes the ahistorical move toward a new beginning, saying, "For a handshake, a grin, a cigarette and half a glass of whiskey you want three hundred years to disappear—and in five minutes! . . . In this light, for instance, I really cannot tell you from Major Rice!"[80]

Near the end of *Les Blancs*, Tshembe, lamenting his involvement in the anticolonial politics of his ancestral home, and its implications for the possibility of returning to his private, comfortable life with his European wife and child, exclaims: "I want to go *home*." When asked if his home is in the mountains of Europe or the mountains where he grew up in Africa, he replies that he no longer knows.[81]

The play's ambiguous and controversial ending reflects well the uncertain endpoint of reconciliation as non-alienation. Far from closing the books, reconciliation as non-alienation is quite open-ended in terms of the substantive kinds of social forms or institutionalized relations that agents may come to endorse and pursue. In the case of settler colonialism, reconciliation as non-alienation is not likely to accommodate the assimilationist dreams of settlers who may accept the inclusion of Indigenous peoples, but only within a predetermined settler constitutional framework. But in contrast to conceptions of reconciliation as closure, reconciliation as non-alienation does not foreclose continued political struggle, and does not assume a homogenizing ideal or a conflict-transcendent form of social unity. For this reason, also, however, such a conceptualization of reconciliation cannot produce a substantive vision of what a reconciled social/political order should look like. In *Les Blancs*, an ally of the anticolonial cause, Madame Neilsen, asks Tshembe if he hates Europeans. He replies, "I have seen your mountains. Europe—in spite of all her crimes—has been a great and glorious star in the night. Other stars shone before it—and will again with it. . . . The heavens, as you taught me, are broad and can afford a galaxy."[82] Although I have said that we cannot offer a substantive vision of what a reconciled world would look like, we could view Hansberry's vision of a galaxy of glorious stars as an apt abstract vision when imagining one kind of world we can hope for. It supports the view that a measure of conditions for non-alienated flourishing for Indigenous peoples in settler colonial states such as Canada, as well as in the wider world, is whether Indigenous peoples can effectively participate as equals in shaping their terms of association "without giving up who they are as indigenous peoples," and whether they are empowered to return Indigenous "ways of knowing the world to their rightful place in the landscape of *human* ideas."[83]

At the same time, it should be acknowledged that conceptualizing reconciliation as a response to the history of human iniquity invites a tragic framing of non-alienation as addressing the challenges of "making possibility out of dispossession,"[84] slavery, genocide, and other socially produced atrocities. As Aimé Césaire has argued, it is impossible to return to a galaxy populated by stars from a precolonial past.[85] Hartman has also reflected on the disappointment of being a Black person trying to return to a place that has not been touched by slavery. Her journey to Ghana to find "home" first reveals to her the difference between the Pan-Africanism of the continent and the Pan-Africanism of the diaspora.[86] Eventually, she identifies a connection through the stories of the stateless—those fugitives from slave raids who fled their villages in search of "free territory." Being at home in the world, according to the "fugitive's dream," did not entail returning, owning, or belonging to a mythical homeland, but entailed that "old identities sometimes had to be jettisoned in order to invent new ones. Your life might just depend on this capacity for self-fashioning."[87] Ghanaian American writer Yaa Gyasi's novel, *Homegoing*, provides an illustrative case of imaginative homemaking in her fictional reconstruction of a family history of eight generations torn apart and indelibly shaped by slavery, colonialism, and racial iniquity. At various times, characters struggle precisely with making possibilities for self-realization in defiance of, as well as out of, their oppressive surroundings.[88] Whatever their degree of success, to create narratives depicting agents' struggles in contexts of genocide, slavery, and dispossession is a powerful exercise of appropriative agency for those whose capacities to appropriate and narrate their own histories were obliterated through "thingification" or genocide. The creative reappropriation and innovation required for self-realization in such contexts invariably will lead to plural paths and boundary-crossing identities of anticolonial and decolonial subjectivity.[89] Reconciliation as nonalienation entails placing the homemaking struggles of the fugitive, the refugee, the border-crosser, the exiled, the oppressed, and the dispossessed at the center, rather than periphery, of our normative conceptions of being at home in this world.

CONCLUSION

The question of reconciliation is about whether and how agents can imagine new selves, another "other," with whom to engage in transformed social relations, in order to create new forms of non-alienated flourishing in mutually non-alienating relations. Some may worry that the ideal of non-alienation is illusory or infeasible, given the impossibility of realizing the idealized subject in conditions of structural oppression and domination. How can non-alienated agents or structures be fashioned out of alienated subjects and conditions? Although agents' social positions and structures are mutually constituted, my view is that even agents in conditions of severe domination and oppression can exercise oppositional agency or resistance. This is not to say that such forms of political agency thereby generate a free or autonomous subject. The exercise of such agency cannot be equated with enjoying structural justice or freedom.[90] Still, agents variously situated in unjust structures can make use of their agency to contribute to challenging and overturning structural injustices through self-transformation and collective action. Agents, individually or collectively, need not be autonomous in any ideal sense to do this, but the more effectively they are able to act from their social positions to dismantle structures of oppression and domination, and to dream new and less alienated ways of self-realization, the more structural freedom their agency will produce that will, in turn, enable them to develop more ideal non-dominated and non-alienated forms of subjectivity. As structures change, new norms and practices of politics will develop or become more visible, giving rise to new challenges that will engender further theoretical innovations about further structural changes. Different waves of feminism illustrate well how structural changes can produce new struggles for reconciliation when agents with new social identities interact in ways that precipitate new social conflicts. We can also evaluate the process of decolonization in this way, to help contextualize the normative significance of historical periods of decolonization, and also make sense of contemporary claims by Indigenous and other subjugated peoples that colonialism is not over.

But achieving reconciliation as non-alienation is not likely with agents as they are. In settler colonial contexts, the collective psychology of settler home ownership that entrenches anti-Indigenous institutions, norms, and practices will need to be relinquished for a new non-alienated politics to be born. In this sense, it is true that the regulative ideal of non-alienation may close off possibilities for some forms of interactional reconciliation; indeed, the ideal of non-alienation reveals just how irreconcilable things may be between contemporary agents, whose social positions and identities are firmly attached to settler colonial images of self and home. Whether it is at the ballot box, in party politics, state agencies, or social movements, in the school lunchroom, corporate boardroom, on the movie screen, in the realm of domestic labor, at the hockey rink or basketball court, in hospital wards, or the halls of academia, the struggles of agents to be at home in the world—and between and within agents over whose home it is, and what kind of home it is, including how much and what kinds of non-dominating and non-alienating spaces are available to different categories of persons and social groups in these worlds—constitute the political struggle for reconciliation. When that struggle is viewed as one that aims at non-alienation, it can open space for alternative, transformed, and more emancipated dreams of reconciliation.

The stakes of the struggle are high. The problem of reconciliation is not only about how far such societies must go to repudiate their racist and genocidal past, but also, relatedly, what they (or we) must do to promote fundamental structural change, both domestically and globally, so that they/we can halt and prevent a racist and genocidal present and future. Reconciliation is a practical political necessity of all appropriative agents to claim the space they need to be able to live, indeed, to breathe. In this sense, the project of reconciliation is not one that can be voluntarily or easily given up by those who are oppressed and dominated in contemporary world politics. To give up on reconciliation, on the struggle to be at home in the world, would be to give up on life itself.[91]

NOTES

An earlier version of this chapter was presented virtually at the conference on "Reconciliation and Repair" of the American Society for Political and Legal Philosophy, September 25, 2020. Thanks to Melissa Schwartzberg and Eric Beerbohm for organizing the conference, and to Saira Mohamed and Ryan Preston-Roeder for their commentaries. Subsequent versions of the paper were presented at the Research Group on Constitutional Studies Works-in-Progress series at McGill University (November 2020), the Newcastle Politics Research Seminar (on zoom November 2020), and the Queen's Legal and Political Philosophy Colloquium (on zoom November 2020). Thanks to all the participants, as well as Arash Abizadeh, Wendell Nii Laryea Adjetey, Yann Allard-Tremblay, Terri Givens, Will Kymlicka, Andreas Leidinger, Jacob Levy, Andrew Lister, Wayne Modest, Saira Mohamed, Ryan Preston-Roeder, Laura Routley, Christa Scholtz, Melissa Schwartzberg, Geoffrey Sigalet, Christine Sypnowich, Benjamin Thompson, Ashwini Vasanthakumar, Yves Winter, and Didier Zúñiga for comments.

1 Derek Chauvin was convicted in April 2021 of second-degree unintentional murder, third-degree murder, and manslaughter, and three other (former) police officers face charges. Police forces in the United States have killed approximately 1,100 people every year since 2013, according to the advocacy and research group, Mapping Police Violence. See Laurence Ralph, "To Protect and to Serve: Global Lessons in Police Reform," *Foreign Affairs*, July 30, 2020. www.foreignaffairs.com.

2 "Take Action for Human Rights: Demand Justice for George Floyd," Amnesty International, www.amnesty.org.

3 It is estimated that 15–26 million people participated in protests in the weeks following Floyd's killing. See Larry Buchanan, Quoctrung Bui, and Jugal K. Patel, "Black Lives Matter May Be the Largest Movement in U.S. History," *New York Times*, July 3, 2020. www.nytimes.com.

4 See, for example, the statement by UN High Commissioner for Human Rights Michelle Bachelet: "Madagascar/ Child Prostitution and Sex Tourism: For All to See, in Total Impunity," Office of the High Commissioner, Human Rights, United Nations, July 26, 2013, www.ohchr.org.

5 Black Lives Matter is a grassroots decentralized global network that was founded in 2013 by Alicia Garza, Patrisse Cullors, and Opal Tometi, in response to the acquittal of George Zimmerman for the shooting death of Trayvon Martin in Sanford, Florida. See "Herstory," Black Lives Matter, https://blacklivesmatter.com.

6 "We have got to have reconciliation. This country has not reconciled its differences with us. We survived slavery but we didn't reconcile. We survived segregation but we didn't reconcile. We're suffering . . . discrimination because we didn't reconcile. It's time for a Department of Reconciliation . . ." Al Green, Representative of the US Congress, June 8, 2020. www.rev.com.

7 Bill Chappell, "Pope Francis Prays for George Floyd, Decries 'The Sin Of Racism,'" NPR, June 3, 2020, www.npr.org.

8 Larry Schooler, "After Floyd Killing, We Need a Truth and Reconciliation Commission on Race and Policing," *USA Today*, 7 June 2020. www.usatoday.com. See also Sarah Souli, "Does America Need a Truth and Reconciliation Commission?," *Politico*, August 16, 2020, www.politico.com.

9 Tom Jackman, "Prosecutors in Three Cities Launch Commissions for Victims of Unjust Policing And Prosecution," *Washington Post*, July 1, 2020, www.washingtonpost.com.

10 Joel Burgess, "In Historic Move, North Carolina City Approves Reparations for Black Residents," *USA Today*, July 16, 2020, www.usatoday.com.

11 The court-mandated settlement was agreed to by the legal counsel for former Residential School survivors, the Assembly of First Nations, and other Indigenous organizations, as well as church bodies, and the Canadian federal government. The Indian Residential Schools Settlement Agreement (IRSSA) provided CAN$1.9 billion to more than 78,000 former students of the residential schools system; CAN$3.233 billion for settling almost 38,000 claims of sexual abuse and serious physical and psychological abuse; CAN$60 million for the Canadian TRC; CAN$20 million for commemorative projects; and CAN$125 million for the Ab-

original Healing Foundation. See "The Indian Residential Schools Settlement Has Been Approved," Residential School Settlement, www.residentialschoolsettlement.ca.

12 Calls to Action, Truth and Reconciliation Commission of Canada, 2012, https://ehprnh2mwo3.exactdn.com.

13 2SLGBTQQIA in this context refers to Indigenous people who identify as "Two-Spirit, transgender, lesbian, bisexual, queer, questioning, intersex, asexual, and/or gender diverse or non-binary." See Canada, *Reclaiming Power and Place: The Final Report of the National Inquiry into Missing and Murdered Indigenous Women and Girls*, Vol. 1a (2019), 447.

14 On genocide, see *Reclaiming Power and Place*, Vol. 1a (2019), 50–54, and 355. On police reforms, see *Reclaiming Power and Place: The Final Report*, Vol. 1b (2019), 192. www.mmiwg-ffada.ca.

15 The Tk'emlúps te Secwépemc First Nation, in British Columbia's Central Interior, announced in May 2021 that using ground-penetrating radar, it had uncovered 215 potential burial sites of children, located near the former Kamloops Indian Residential School. Weeks later, the Cowessess First Nation announced the discovery of 751 unmarked graves at a cemetery near the former Marieval Indian Residential School in Saskatchewan. Others have been in located in Cranbrook, B.C. and Penelakut, B.C. On the work of Indigenous archaeologist Kisha Suprenant and her team, see CBC Radio, *The Current*, June 25, 2021. www.cbc.ca.

16 "Murray Sinclair Calls for Inquiry into Residential School Burial Sites, More Support for Survivors," CBC Radio, *The Current*, June 2, 2021, www.cbc.ca.

17 Although there are continuing legal battles over the federal government's failure to provide equitable child and family services to Indigenous children, the Canadian government, the Assembly of First Nations, and the plaintiffs in two class action suits achieved a final settlement agreement in July 2022, the largest in Canadian history. It includes CAN $20 billion for compensation, as well as CAN $20 billion to reform the on-reserve child welfare system. https://fncaringsociety.com.
After a week-long "penitential pilgrimage" of reconciliation between the Catholic Church and Indigenous people in Canada in July 2022, Pope Francis concluded on his flight back to Rome that the residential school system and forced assimilation policies constituted "genocide." See Ka'nhehsí:io Deer, "Pope Says Genocide Took Place at Canada's Residential Schools," CBC, July 30, 2022. www.cbc.ca. For an investigative report on the Catholic Church in Canada, see Tavia Grant and Tom Cardoso, "The Catholic Church in Canada Is Worth Billions, a *Globe* Investigation Shows. Why Are Its Reparations for Residential Schools So Small?" *The Globe and Mail*, August 7, 2021. www.theglobeandmail.com.

18 Sheryl Lightfoot, "Settler-State Apologies to Indigenous Peoples: A Normative Framework and Comparative Assessment," *Native American and Indigenous Studies* 2 (2015): 15–39 at 36.

19 "Alberta RCMP Launch Reconciliation Strategy," Royal Canadian Mounted Police, June 19, 2020, www.rcmp-grc.gc.ca.

20 Nicole Narea, "Amid Calls for His Removal, Trump Says He'll Support the Transition to a 'New Administration,'" Vox, January 7, 2021, www.vox.com.

21 See Catherine Lu, *Justice and Reconciliation in World Politics* (Cambridge: Cambridge University Press, 2017).

22 Rahel Jaeggi, *Alienation*, trans. F. Neuhouse and A. E. Smith (New York: Columbia University Press, 2014), xxi and 22, 2, 36, and 37.

23 For a development of alienation along more Kantian lines, where alienation denotes a condition of agents who have lost or are denied their standing as morally autonomous agents (and hence are dominated), see Rainer Forst, "Noumenal Alienation: Rousseau, Kant and Marx on the Dialectics of Self-Determination," *Kantian Review* 22, 4 (2018): 523–551. The Kantian-Forstian approach makes alienation practically synonymous with unjust domination, entailing a violation of rights. Such alienation would be redressed through redressing injustice; and reconciliation as a response to such alienation would become synonymous with justice. Jaeggi's account of alienation is thus more appropriate for my construction of reconciliation as a distinct moral striving from justice. For further elaboration, see my "The Right to Justification and the Good of Nonalienation," in *Justification and Emancipation: The Political Philosophy of Rainer Forst (Penn State Series in Critical Theory)*, ed. Amy Allen and Eduardo Mendieta (University Park: Penn State University Press, 2019), 76–92.

24 "Transitional justice" became the label for "the set of institutions, policies, and practices designed to deal with atrocities and major politically motivated human rights violations in the process, anticipation, or aftermath of regime change or violent conflict." Leslie Vinjamuri and Jack Snyder, "Law and Politics in Transitional Justice," *Annual Review of Political Science* 18, 1 (2015): 303–327. See also Pablo de Greiff, "Theorizing Transitional Justice," in *Transitional Justice*, ed. Melissa Williams, Rosemary Nagy, and Jon Elster (New York: NYU Press, 2012), 31–77.

25 Elizabeth Kiss, "Moral Ambitions within and Beyond Political Constraints," in *Truth v. Justice: The Morality of Truth Commissions*, ed. Robert I. Rotberg and Dennis Thompson (Princeton, NJ: Princeton University Press, 2000), 68–98.

26 The South African Truth and Reconciliation Commission put forth the claim that the road to reconciliation required a truthful accounting of

the past. The achievement of reconciliation was associated with achieving national unity, the well-being of all citizens, and civic peace. See "Promotion of National Unity and Reconciliation Act 34 of 1995," Government of South Africa, www.justice.gov.za.

27 Nikolay Koposov, *Memory Laws, Memory Wars: The Politics of the Past in Europe and Russia* (Cambridge: Cambridge University Press, 2018), 10.

28 Barry Buzan and George Lawson, *The Global Transformation: History, Modernity and the Making of International Relations* (Cambridge: Cambridge University Press, 2015), 124. See also Edward Keene, *Beyond the Anarchical Society: Grotius, Colonialism and Order in World Politics* (Cambridge: Cambridge University Press, 2002).

29 See also the Maryland Lynching Truth and Reconciliation Commission, Maryland.Gov, 2019, https://msa.maryland.gov.

30 Ronald W. Walters, *The Price of Racial Reconciliation* (Ann Arbor: University of Michigan Press, 2008), 130.

31 Kim Harrisberg, "Thousands Have Attended Black Lives Matter Demonstrations in Cape Town, Pretoria and Johannesburg to Protest Violence by Security Forces Implementing the Lockdown—and Prior to the Pandemic—Directed Mainly at Poor, Black Communities," Reuters, June 9, 2020, www.reuters.com.

32 Courtney Jung, "Reconciliation: Six Reasons to Worry," *Journal of Global Ethics* 14, 2 (2018): 252–265 at 262.

33 Rauna Kuokkanen, "Reconciliation as a Threat or Structural Change? The Truth and Reconciliation Process and Settler Colonial Policy Making in Finland," *Human Rights Review* 21 (2020): 293–312. In this case, reconciliation efforts will examine policies of "dispossession of land and resources, legacy of residential schools, language and identity theft, forced conversion to Christianity, destruction and defamation of Sámi spirituality and sacred sites, and active engagement in racial biology research as recently as in the late 1960s in which Sámi were measured and categorized."

34 Glen Sean Coulthard, *Red Skin, White Masks: Rejecting the Colonial Politics of Recognition* (Minneapolis: University of Minnesota Press, 2014), 109.

35 See Jung, "Reconciliation: Six Reasons to Worry," for a trenchant review of the concerns of Indigenous scholars and activists about the limits and dangers of engaging in practices of reconciliation proposed by settler states. See also Alasia Nuti, "On Structural Injustice, Reconciliation, and Alienation," *Critical Review of International Social and Political Philosophy* 23, 4 (2020): 427–434.

36 See Lu, *Justice and Reconciliation*, chap. 6 for an elaboration of these critiques.

37 See Andrew Schaap, "Reconciliation as Ideology and Politics," *Constellations* 15, 2 (2008): 249–264 at 249, for a similar Gramscian form of critique that does not view political ideas or concepts as intrinsically true or false, reactionary or radical, but as potentially emancipatory. See also Catherine Lu, "Structural Injustice and Alienation: A Reply to My Critics," *Critical Review of International Social and Political Philosophy* 23, 4 (2020): 441–452.

38 Lu, *Justice and Reconciliation*, 35, 118.

39 Lu, *Justice and Reconciliation*, 182–216.

40 See Michael O. Hardimon, "The Project of Reconciliation: Hegel's Social Philosophy," *Philosophy and Public Affairs* 21, 2 (1992): 165–195.

41 According to Charles Taylor, a social imaginary entails "the ways that people imagine their social existence, how they fit together with others, how things go on between them and their fellows, the expectations that are normally met, and the deeper normative notions and images that underlie these expectations." Social imaginaries feature a common understanding among ordinary people "that makes possible common practices and a widely shared sense of legitimacy." According to Taylor, the "Western social imaginary" consists of three cultural forms, located in the economy, the public sphere, and self-governance. See Charles Taylor, *Modern Social Imaginaries* (Durham, NC: Duke University Press, 2003), 23.

42 Elizabeth Pleck, *Domestic Tyranny: The Making of Social Policy Against Family Violence from Colonial Times to the Present* (New York: Oxford University Press, 1987), 8.

43 Maykel Verkuyten and Borja Martinovic, "Collective Psychological Ownership and Intergroup Relations," *Perspectives on Psychological Science* 12, 6 (2017): 1021–1039 at 1022. See also Monica Duffy Toft, "Territory and War," *Journal of Peace Research* 51 (2014): 185–198.

44 Hilary Pilkington, "Going Home? The Implications of Forced Migration for National Identity Formation in Post-Soviet Russia," in *The New Migration in Europe: Social Constructions and Social Realities*, ed. Khalid Koser and Helma Lutz (New York: St. Martin's Press, 1997), p. 88.

45 See Anna Stilz, "Decolonization and Self-Determination," *Social Philosophy and Policy* 32, 1 (2015): 1–24; and Anna Stilz, *Territorial Sovereignty: A Philosophical Exploration* (Oxford: Oxford University Press, 2019).

46 Duncan Bell, "Founding the World State: H. G. Wells on Empire and the English-Speaking Peoples," *International Studies Quarterly* 62 (2018): 867–879 at 871. See also Duncan Bell, *Dreamworlds of Race: Empire and the Utopian Destiny of Anglo-America* (Princeton: NJ: Princeton University Press, 2020).

47 Eric D. Weitz, "From Vienna to the Paris System: International Politics and the Entangled Histories of Human Rights, Forced Deportations, and Civilizing Missions," *American Historical Review* 113, 5 (2008): 1313–1343 at 1328.

48 Adom Getachew, *Worldmaking after Empire: The Rise and Fall of Self-Determination* (Princeton, NJ: Princeton University Press, 2019).

49 See Patrick Wolfe, "Settler Colonialism and the Elimination of the Native," *Journal of Genocide Research* 8, 4 (2006): 387–409.

50 In the United States, Congress in 1913 planned a monument to the "departed race," to be built on Staten Island, New York. According to President William Howard Taft, the statue to commemorate the expected extinction of Indigenous people "tells the story of the march of empire and the progress of Christian civilization to the uttermost limits." See Bruce Duthu, *American Indians and the Law* (New York: Penguin, 2008), xxiii.

51 Robert Nichols, "Indigenous Peoples, Settler Colonialism, and Global Justice," in *Empire, Race and Global Justice* ed. Duncan Bell (Cambridge: Cambridge University Press, 2019), 228–250 at 249.

52 See Catherine Lu, "Decolonizing Borders, Self-Determination, and Global Justice," in *Empire, Race and Global Justice*, ed. Duncan Bell (Cambridge: Cambridge University Press, 2019), 251–272 at 271.

53 Frantz Fanon, *Black Skin, White Masks* (New York: Grove Press, 1952).

54 Aimé Césaire, *Discourse on Colonialism* [1950] (New York: Monthly Review Press, 2000), 42.

55 "The final and worst psychological impact [of colonialism] has been the generation of a deep feeling of inferiority as well as the loss of a sense of human dignity among Africans. Both complexes were surely the outcome not only of the wholesale condemnation of everything African already referred to but, above all, of the practice of racial discrimination and the constant humiliation and oppression to which Africans were subjected throughout the colonial period." See A. Adu Boahen, *African Perspectives on Colonialism* (Baltimore, MD: Johns Hopkins University Press, 1987), 108.

56 Christina Sharpe, *In the Wake: On Blackness and Being* (Durham, NC: Duke University Press, 2016), 14.

57 Sharpe, *In the Wake: On Blackness and Being*, 7.

58 Saidiya Hartman, *Lose Your Mother: A Journey Through the Atlantic Slave Route* (New York: Farrar, Straus and Giroux, 2007), p. 197. See also Dionne Brand, *A Map to the Door of No Return: Notes to Belonging* (Toronto: Vintage Canada), 2011. Brand's book begins with her account of a "tear in the world" that opened when she was thirteen, generated by her grandfather's inability to tell her about her family's origins: "We were not from

the place where we lived and we could not remember where we were from or who we were" (p. 5).

59 Leanne Simpson, *Dancing on Our Turtle's Back: Stories of Nishnaabeg Re-Creation, Resurgence and a New Emergence* (Winnipeg: Arbeiter Ring Publishing), 2011, 17.

60 "Canadians are most likely to believe that Indigenous Peoples (77%), Black people (73%), and South Asians (75%) experience discrimination often or occasionally; by comparison, fewer—although still a majority—(54%) believe this is the case for Chinese people in Canada. Very few (5%) say that racialized Canadians never experience discrimination." Also, "Majorities of Canadians who are Black (54%) or Indigenous (53%) have personally experienced discrimination due to race or ethnicity from time to time if not regularly. Such experience is also evident but less widely reported by those who are South Asian (38%), Chinese (36%), from other racialized groups (32%), or White (12%)." Keith Neuman, "Race Relations in Canada 2019 Survey," Environics Institute, December 10, 2019. The most significant change in the 2021 survey is an increased perception of racism against Chinese people (70%), likely prompted by reports of increased anti-Asian racism during the COVID-19 pandemic. www.environicsinstitute.org.

61 Kathleen Harris, "Canada Loses Its Bid for Seat on UN Security Council," CBC, June 17, 2020, www.cbc.ca.

62 Canadian Museum of Human Rights, Summary of the 2018–2019 to 2022–2023 Corporate Plan, https://humanrights.ca. Following a report that found "pervasive and systemic racism" in the operation of the museum itself, a change in leadership resulted in a changed mandate; see "About," Canadian Museum of Human Rights, https://humanrights.ca.

63 For a brief history of the museum's changes on recognizing the Indian Residential School system as genocide, see David MacDonald, *The Sleeping Giant Awakens: Genocide, Indian Residential Schools, and the Challenge of Conciliation* (Toronto: University of Toronto Press, 2019), 167–171.

64 Fanon, *Black Skin, White Masks*, 206.

65 See my "The Right to Justification and the Good of Nonalienation," in *Justification and Emancipation*, 86.

66 Coulthard, *Red Skin, White Masks*, 39.

67 See Simpson, *Dancing on Our Turtle's Back*, 17.

68 Audra Simpson, *Mohawk Interruptus: Political Life Across the Borders of Settler States* (Durham, NC: Duke University Press, 2014).

69 See Coulthard, *Red Skin, White Masks*.

70 See Matt James, "The structural injustice turn, the historical injustice dilemma and assigning responsibility with the Canadian TRC Report," *Canadian Journal of Political Science* 43 (2021): 374–396.

71 Quoted in *The Nation*, January 2017. Sebastian Faber, "Is Dutch Bad Boy Thierry Baudet the New Face of the European Alt-Right?," www.thenation.com. According to Ben Margulies, the FvD "unites the centre-right's favoured cultural identity and economic policies with far-right racism, authoritarianism and xenophobia in a single party." Margulies, "Why Europe Should Worry about Thierry Baudet," *EUROPP—European Politics and Policy* / LSE Blog, April 24, 2019: https://blogs.lse.ac.uk.

72 Roger Scruton, "Oikophobia," *Journal of Education* 175, 2 (1993): 93–98. It has also been instrumental in Scruton's endorsement of Brexit and criticisms of the European Union. See Roger Scruton, *England and the Need for Nations* (London: Civitas, Institute for the Study of Civil Society, 2006), 33–38.

73 Scruton, "Oikophobia," 94.

74 Scruton, "Oikophobia," 97.

75 Simon Keller, "Patriotism as Bad Faith," *Ethics* 115 (2005): 563–592.

76 Scruton, "Oikophobia," 96.

77 See Iris Marion Young, *Justice and the Politics of Difference* (Princeton, NJ: Princeton University Press, 1990), 38.

78 Lorraine Hansberry was born in 1930, in Chicago, Illinois, and died of cancer in 1965. *Les Blancs* was incomplete before her death in 1965, and finalized posthumously in 1972. Hansberry attended the New School for Social Research in New York, studied under W.E.B. Du Bois (1868–1963), and worked for *Freedom*, Paul Robeson's Black newspaper (1950– 1953). In 1957, she wrote under a pseudonym to a feminist magazine, *The Ladder*, about feminism and homophobia, to avoid discrimination. Her most well-known play is *A Raisin in the Sun*. See Joy L. Abell, "African/American: Lorraine Hansberry's *Les Blancs* and the American Civil Rights Movement," *African American Review* 35, 3 (2001): 459–470.

79 Lorraine Hansberry (1930–65), *Les Blancs* in *Les Blancs: The Collected Last Plays* (New York: Vintage Books, 1972), Act 1, Scene 3, p. 71 (italics mine).

80 Ibid., 74.

81 Hansberry, *Les Blancs*, Act 2, Scene 8, 126.

82 Ibid., 125.

83 Dale Turner, *This Is Not a Peace Pipe: Towards a Critical Indigenous Philosophy* (Toronto: University of Toronto Press, 2006), 117, emphasis mine.

84 Hartman, *Lose Your Mother*, 7.

85 Césaire, *Discourse on Colonialism*, 44–45.

86 Hartman, *Lose Your Mother*, 218.

87 Ibid.

88 Yaa Gyasi, *Homegoing* (Toronto: Anchor Canada, 2016), 99.

89 See Wendell Nii Laryea Adjetey, *Cross-Border Cosmopolitans: The Making of a Pan-African North America* (Chapel Hill: University of North Carolina Press, 2023), chap. 2.

90 See Jennifer Einspahr, "Structural Domination and Structural Freedom: A Feminist Perspective," *Feminist Review* 94, 1 (2010): 1–19.

91 For a poignant depiction of such a struggle for an Indigenous girl and her family, see Tracy Lindberg, *Birdie* (Toronto: Harper Collins, 2015).

2

RECONCILIATION AND THE MILITARY

SAIRA MOHAMED

In the dying days of the Trump administration, the pages of news-
papers and magazines began to publish calls for some form of
reckoning with the past four years of abuses. Proposals for truth
and reconciliation commissions emerged alongside debates about
whether prosecutions would help or hinder healing. These pieces
overflowed with the many transgressions that could or should be
addressed: separation of children from their parents at the border
and their detention in ghastly conditions; the sabotage and rejec-
tion of opportunities to mitigate the destruction of the pandemic;
the use of the office of the presidency as an opportunity to make
a buck; the president's early hints at the possibility that he would
not support a peaceful transition of power, followed by the series
of baseless lawsuits, followed by the innuendo and encouragement
of those who launched an insurrection when it was clear that the
courts would not help him.[1] The language of trauma was used to
describe the nation as a whole—trauma exacerbated, of course,
by the hundreds of thousands of deaths and sickness and fear and
isolation brought on by the pandemic, but it was trauma created
by a destructive president long before disease brought the world
to its knees.[2]

In the accounting of these offenses, there was little mention
of the military.[3] Service members were not included in the list of
groups who had been abused; the military was not included in the
list of institutions that needed healing. Perhaps this omission is
unsurprising, a reflection of the simple fact that American service
members had not suffered to the same degree or in the same way
as so many other populations under the Trump administration.

They were not torn from their children; they were not targeted (even if they were mocked);[4] they were not tangled in a web of perjury or obstruction or corruption.[5] But still, they were exploited and treated as instruments, with military and political leaders putting service members in positions that they simply should not have been in, deploying soldiers in order to achieve their own improper ends, and publicly toying with ideas of using service members to violate human and constitutional rights at home and overseas. When observers responded, they did so not by condemning these abuses, but by emphasizing service members' obligations to disobey any illegal orders, and they decried the "politicization" of the military—as if the main problem of asking service members to violate the law was that it brought them too close to politics. And thus, despite the uniformity and seeming justifiability of the failure of the truth and reconciliation commentariat to mention them, this chapter argues that the institutional betrayals experienced by the members of the military—both under Trump and even before—are ripe for examination under a framework of reconciliation.[6]

For those who study it and for those who live it, the notion that there can be reconciliation after conflict represents, in various views, a political reality, a fanciful hope, a naïve and conservative façade, or an ideal to strive for. In her insightful essay, "Reconciliation as Non-Alienation: The Politics of Being at Home in the World," Catherine Lu helps us sort through the question of what reconciliation is and whether it should be valued by providing an illuminating examination of reconciliation as a process that addresses the social condition of alienation. Focusing on reconciliation "in structural terms," rather than as a "quality[] of interactional relationships,"[7] Lu offers the reader not only a precise and careful clarification of the concept of reconciliation, but also a defense of it. Defining reconciliation as being "at home in the world," Lu explains that reconciliation functions as part of a "regulative political ideal . . . aimed towards the creation of a mutually affirmable and affirmed social/political order that can support the flourishing of non-alienated agents."[8] Under conditions of reconciliation through disalienation, agents can "becom[e] free and equal authors of their social structures."[9]

This chapter reckons with Lu's vision of structural reconciliation as a framework for understanding how service members who have been betrayed by leadership might one day again see themselves as part of the military and non-military institutions to which they belong. It begins by sketching the contours of the long-standing, dominant approach for understanding distortion of the relationship between the military and civilian leadership in the United States: politicization, or the risk of involving the military or members of the military in politics. To be sure, some scholars of civil-military relations recently have questioned the wisdom of the politicization framework and encouraged greater consideration of the benefits of a politicized military. But both the politicization literature and critiques of it, this chapter contends, continue the long tradition in the American military of seeing military service members as resources rather than as human agents. As a result, they neglect and deny that members of the military can be exploited (and should not be exploited) by the government they serve. The chapter then turns to reconciliation and argues that it offers a path toward non-alienation, with the potential not only to restore military institutions, but also to transform them by creating space for recognizing the dignity of service members, individuals who in conventional legal, political, and cultural framings are typically represented as mere instruments of the state, who by definition cannot be abused. The chapter closes by exploring how the possibilities of a reconciliation framework may be impeded by the concept's stubborn and persistent identification of a perpetrator on one side and a victim on the other. Because of the challenges to identifying service members—especially those who have committed or contributed to war crimes or other wrongs—as "victims," the framework of reconciliation may continue to be a far-off ideal for addressing alienation in the military.

POLITICIZATION

The primary framework in the United States for understanding and assessing the relationship between the country's leadership and the military is politicization. A politicized military is one that is loyal to party or to partisan causes. American civil-military relations are built around an idol of non-politicization, and an expectation that the military serves the Constitution and democratically elected officials, who in turn must devote themselves to country before party.[10]

The American model of non-politicization has drawn significantly from Samuel Huntington's *The Soldier and the State,* written
before his perhaps more (in)famous *The Clash of Civilizations.* Huntington put forward what he called a model of "objective control,"
under which the military focuses on the "management of violence,"
while the civilian branches of government preserve control over
policy.[11] The military respects civilian authority over policy decisions and political struggles, and civilian authorities respect the
military's control over battlefield decision-making. "The antithesis
of objective civilian control," writes Huntington, "is military participation in politics."[12]

The objective control model has come under increased scrutiny
and even attack in recent years. Political scientist Risa Brooks draws
attention to recent survey research showing that members of the
military themselves are questioning the model. One 2013 survey of
veterans who had served at high levels, conducted by Kori Schake
and Jim Mattis, found that 63 percent of respondents agreed with
the statement that resignation was appropriate in response to an
"'unwise'" order.[13] In the late 1990s, only 28 percent of respondents
had supported resignation in those circumstances.[14] At less senior
levels, too, resistance to entanglement of politics and the military
has waned. Brooks notes that more than 40 percent of respondents to a 2015–2016 survey of West Point cadets and National
Defense University officers reported that "their military friends
often talked about politics on social media."[15] One-third said they
had "seen their friends in the military make rude comments about
the president on social media sites."[16] Brooks not only argues that
the descriptive accuracy of the apolitical norm is deteriorating; she
also argues that it ought to be questioned because it compromises
strategic interests and military effectiveness.[17] Mara Karlin and Jim
Golby, too, challenge the wisdom of the politicization model. They
argue that "[t]he military is far too important in American society
for it to be apolitical." Instead, military leaders should "be able to
engage on political issues," and what should be avoided is a military that embraces "partisanship, institutional endorsements, and
electoral influence."[18]

Although these critiques have had some traction in academic
and policy circles, their very existence offers a hint of the power of
The Soldier and the State and its central framing of non-politicization

of the military. According to Major General William Rapp, the book "has defined civil-military relations for generations of military professionals. Soldiers have been raised on Huntingtonian logic and the separation of spheres of influence since their time as junior lieutenants."[19] In the pages of the *New York Times*, Gary Bass described *The Soldier and the State* as "by far the most influential book on the subject" of civil-military relations.[20] In his first graduation addresses to the military service academies, then-Secretary of Defense Robert Gates advised the cadets that they would "have a responsibility to communicate to those below [them] that the American military must be nonpolitical."[21] The frame of politicization has been embraced by the public, too. When, during a protest in the summer of 2020, Marine veteran Todd Winn stood outside the Utah Capitol wearing his dress blues with his mouth covered by tape that read "I Can't Breathe,"[22] and when Representative Tom Malinowski posted a photo on Twitter of an individual wearing a Marine Corps uniform at a Black Lives Matter rally[23]— accompanying the image only with the text "America."—social media commenters were quick to warn against the dangers of a political military.

Meanwhile, discussions of the dangers of politicization of the military reached new heights of urgency under President Trump, who "broke[] new ground in trampling the norms and regulations that restrict the political behavior of service members."[24] And so, when President Trump embraced the use of the military to squelch protests in early June 2020, it may come as no surprise that the concern this generated primarily was about the risk of politicizing the military. Indeed, retired military and diplomatic officials published an open letter urging protection of the military's "apolitical" tradition.[25] The letter, signed by 612 former ambassadors, generals, admirals, and other senior officials, noted that "[t]he professionalism and political neutrality of the U.S. military have been examples for people around the world" and are "among our nation's greatest assets in protecting Americans and asserting American interests across the globe." They rejected the Trump administration's characterization of peaceful protest as a "battlespace" that must be "dominated,"[26] and they warned of the dangers that would result from "[m]isuse of the military for political purposes."

The letter justified its focus on the dangers of politicization of the military primarily by reference to the impact of a politicized military on the country and on the world. The writers expressed concern, too, for the service members themselves—the "U.S. military assets," as they were called in the letter—though not for their experience. Instead, the concern was for their appearance: "The stationing of D.C. Air National Guard troops in full battle armor on the steps of the Lincoln Memorial is inflammatory and risks sullying the reputation of our men and women in uniform in the eyes of their fellow Americans and of the world."[27] The consequence of politicization was damage to the reputation of the military as protectors of democracy, free from the taint of politics. Ultimately, the grievances the letter expressed about politicization were framed in terms of the possible future consequences for politics and security—concern for American interests, concern for American reputation. There was no acknowledgment that in those acts that the letter described as politicization, there was wrongdoing that needed to be rectified, or betrayal that demanded restoration.

The politicization framing dominated expressions of remorse following the incident, too. Soon after the protests, the former Chairman of the Joint Chiefs of Staff, Mark Milley, expressed regret for his role in the photos taken of President Trump in front of St. John's Episcopal Church after the area around Lafayette Square, the public park just north of the White House, was forcibly cleared of protesters on June 1, 2020. In a graduation speech for the National Defense University, Milley noted that the procession from the White House and the subsequent photographs—Trump with an upside-down Bible in hand, Milley in combat uniform, alongside the Attorney General and the Secretary of Defense—"sparked a national debate about the role of the military in civil society." Milley continued, "I should not have been there. My presence in that moment, and in that environment, created the perception of the military involved in domestic politics."[28] The overwhelming consensus was that the transgression that had been committed was a violation of the sacred norm of the apolitical military.[29] Meanwhile, in these many analyses of what went wrong at Lafayette Square, and how to avoid its recurrence, the experience of the service members who had to fall in line and abide the transgressions of their leaders was nowhere to be found.

Betrayal

Whereas political, diplomatic, and military leaders in the summer of 2020 observed the wrong of politicization, service members who were stationed at protests experienced a wrong as well. But they were troubled not simply about the politicization of the military. Instead, their experience was one of betrayal—betrayal that arose out of the decisions of leaders to deploy the military in order to violate the rights of protesters, and to enhance the reputation of the president, rather than to respond appropriately to security needs. One DC National Guard member who spoke to Politico said, "As a military officer, what I saw was more or less really f—ed up." He and other Guard members disputed the White House statement that the protesters were violent and insisted that they remained peaceful, even if loud. He commented, "A lot of us are still struggling to process this, but in a lot of ways, I believe I saw civil rights being violated in order for a photo op." He continued, "I'm here to support and defend the Constitution of the United States and what I just saw goes against my oath and to see everyone try to cover up what really happened. . . . What I saw was just absolutely wrong."[30]

I focus here on one incident under one president at a time of particular turbulence in the country. But the experience of service members at Lafayette Square is not unique. The language used by this individual recalls the words that military members have been using for decades. It recalls the words of those who were sent to Iraq, only to learn later that there were no weapons of mass destruction, that they had been deceived by those they were trained to trust and obey, that the deaths and injuries that they caused and that they endured were for naught.[31] It recalls the words of those who were ordered or encouraged to torture prisoners, who were told by their leaders to take the gloves off, to obtain intelligence no matter what it took, who were later called "bad apples" by those same leaders when the abuses of Abu Ghraib and Bagram and Guantánamo came to light, who emerged feeling guilt and shame and anguish over what they had done,[32] who emerged convinced that they are forever "irredeemable."[33] These are words that expose an expectation by service members that the military should not be used for improper ends—an expectation that, as I have addressed in separate writing, is reflected both in the military's consistent pronouncements that service members can and should trust and obey their superiors, and in the law's valorization of the relationship of subordinate to superior in the military.[34] And they are words that seek to articulate that when the military is used for improper ends, it is wrong not because it is a violation of the principle against politicization of the military, as so many would characterize it, not because of the political or security implications, but rather because it is a betrayal of the vital trust that should exist between leadership—both military and political leadership—and the military.

The words used to describe that moment in Lafayette Square—and the words of so many service members beyond that moment—reflect Jonathan Shay's concept of moral injury, defined as a "betrayal of what's right . . . by someone who holds legitimate authority."[35] Shay, a psychiatrist, began his exploration of moral injury with a study of the similarities between combat veterans of the Vietnam War, whom Shay had been treating, and Homer's depiction of Achilles in the *Iliad*. For Shay and other researchers studying moral injury, post-traumatic stress disorder (PTSD) resulting from combat exposure, which was already well known, could not capture combat veterans' feelings of guilt and shame, nor could it explain much of the damage to veterans' lives that had arisen from the experience and aftermath of war, and, in many cases, the suicides that ended their lives.[36] PTSD was about a heightened fear response to threatening events, but what Shay and others were seeing was different. It was destruction of character. And it was brought on by a sense on the part of the veterans that they had been betrayed by those who were supposed to do right, whom they were supposed to trust—and under the law, were obligated to trust.[37]

In the years since Shay's initial explorations of veterans' experiences of betrayal, the concept of moral injury has expanded to describe more broadly, in the words of philosopher Nancy Sherman, the "experiences of serious inner conflict" that "arise from . . . transgressive commissions and omissions perpetrated by oneself or others."[38] Whereas Shay originated the concept of moral injury by focusing on what he calls "leadership malpractice,"[39] other researchers include in their concept of moral injury the consequences of an individual's own choices to engage in conduct that

violates their sense of right and wrong. Whereas for Shay "the violator is a powerholder," for others like Brett Litz, another pioneer
in moral injury research, "the violator is the self."[40] The two experiences may overlap, and a person may experience moral injury
both because they have been betrayed by the leaders whom they
expected to behave in accordance with "what's right," and because
they have betrayed their own assessment of "what's right."[41]

Viewing the experiences of the service members at Lafayette
Square through the lens of moral injury exposes the deficiencies
of politicization as the core reference point by which to assess the
treatment of the military. The experiences described by service
members that have been identified as moral injury simply cannot
be captured by the framework of politicization, for the problem
is not the blurring of the line between military and politics, as
the former generals and the ambassadors and cabinet secretar-
ies would have it. The problem is using the military for improper
ends, putting service members in positions that are supposed to
be honorable but ultimately are violations of international law or
the Constitution or the shared ethical and moral codes of social
and military life.

RECONCILIATION

Viewing the experiences of service members through the frame of
moral injury, rather than politicization, opens the door to thinking about the possibilities of reconciliation. Over the last three
decades during which researchers, practitioners, and laypersons
have struggled to understand how and whether individuals and
communities can emerge from conflict, the meaning of "reconciliation" has often gone unsaid. Writing of South Africa, for example,
James L. Gibson notes that one of two "themes [that] dominate
contemporary discussions of the truth and reconciliation process"
is that "no-one seems to know what 'reconciliation' means."[42] In the
midst of this fog emerges Catherine Lu's distinct account of reconciliation as a reckoning with alienation, or the "experiences of
disconnection, disruption or distortion in 'the structure of human
relations to self and world' and 'the relations agents have to themselves, to their own actions, and to the social and natural worlds.'"[43]
Lu's account defines reconciliation as a process; in contrast to the

conventional view of reconciliation as closure, reconciliation as non-alienation is "open-ended in terms of the substantive kinds of social forms or institutionalized relations that agents may come to endorse and pursue," and it may involve "continued political struggle."[44]

Reconciliation in Lu's vision consists of the ability to see oneself in social and political institutions. Lu describes the social or political home as "the setting that organizes meaning, coherence, and stability in individuals' social existence, and the basis from which they flourish or flounder,"[45] and she reflects on the complete and unavoidable ways in which a person's identity and agency are tied up in their understandings of home. The account is ultimately about the political possibility of reconciliation, and even short of reconciliation, the capacity for expressions of "oppositional agency or resistance" through which individuals can "make use of their agency to contribute to challenging and overturning structural injustices through collective action."[46]

To the extent that reconciliation is considered in the context of service members, it is conventionally an individual, therapeutic model, one that focuses on the steps that can be taken toward healing and forgiveness (typically of the self).[47] Indeed, explorations of moral injury in service members have predominantly been pursued through the fields of psychology and psychiatry.[48] Lu's work distinguishes these therapeutic models as "inappropriate for conceptualizing reconciliation as a political project."[49] "Should we consider reconciliation achieved if all victims overcome their traumas through counseling?" she asks.[50] Surely not; "personal psychological healing . . . may be worthwhile but cannot account for the moral/political value of reconciliation," for reconciliation as a political project requires not "deep social unity that depends on . . . sentimental transformations" (of, say, hatred against perpetrators), but rather transformations of social or political structures that produce alienation.[51] The therapeutic approach to the problem of moral injury in the military thus may resolve the immediate concern of the despair and suffering that have been so pervasive in members of the military. But it is not responsive to the larger political problems that arise out of and are reflected in a long-standing and persistent model of civil-military relations that concerns itself primarily with politicization, that lacks a vocabulary for identifying service members as rights holders and not mere instruments of the state, and that fails to recognize the betrayals of trust that are perpetrated when leaders exploit the military for improper ends.

Viewing the experience of military service members through the framework of reconciliation and alienation thus opens a door to understanding military exploitation and betrayal as a structural problem that ultimately is rooted in the notion that soldiers are cannon fodder, tools to be used by the state, rather than persons in their own right. And the framework of reconciliation and alienation allows for a reimagining of both the problem and the solution: Whereas the politicization framework sees only separation of military and politics as the necessary solution, the alienation and reconciliation framework suggests that the betrayal experienced by service members could be addressed through a process of reckoning with the abuses of power and authority that have achieved the instrumentalization of service members for improper ends—namely, violations of rights, illegal war, and illegal methods of war—through improper means—namely, the gutting of legal checks on such ends and a politics of fear.[52] The restoration of social trust—conceived in most work on moral injury at an individual level—emerges as a goal of political transformation.[53] And the political project of reconciliation would allow for an assertion of a more radical vision of the military service member not as an extension of the state, not as an instrument of the state, but instead as an autonomous agent who enjoys a right not to be exploited by the state that they serve.

Consider, for example, a reconciliation process that addresses the US torture program. Military service members, as well as other individuals outside the military, have shared their experiences of disaffection, anguish, guilt, shame, and betrayal after they participated in torture and other abuses during interrogation of individuals detained under the guise of the war on terror.[54] And still, no process of reckoning has occurred. There have been no prosecutions of the leaders who formulated the program, who devised the specious legal justifications for it, who authorized abusive interrogation methods, who willfully neglected opportunities to rein in the use of illegal tactics.[55] Blame and legal responsibility have been placed on the shoulders of a few lower-level individuals, on "bad apples."[56] The Obama administration declined to prosecute or otherwise seek accountability for those who crafted and implemented the torture program, citing a "need to look forward as opposed to looking backwards."[57] The Trump administration launched an attack on the International Criminal Court (ICC) when it authorized an investigation into torture perpetrated in Afghanistan by American personnel, as well as abuses committed by members of the Taliban.[58] The Biden administration has taken a less overtly hostile stance toward the ICC, but it maintains that the Court should not investigate Americans, even while it voices support for accountability efforts targeting nationals of other countries.[59] The message from the country's leadership is that what happened is in the past, that nothing more needs to be corrected.

The political promise of reconciliation thus lies in its capacity to force the questions of betrayal back into existence. The goal, as Lu reminds us, is not closure; reconciliation instead offers a justified demand for a reckoning with the dynamics of power within these institutions, an opportunity to question and, indeed, reject the refusal to hold accountable those who twisted their positions of authority to use those subordinate to them to commit transgressions of law and morality. Reconciliation offers an opportunity to name the wrong, though not the wrong of torture itself; that much has been named, even if not enough has been done to disclaim it, to punish it, to restore those who were its victims, and to ensure that the United States does not embrace it again. The wrong that has *not* been named is the wrong that was done to every person who was invited to carry out torture in the name of the country, and to every person who accepted the invitation and emerged from it broken.

CHALLENGES

To be sure, the prospects for reconciliation for the military face formidable challenges, including, as I address in other work, the foundational reluctance in American law, politics, and culture to see the soldier as separate from the state, and to see the soldier as an individual, rather than as a resource to be used however the state pleases.[60] Beyond this, to orient the relationship between soldier and state as one appropriate for the framework of reconciliation runs into the further challenge that, for all its forms, reconciliation is typically imagined to involve an interaction between two sides—victim and perpetrator, citizenry and regime—whether conceived as individuals or as collectives.[61]

Casting service members in the role of victim runs into the roadblock of the insistence on innocence in victims, victims free of the taint of perpetration or complicity in wrongdoing.[62] As Mark Drumbl writes, "victims are to be pure and ideal; perpetrators are to be unadulterated and ugly."[63] Moreover, as Ross McGarry and Sandra Walklate explore, "the social and cultural expectations traditionally associated with soldiering do not lend themselves easily to the connotations of victimisation that imply vulnerability, weakness and passivity."[64] A soldier is a model of a "'non-victim' endowed with the capacity for the use of brute force and resilience."[65]

Lu of course acknowledges the limits of reconciliation; the concern here is not with her model, but rather with the dominant frames for understanding not only reconciliation, but also victimhood and the military.[66] And in applying Lu's framework, we should be wary of a concept of reconciliation that neglects the nature of alienation "as critique of a social condition, in which subjects either have lost or are denied their standing as morally autonomous agents . . . , or have lost or are deprived of their appropriate agency to participate meaningfully in the meaning of the social order."[67] The point is not to imagine reconciliation as a way forward in one's fanciful vision of what would have happened if Donald Rumsfeld had sought redemption for telling interrogators to "take the gloves off" or refusing to restrain those under his authority from using abusive interrogation techniques.[68] But reconciliation, freed of the constraints imposed by its traditional expectations of victim and perpetrator, can offer a way forward in members of the armed services from the prevailing understanding of them as mere instruments of the state, an opportunity to assert their humanity in productive ways. In scholarship and case law there are glimmers of recognition that soldiers are human, too: recognition of human rights claims for negligent failures to properly equip soldiers in combat;[69] requirements of states to protect wounded soldiers;[70] proposals that states are right to prioritize the lives of their soldiers above the lives of others.[71] To grant the soldier the privilege of reconciliation is not only to acknowledge the wrong of alienation and of its roots, but to acknowledge that the soldier is a category of person who can be wronged and should not be, who can be exploited and should not be, who can be and must be recognized as separate from the state.[72]

A final concern might be the risk that acknowledging these betrayals may exacerbate divisions and threaten the delicate system of discipline and obedience on which the American military relies. This is indeed a risk, as is any widening of the acknowledgment of service members' humanity and autonomy. But betrayal and moral injury are themselves risks to military discipline. Service members have deserted because they lost trust in their superiors— and themselves—after being ordered to engage in torture, and they have chosen to leave behind their military careers because of these betrayals.[73] For those who stay, the disaffection that comes from moral injury undermines the capacity of many to believe in the legitimacy of the chain of command. The loss of social trust endured by those experiencing moral injury is itself a risk to military discipline, which is properly built not on blind obedience but on deserved loyalty.

CONCLUSION

A truth and reconciliation commission for the Trump era may not be forthcoming anytime soon. But acknowledgment of the wrongs perpetrated by leaders against the military is nonetheless crucial, whether it comes from leaders or from someone else. That is, although perpetrators "are in the most significant position" to "retract[] . . . messages of insult," third parties, too, can contribute to the political work of reconciliation.[74] A recognition by journalists, by political commentators, by the citizenry, that the president not only "politicized" the military, but also exploited its members, when he trotted them out to harass peaceful protesters, is a start. An acknowledgment that the mental health crisis engulfing veterans is in part attributable to leaders who have long betrayed them is a start. The outcome might be not only a country more attuned to the many dimensions of a leader's abuse of authority, but also a country more willing to see soldiers as people. That may be, moreover, a country perhaps less willing to go to war, perhaps less willing to ignore the impact of war on service members. In that regard, alienation might be seen as ultimately productive, a status that can generate acknowledgment of a wrong and trigger movement toward overcoming it, for it transforms what might otherwise be individual feelings of disorientation, hopelessness, and anguish—individual feelings that are understood to merit only isolated treatment—into a political status that demands fresh thinking about the nature of authority and exploitation.

NOTES

1 See, e.g., Jill Lepore, "Let History, Not Partisans, Prosecute Trump," *Washington Post*, Oct. 18, 2020, www.washingtonpost.com (describing the "litany" of Trump administration "wrongdoing," including "corruption, fomenting insurrection, separating parents and children at the border, and violently suppressing political dissent").

2 See, e.g., Masha Gessen, "Why America Needs a Reckoning with the Trump Era," *New Yorker*, Nov. 10, 2020, www.newyorker.com; Jeremy Adam Smith, "Can We Recover from the Trauma of the Trump Years?," *Greater Good Magazine* (Feb. 9, 2021), https://greatergood.berkeley.edu.

3 For a notable exception, see Gessen, "Why America Needs a Reckoning" (including " seeing American troops used against protesters" in a list of traumas of the prior four years).

4 See Jeffrey Goldberg, "Trump: Americans Who Died in War Are 'Losers' and 'Suckers,'" *The Atlantic*, Sept. 3, 2020, www.theatlantic.com.

5 See Omar G. Encarnación, "Truth After Trump: The Case for a Truth Commission in the United States," *Foreign Policy*, Nov. 30, 2020, https://foreignpolicy.com (discussing child separation, as well as "compelling" cases for charges of "perjury [for offering false testimony to the special counsel investigating Russian interference in the 2016 general elections]; public corruption [for using the presidency to enrich himself]; and obstruction of justice [for firing FBI Director James Comey]").

6 See Carly Parnitzke Smith and Jennifer J. Freyd, "Dangerous Safe Havens: Institutional Betrayal Exacerbates Sexual Trauma," *Journal of Traumatic Stress* 26 (February 2013): 119–124, https://doi.org/10.1002/jts.21778; Carly Parnitzke Smith and Jennifer J. Freyd, "Institutional Betrayal," *American Psychologist* 69, no. 6 (2014): 575, 578, https://doi.org/10.1037/a0037564.

7 Lu, "Reconciliation as Non-Alienation."

8 Lu, "Reconciliation as Non-Alienation."

9 Lu, "Reconciliation as Non-Alienation."

10 See Samuel Huntington, *The Soldier and the State: The Theory and Politics of Civil-Military Relations* (Cambridge, MA: Belknap Press, 1957);

Richard H. Kohn, "Tarnished Brass: Is the U.S. Military Profession in Decline?," *World Affairs* 171, no. 4 (Spring 2009): 77.

11 Huntington, *Soldier and the State*, 13, 83. "Objective control" is to be distinguished from "subjective control," which "achieves its end by civilianizing the military, making them the mirror of the state." Huntington, *Soldier and the State*, 83.

12 Huntington, *Soldier and the State*, 83.

13 Risa Brooks, "Paradoxes of Professionalism: Rethinking Civil-Military Relations in the United States," *International Security* 44, no. 4 (Spring 2020): 18, https://doi.org/10.1162/isec_a_00374 (citing Jim Golby, Lindsay P. Cohn, and Peter D. Feaver, "Thanks for Your Service: Civilian and Veteran Attitudes After Fifteen Years of War," in *Warriors and Citizens: American Views of Our Military*, ed. Kori Schake and Jim Mattis [Stanford, CA: Hoover Institution Press, 2016], 123).

14 Brooks, "Paradoxes of Professionalism," 18.

15 Brooks, "Paradoxes of Professionalism," 22 (citing Heidi A. Urben, *Like, Comment, Retweet: The State of the Military's Nonpartisan Ethic in the World of Social Media* [Washington, DC: National Defense University Press, 2017], 24).

16 Brooks, "Paradoxes of Professionalism," 23 (citing Urben, *Like, Comment, Retweet*, 35).

17 Brooks, "Paradoxes of Professionalism," 34.

18 Jim Golby and Mara Karlin, "The Case for Rethinking the Politicization of the Military," *Brookings*, June 12, 2020, www.brookings.edu; see also Andrew J. Bacevich, "Discord Still: Clinton and the Military," *Washington Post*, Jan. 3, 1999, www.washingtonpost.com ("The dirty little secret of American civil-military relations," he writes, is "that the commander in chief does not command the military establishment; he cajoles it, negotiates with it, and, as necessary, appeases it").

19 William E. Rapp, "Civil-Military Relations: The Role of Military Leaders in Strategy Making," *Parameters* 45, no. 3 (Autumn 2015): 1, https://press.armywarcollege.edu, quoted in Brooks, "Paradoxes of Professionalism," 9; see also Rebecca L. Schiff, *The Military and Domestic Politics: A Concordance Theory of Civil-Military Relations* (New York: Routledge, 2009), 36 (noting "[s]cholars' unwavering allegiance to Huntington" and commenting that "[o]ne real problem . . . is that no one wants to challenge Huntington's separation theory"); Gary J. Bass, "Should We Worry About Trump's Fawning Admiration of the Military?," *New York Times*, June 29, 2018, www.nytimes.com (calling *The Soldier and the State* "by far the most influential book on the subject" of civil-military relations and claiming it is "seen as essential even by its critics").

20 Bass, "Trump's Fawning Admiration of the Military."

21 See Robert M. Gates, "Air Force Academy Commencement" (Air Force Academy, CO, May 30, 2007), 2007 WLNR 26628010; Robert M. Gates, "United States Naval Academy Commencement" (Annapolis, MD, May 25, 2007), 2007 WLNR 26628000; see also Robert M. Gates, "Evening Lecture at the U.S. Military Academy (West Point, N.Y.)" (West Point, NY, April 21, 2008), 2008 WLNR 25536834.

22 Caitlin O'Kane, "Marine Veteran Stands Outside in the Heat for Hours with the Words 'I Can't Breathe' Taped Over His Mouth," *CBSNews*, June 8, 2020, www.cbsnews.com.

23 See Tom Malinowski (@Malinowski), "America.," Twitter, June 6, 2020, 9:54 a.m., https://twitter.com/Malinowski/status/1269311653524516867; see also Golby and Karlin, "Case for Rethinking" (discussing Malinowski's tweet and varied reactions, including those who "assert[ed] that he was standing up for human dignity" and those who "roundly criticized him for violating the military's 'apolitical' norm by protesting in the garb of the institution he ostensibly represents").

24 Bass, "Trump's Fawning Admiration of the Military"; see Jim Golby, "Uncivil-Military Relations: Politicization of the Military in the Trump Era," *Strategic Studies Quarterly* 15, no. 2 (Summer 2021): 168, www.airuniversity.af.edu (finding, in study of 1981 to 2020, that Trump's politicization of the military was "unique").

25 "The Strength of America's Apolitical Military," *Just Security* (blog), June 5, 2020, justsecurity.org/70608/the-strength-of-americas-apolitical-military/.

26 Thomas Gibbons-Neff et al., "Former Commanders Fault Trump's Use of Troops Against Protesters," *New York Times*, June 2, 2020, www.nytimes.com (quoting Defense Secretary Mark T. Esper's statement about protests that "[w]e need to dominate the battle space").

27 "Strength of America's Apolitical Military."

28 Dan Lamothe, "Pentagon's Top General Apologizes for Appearing Alongside Trump in Lafayette Square," *Washington Post*, June 11, 2020, www.washingtonpost.com.

29 See, for example, Greg Rienzi, "Veering Toward a Civilian-Military Crisis," *Hub*, June 30, 2020, https://hub.jhu.edu (discussing expert views during panel on Lafayette Square at the School of Advanced International Studies at Johns Hopkins University); Robert Kagan, "The Battle of Lafayette Square and the Undermining of American Democracy," *Washington Post*, June 3, 2020, www.washingtonpost.com.

30 Daniel Lippman, "'What I Saw Was Just Absolutely Wrong': National Guardsmen Struggle with Their Role in Controlling Protests," *Politico*, June 9, 2020, www.politico.com.

31 See Nancy Sherman, *The Untold War: Inside the Hearts, Minds, and Souls of Our Soldiers* (New York: W.W. Norton, 2010), 41 (describing, based on interviews with soldiers, the uniform sentiment that when "willingness to serve [is] exploited for a cause that is unworthy or for a war grounded in unjustified fear or waged for a pretext," "the betrayal felt is profound," "a rupture of the deepest kind of trust and care").

32 See Laura Blumenfeld, "The Tortured Lives of Interrogators," *Washington Post*, June 4, 2007, www.washingtonpost.com; Lydia DePillis, "This Is What It Feels Like to Torture," *Washington Post*. Dec. 11, 2014, www.washingtonpost.com.

33 Ashley Gilbertson, "The Life and Lonely Death of Noah Pierce," *Virginia Quarterly Review*, Fall 2008, www.vqronline.org (quoting Jonathan Shay).

34 See Saira Mohamed, "Abuse by Authority: The Hidden Harm of Illegal Orders," *Iowa Law Review* 107, no. 5 (2022): 2230–2237.

35 Jonathan Shay, "Moral Injury," *Psychoanalytic Psychology* 31, no. 2 (2014): 183, https://psycnet.apa.org/doi/10.1037/a0036090. Shay's definition of moral injury is different from that of other clinician-researchers who study moral injury arising out of a betrayal of one's own self. See Brett T. Litz et al., "Moral Injury and Moral Repair in War Veterans: A Preliminary Model and Intervention Strategy," *Clinical Psychology Review* 29, no. 8 (December 2009): 695–706, https://doi.org/10.1016/j.cpr.2009.07.003; see also Shay, "Moral Injury," *Psychoanalytic Psychology*, 184 (distinguishing his model from that of Litz and co-authors).

36 See Jonathan Shay, "Moral Injury," *Intertexts* 16, no. 1 (Spring 2012): 58, https://doi.org/10.1353/itx.2012.0000; Shay, "Moral Injury," *Psychoanalytic Psychology*, 184; Shira Maguen and Brett Litz, "Moral Injury in Veterans of War," *PTSD Research Quarterly* 23, no. 1 (2012): 1, www.vva1071.org; see also Craig J. Bryan et al., "Moral Injury, Posttraumatic Stress Disorder, and Suicidal Behavior Among National Guard Personnel," *Psychological Trauma: Theory, Research, Practice, and Policy* 10, no. 1 (2018): 36–45, https://doi.apa.org/doi/10.1037/tra0000290 (studying differences between PTSD and moral injury).

37 Jonathan Shay, *Achilles in Vietnam: Combat Trauma and the Undoing of Character* (New York: Scribner, 1994), 23–38; see Shay, "Moral Injury," *Intertexts*, 60 (noting that "[w]e have been carefully taught a belief about stable good character in adulthood" and that "[t]he trouble with this lovely idea is that it's not true").

38 Nancy Sherman, *Afterwar: Healing the Moral Sounds of Our Soldiers* (Oxford: Oxford University Press, 2015), 8; see also Maguen and Litz, "Moral Injury in Veterans of War," 1.

39 Jonathan Shay, "Casualties," in *The Modern American Military* ed. David M. Kennedy (Oxford: Oxford University Press, 2013), 302–303.

40 Shay, "Moral Injury," *Psychoanalytic Psychology*, 183.

41 Jonathan Shay, *Odysseus in America: Combat Trauma and the Trials of Homecoming* (New York: Scribner, 2002), 151.

42 James L. Gibson, "Overcoming Apartheid: Can Truth Reconcile a Divided Nation?," *Politikon: South African Journal of Political Studies* 31, no. 2 (2004): 132, https://doi.org/10.1177%2F0002716205282895; see also, e.g., Harvey M. Weinstein, "Editorial Note: The Myth of Closure, The Illusion of Reconciliation: Final Thoughts on Five Years as Co-Editor-in-Chief," *International Journal of Transitional Justice* 5, no. 1 (March 2011): 5, https://doi.org/10.1093/ijtj/ijr002 ("[T]the problem lies in the multiple meanings of an imprecise term. Virtually every academic paper on the subject begins with this problem of imprecision and definition.").

43 Lu, "Reconciliation as Non-Alienation," quoting Rahel Jaeggi, *Alienation*, trans. Frederick Neuhouser and Alan E. Smith, ed. Frederick Neuhouser (New York: Columbia University Press, 2014), 220.

44 Lu, "Reconciliation as Non-Alienation."

45 Lu, "Reconciliation as Non-Alienation."

46 Lu, "Reconciliation as Non-Alienation."

47 See, e.g., Rita Nakashima Brock and Gabriella Lettini, *Soul Repair: Recovering from Moral Injury After War* (Boston: Beacon Press, 2015).

48 Nancy Sherman's work is a notable contribution outside of these fields. See Sherman, *Afterwar*.

49 Catherine Lu, *Justice and Reconciliation in World Politics* (Cambridge: Cambridge University Press, 2018), 186.

50 Lu, *Justice and Reconciliation*, 186.

51 Lu, *Justice and Reconciliation*, 186.

52 The political project of reconciliation opens space for critiques such as those of Robert Emmet Meagher, who argues that the existence of moral injury demands that we question the legitimacy of just-war theory. See Robert Emmet Meagher, *Killing from the Inside Out: Moral Injury and Just War* (Eugene, OR: Cascade Books, 2014).

53 See Shay, *Odysseus in America*, 151 (defining "social trust" as "the expectation that power will be used in accordance with 'what's right'" and explaining that "[w]hen social trust is destroyed, it is not replaced by a vacuum, but rather by a perpetual mobilization to fend off attack, humiliation, or exploitation, and to figure out other people's trickery"); see also Thomas E. Ricks, "Modern Soldiers from Ancient Texts," *Washington Post*, Sept. 17, 2004, www.washingtonpost.com/ (discussing Shay's vision of "cohesion" and "mutual trust").

54 See, for example, Eric Fair, *Consequence: A Memoir* (New York: Henry Holt, 2016); Joshua E. S. Phillips, *None of Us Were Like That Before: American Soldiers and Torture* (London: Verso, 2012); Justine Sharrock, *Tortured: When Good Soldiers Do Bad Things* (Hoboken, NJ: John Wiley and Sons, 2010); Blumenfeld, "Tortured Lives of Interrogators."

55 See Human Rights Watch, *Getting Away with Torture* (2011), hrw.org/report/2011/07/12; Philippe Sands, *Torture Team: Rumsfeld's Memo and the Betrayal of American Values* (New York: Palgrave Macmillan, 2008), 205–208.

56 See Peter Rowe, "Military Misconduct During International Armed Operations: 'Bad Apples' or Systemic Failure?," *Journal of Conflict and Security Law* 13, no. 2 (Summer 2008): 165, https://doi.org/10.1093/jcsl/krn024; Toy-Fung Tung, "Just War Claims: Historical Theory, Abu Ghraib, and Transgressive Rhetoric," in *International Criminal Justice: Critical Perspectives and New Challenges*, ed. George Andreopoulos, Rosemary Barberet, and James P. Levine (New York: Springer, 2011), 53.

57 David Johnson and Charlie Savage, "Obama Reluctant to Look into Bush Programs," *New York Times*, Jan. 11, 2009, www.nytimes.com.

58 Lara Jakes and Michael Crowley, "U.S. to Penalize War Crimes Investigators Looking into American Troops," *New York Times*, June 11, 2020, www.nytimes.com.

59 Pranshu Verma and Marlise Simons, "Reversing Trump, Biden Repeals Sanctions on Human Rights Prosecutor," *New York Times*, April 2, 2021, www.nytimes.com.

60 See Saira Mohamed, "Cannon Fodder, or a Soldier's Right to Life," *Southern California Law Review* 95, no. 5 (forthcoming 2022): 27–32 (manuscript on file with author).

61 See, e.g., Johan Galtung, "After Violence, Reconciliation, and Resolution: Coping with Visible and Invisible Effects of War and Violence," in *Reconciliation, Justice, and Coexistence: Theory and Practice*, ed. Mohammed Abu-Nimer (Lanham, MD: Lexington Books, 2001), 3 (describing reconciliation as "the process of healing the traumas of both victims and perpetrators after the violence, providing a closure of the bad relation"); Jens Meierhenrich, "Varieties of Reconciliation," *Law and Social Inquiry* 33, no. 1 (Winter 2008): 207, https://doi.org/10.1111/j.1747-4469.2008.00098.x (discussing the "intersubjective" nature of reconciliation, which necessarily involves "action . . . from perpetrators *as well as* victims," "wrongdoers *as well as* those wo have been wronged"). Indeed, the South African Truth and Reconciliation Commission (TRC)—often considered the gold standard for reconciliation processes—required participants to decide prior to their testimony whether to register as victims, in which case they would give testimony to the Human Rights Violations Committee, or as perpetrators, in which case they would testify to the Amnesty Committee.

See Claire Moon, *Narrating Political Reconciliation: South Africa's Truth and Reconciliation Commission* (Lanham, MD: Lexington Books, 2009), 58 (describing these arrangements and noting that "[t]his fundamental division in the mechanisms of the Commission structured the identities of those submitting to its authority prior to public hearings which further reinforced, perpetuated and legitimized these already established identities as the central protagonists of South Africa's new historical account"). One of the significant critiques of reconciliation, in turn, is that it improperly divides the world into these narrow categories. Some of these critiques take the position that categories beyond victim and perpetrator merit recognition. Mahmood Mamdani argued at the time of the South African TRC that it should have addressed the responsibility of not only perpetrators of crimes within the apartheid system, but also beneficiaries of that system. Mahmood Mamdani, "Reconciliation without Justice," *Southern African Review of Books* (November/December 1996): 3–5. Others, meanwhile, challenge the content of those categories and their implications for social repair. For example, Robert Meister challenges the very distinction within post–Cold War discourse between perpetrators and "beneficiaries . . . who received material and social advantage from the old regime." Robert Meister, *After Evil: A Politics of Human Rights* (New York: Columbia University Press, 2011), 26. Laurel Fletcher and Harvey Weinstein draw attention to the failure of trials to address the responsibility of those bystanders who are seen as having done "nothing," and the consequent limitations of trials to contribute to reconciliation. Laurel E. Fletcher and Harvey M. Weinstein, "Violence and Social Repair, Rethinking the Contribution of Justice to Reconciliation," *Human Rights Quarterly* 24, no. 3 (August 2002): 573–639, https://doi.org/10.1353/hrq.2002.0033.

62 See Christine Schwöbel-Patel, "The 'Ideal' Victim of International Criminal Law," *European Journal of International Law* 29, no. 3 (August 2018): 709–718, https://doi.org/10.1093/ejil/chy056; Trudy Govier, *Victims and Victimhood* (Peterborough, ON: Broadview Press, 2015): 23 ("One must not deserve the harm imposed by the damaging act itself, even though one might have acted so as to create the context in which the act occurred").

63 Mark A. Drumbl, "Victims Who Victimize," *London Review of International Law* 4, no. 2 (2016): 218–219, https://doi.org/10.1093/lril/lrw015.

64 Ross McGarry and Sandra Walklate, "The Soldier as Victim: Peering Through the Looking Glass," *British Journal of Criminology* 51, no. 6 (November 2011): 904, https://doi.org/10.1093/bjc/azr057.

65 McGarry and Walklate, "Soldier as Victim," 904.

66 See Lu, *Justice and Reconciliation*, 63–87.

67 Lu, "Reconciliation as Non-Alienation."

68 See Richard A. Serrano, "Prison Interrogators' Gloves Came Off Before Abu Ghraib," *Los Angeles Times,* June 9, 2004, www.latimes.com; Albert T. Church, III, "Executive Summary," in *Review of Department of Defense Interrogation Operations and Detainee Interrogation Techniques* (March 11, 2005), 5–7, 10, https://web.archive.org. Cf. Timothy Bewes, "Alienation," in *The Bloomsbury Companion to Marx,* ed. Imre Szeman and Jeff Diamanti (London: Bloomsbury Academic, 2019), 263 ("Holding back from defining what one means by a 'complete,' 'successful' or 'undistorted' relation to the self, however, or the content of the 'good life,' far from avoiding the risks of essentialism, opens up such terms to the imperialist or theological conceptions or anyone who might lay claim to them. Do western military leaders feel less than 'complete' when they order drone strikes in Yemen or Afghanistan?").

69 See *Smith v. Ministry of Defence,* [2013] UKSC 41, ¶¶ 13–15.

70 See, e.g., Geneva Convention for the Amelioration of the Condition of the Wounded and Sick in Armed Forces in the Field, art. 12, Aug. 12, 1949, 6 U.S.T. 3114.

71 See, e.g., Asa Kasher and Amos Yadlin, "Assassination and Preventive Killing," *SAIS Review of International Affairs* 25, no. 1 (Winter–Spring 2005): 50, https://doi.org/10.1353/sais.2005.0011.

72 On acknowledgment as a feature of reconciliation, see Trudy Govier, "What Is Acknowledgement and Why Is It Important?," in *Dilemmas of Reconciliation,* ed. Carol A. L. Prager and Trudy Govier (Waterloo, ON: Wilfrid Laurier University Press, 2003), 71 (describing acknowledgment as "a kind of *avowal* that amounts to a spelling out or marking of what we know"); Margaret Urban Walker, *Moral Repair: Reconstructing Moral Relations After Wrongdoing* (New York: Cambridge University Press, 2006); Lawrence Weschler, *A Miracle, A Universe: Settling Accounts with Torturers* (Chicago: University of Chicago Press, 1998), 4.

73 Camilo Mejía, *Road from Ar Ramadi: The Private Rebellion of Staff Sergeant Camilo Mejía* (New York: New Press, 2008): 44–55.

74 Trudy Govier, "A Dialectic of Acknowledgment," in *Reconciliation(s): Transitional Justice in Postconflict Societies,* ed. Joanna R. Quinn (Montreal: McGill-Queen's University Press, 2009), 48.

3

SOURCES OF SHAME, IMAGES OF HOME

RYAN PRESTON-ROEDDER

In "Reconciliation as Non-Alienation: The Politics of Being at Home in the World," Catherine Lu aims, we might say, to rescue the concept and practice of reconciliation. Reconciliation is central to many people's understanding of how we should respond to political catastrophes and to grave structural injustice. From the Truth and Reconciliation Commission assembled in South Africa after the apartheid system of racial segregation was overturned, to the Commission assembled in Canada to examine wrongs committed in the Indian residential school system, to the campaigns for reconciliation and national healing in the United States in the aftermath of the police killing of George Floyd, calls for reconciliation have accompanied calls for justice.[1] Nevertheless, theorists have raised trenchant criticisms of reconciliation, arguing that reconciliation is incompatible with the demands of justice, or that it imposes excessive burdens on those who are victimized or oppressed. Lu aims to develop a novel conception of reconciliation that avoids these criticisms and accounts for reconciliation's distinctive significance. Put briefly, she claims that reconciliation aims to address agents' alienation from the unjust social institutions and practices that structure their lives; it aims, in other words, to enable these agents to *be at home* in their social worlds.

In these comments, I will present two kinds of challenges that Lu's account faces. Both challenges have their source in forms of shame and fear that are apt to discourage socially privileged agents from participating in the process of reconciliation that Lu describes. To be clear, I present these challenges in a constructive spirit. The idea of being at home in one's social world, which

64

Lu develops in her chapter, is undoubtedly important, and Lu's application of this idea to questions concerning the nature and significance of reconciliation is highly illuminating. My hope is that thinking through responses to the challenges that I discuss will deepen our understanding of the grounds for engaging in reconciliation at all, the relation between our ideals of reconciliation and our ideals of justice, and the burdens that may be associated with the pursuit of these ideals.

RESCUING RECONCILIATION

Lu's project of rescuing reconciliation has both critical and constructive dimensions. The first, critical dimension, which Lu develops in detail in her book *Justice and Reconciliation in World Politics*,[2] involves identifying what has been "deficient in contemporary ideas, discourses, and practices of reconciliation."[3] On the one hand, Lu argues that some conceptions of reconciliation may be rightly criticized because they demand too little of the prevailing social order. More precisely, these conceptions fail to call for the punishment of wrongdoers, the compensation of victims, or—crucially—the "structural transformation" of unjust societies.[4] For example, consider a society that is working through the aftermath of its legal enforcement of racial segregation, and suppose that this society creates a truth and reconciliation commission to facilitate the transition to a more just and stable regime. If the commission focuses on acknowledging past wrongs and "closing the books" on past injustice, but it neglects the task of overturning "oppressive and dominating practices, conditions, and relations in contemporary social structures," then it employs a conception of reconciliation that demands too little of the unjust society in which it operates.

On the other hand, some conceptions of reconciliation demand too *much*, whether morally or psychologically, from victims of injustice; in particular, they call on victims to sacrifice their "individual rights, needs, and interests" in order to serve the aims of reconciliation.[5] Such conceptions may make these excessive demands because they focus, inappropriately, on achieving "a kind of social unity" that leaves too little room for "disagreement and dissent," or because they focus, inappropriately, on achieving some apolitical, medicalized form of "individual psychological healing" from the "traumatic experiences" associated with political catastrophes.[6] For example, a process of reconciliation that calls on the survivors of genocide to forgive the perpetrators for the sake of some rarefied ideal of social unity may be criticized on these grounds. A survivor of Rwandan genocide, whom Lu quotes in her discussion, criticizes such a conception when he states that "I don't understand this word 'reconciliation' . . . If a person comes to ask for my forgiveness, I will pardon him after he has resuscitated the members of my family that he killed."[7]

In light of these criticisms, we might ask why we should care about reconciliation at all. In Lu's words, "what value does reconciliation have that is distinct from justice? Especially in cases of clear wrongdoing, why not just focus on justice instead?"[8] These important questions, to which I will return later on, frame Lu's discussion in "Reconciliation as Non-Alienation," and they bring us to the second, constructive dimension of her project. Lu points out that there is nothing essential to the concept of reconciliation "that renders it inevitably regressive, rather than emancipatory."[9] Furthermore, many people in societies throughout the world already understand their moral and political obligations to the victims of injustice in terms of reconciliation. So, she argues, we have good reason to "provide an alternative, more normatively and politically cogent reconstruction of reconciliation"; we have reason, that is, to rescue the concept of reconciliation, rather than abandon it.[10]

Lu proceeds by distinguishing justice from reconciliation and then developing her novel and illuminating account of the latter. Put roughly, while promoting justice in the wake of political catastrophe involves rectifying certain kinds of agential and structural *in*justice, reconciliation involves "responding to various kinds of alienation" that are revealed or produced by such injustice.[11] Drawing on the work of Rahel Jaeggie, Lu describes alienation as a kind of disruption of our capacity to identify with the lives we lead—a disruption of our capacity to express ourselves, and to see ourselves reflected, in what we do. Lu is fundamentally concerned with what she calls "structural alienation," a kind of "estrangement from the social/political order" that arises when unjust institutions and practices "define in objectionable ways" the social identities and roles that we can inhabit, the forms of agency that are available to us, and the aspirations that we might pursue.[12] Such alienation undermines our capacity to flourish and to participate in our society in meaningful ways. On Lu's view, reconciliation is a process that aims primarily to fashion new or altered institutions and practices, and thereby remedy agents' structural alienation from their social and political order.

As it is commonly understood and valued, reconciliation involves repairing damaged relationships among agents or social groups that were previously at odds. Lu's account preserves this vital feature by stating that reconciliation proceeds by way of a "reparatory dialogue between the contemporary inheritors of an unjust past."[13] More precisely, the politics of reconciliation involves a kind of open-ended debate between victims and perpetrators of political catastrophe, or between those who are marginalized and those who are privileged by unjust social and political institutions and practices. Participants in this debate offer, from the standpoint of whatever social position they occupy, narratives and images of their society, including representations of the society's history, its professed ideals and the success or failure of its efforts to realize those ideals, the identities and roles that are available in the society, and so on. To use one of Lu's central metaphors, these participants offer different, and sometimes wildly discordant, conceptions of their society as a kind of *home*—a setting that grounds the "meaning, coherence, and stability" of their social lives and supplies much of the background in light of which they develop and pursue their aspirations. As they confront and respond to one another's representations of home, "agents who participate in the project of reconciliation embark on remaking and potentially transforming" their social world in a manner that remedies their alienation from that world.[14]

Although participating in this sort of reparatory dialogue can bring the promise of a new and better social world, it can also involve a considerable cost, namely, the loss of one's identity. As Lu points out, engaging in a struggle over narratives and images of one's social and political home can involve confronting profoundly unsettling representations of that home, and of one's place in it. In particular, when agents who occupy privileged social positions, and who assume that their society's grave injustices are confined to the remote past, engage in such a struggle, they must confront the searing narratives and images of their social world—and of *themselves*—that issue from their marginalized counterparts.

Consider, for example, James Baldwin's discussion, in *The Fire Next Time*, of White Americans' aversion to clear-eyed narratives of their country's subjugation of Black people. Baldwin notes that many White Americans associate their racial identity with "hard work and good clean fun and chastity and piety and success," and they maintain this image of themselves by "brainwash[ing]" themselves into believing that their Black compatriots, who are "treated like animals," are essentially inferior, and therefore "*deserve* to be treated like animals."[15] To engage seriously in any form of racial reconciliation, these White Americans would have to begin by recognizing Black people's humanity and looking honestly at Black Americans' subjection to lynching and mob violence, at their subjection to police brutality and unjust incarceration, and at their systematic exclusion from opportunities to gain decent housing, health care, education, and employment. To these White Americans, this initial step would feel like waking up one morning "to find the sun shining and all the stars aflame"; it would be "terrifying because it so profoundly attacks one's sense of one's own reality."[16] More generally, the sort of struggle over narratives and images of home that is, on Lu's view, central to the process of reconciliation poses a grave threat to privileged agents' understanding of themselves and their social world, and so engaging in this sort of struggle is apt to arouse such agents' shame and fear. I now want to discuss two kinds of challenges that Lu's account faces in virtue of this threat.

TRANSFORMATION WITHOUT RECONCILIATION?

The first challenge concerns the grounds for engaging in the process of reconciliation at all, given Lu's characterization of that process. On her view, reconciliation aims to enable agents who are alienated from their social and political order to develop suitable narratives and images of their social world and to draw on these representations of home in order to lead lives with which they can identify. And—crucially—this process proceeds by way of a reparatory dialogue between agents who are marginalized within the unjust order and agents who occupy more privileged social

positions. But, in light of privileged agents' aversion to such dialogue, there may be a broad range of cases in which marginalized
agents would be best able to develop and employ suitable narratives
and images if they abandoned or limited the attempt to communicate with their privileged counterparts and focused instead on
generative dialogue with one another. In such cases, we might ask
why any of us, especially those who are marginalized, should care
about reconciliation as Lu understands it.

To clarify the kinds of cases that I have in mind, I will consider some historical examples of Black American communities
that developed narratives and images of home, employed these
representations in ways that mitigated—in limited but important
respects—their alienation from their social world, and did so
without engaging in the relevant sort of struggle with more privileged communities. In his essay collection *Shadow and Act*, Ralph
Ellison notes that he and other Black boys in the community in
which he grew up, namely, Oklahoma City during the early 1900s,
drew on music and literature to fashion new identities and aspirations.[17] Spurred on by their "voracious reading," their exposure
to the "exuberantly creative" improvisation of southwestern jazz
musicians, and their observation of local Black preachers, bootleg-
gers, businesspeople and so on, Ellison and his childhood friends
improvised "patterns to live by."[18] Indeed, they developed conceptions of their own possibilities that "went against the barbs and over
the palings of almost every fence which those who controlled the
social and political power had erected to restrict our roles in the
life of the country."[19] This sort of improvisation enabled Ellison and
his companions to "humanize" their social circumstances and—
crucially—to "evoke a feeling of being at home in the world."[20]

To take a different, and normatively more fraught, example, the
Nation of Islam—a Black nationalist organization founded in the
United States—developed an elaborate set of religious myths and
symbols; and during the 1950s and '60s, many Black Americans
appealed to these myths and symbols in order to craft and adopt
new social identities, roles, and aspirations.[21] Put briefly, the Nation
taught that Black Americans, who had been cut off from knowledge
of their lofty history, were experiencing a kind of "hell" on earth,
and White people, who occupied positions of social and political
power, functioned as a kind of "devil" in that hell.[22] However, God,

who was Black, would soon end White people's reign and make Black Americans whole.[23] Many Black Americans embraced these myths and symbols and appealed to them to fashion new ways of living. Taking note of such transformations, Baldwin claims, in *The Fire Next Time*, that the Nation was

> able to do what generations of welfare workers and committees and resolutions and reports and housing projects and playgrounds have failed to do: to heal the drunkards and junkies, to convert people who have come out of prison and to keep them out, to make men chaste and women virtuous, and to invest both the male and the female with a pride and a serenity that hang about them like an unfailing light.[24]

More broadly, the Nation supplied interpretive resources that marginalized Black Americans used to transform their lives, and to create something new with which they could identify.

Finally, during the late 1960s and early '70s, the Black Panther Party produced visual art, introduced language, and embodied narratives and images that enabled its members to craft and adopt new identities and aspirations. Founded in Oakland, California—a city in which Black residents faced "residential segregation, poverty, unemployment, and police brutality"—the Panthers worked to promote Black Americans' liberation.[25] The Panthers exposed community members to transformative art and language through a newspaper that they published and distributed throughout the United States. In addition to presenting a program for Black liberation and reporting on progressive activism, the paper included visual art that depicted the beauty and humanity of ordinary Black people— everyone "from the Christian to the brother on the block"—and depicted resistance to oppression.[26] Furthermore, the paper supplied alternative representations of the police who terrorized Black communities, depicting these police as "pigs" who were to be ridiculed rather than feared.[27] Finally, by developing community programs that provided food, medical care, community defense, legal aid, and education, the Panthers embodied narratives and images of Black self-determination. Elaine Brown, who chaired the Party in the 1970s, explains in an interview that the aim of these programs was not merely to meet community members' material needs, but also "to influence the minds of people, to understand . . . that if they could get food, that maybe they would want clothing, and maybe they'd want housing, and maybe they'd want land, and maybe they would ultimately want some abstract thing called freedom."[28] As with Ellison and his friends' early improvisation and the Nation of Islam's ministry, reflecting on the Panthers' programs helps us understand how marginalized agents might develop transformative narratives and images of home, without engaging in the sort of struggle with more privileged agents that, on Lu's view, is central to reconciliation.

My discussion of these examples has an important caveat. Members of the marginalized Black communities that I described were able to generate transformative representations of home, but they were able to *use* these representations to reshape themselves and their social worlds only in limited respects and for limited periods. Indeed, all three of the communities that I described were debilitated by unjust actions and policies: Thriving Black communities in Oklahoma during the early twentieth century were subject to lynching, the violence of White mobs, and legally enforced racial segregation;[29] and members the Nation of Islam and the Black Panther Party were harassed, systemically misled, imprisoned, and even assassinated by American law enforcement agencies.[30] Members of these communities could not fully or stably realize the transformative potential of their representations of home because these injustices were not substantially remedied.

This caveat helps shape my formulation of this first challenge. On Lu's view, reconciliation—which aims to address agents' alienation from their social order, and which proceeds by way of debate between the oppressed and the privileged—is distinct from justice, which aims, in the wake of political catastrophe, to remedy agential and structural *in*justice. In the cases I am now considering, the most reliable way for marginalized agents to develop transformative representations of home may be to forgo or substantially limit interpretive struggles with their privileged counterparts and to focus instead on communicating with one another; but, in virtue of the injustice that these marginalized agents endure, their efforts to use such representations to reshape themselves and their societies may be thwarted. In such cases, we might ask—adapting a question that Lu uses to frame her own discussion—why we should care about the process of reconciliation that Lu describes. Why not (1) call on these marginalized agents to develop transformative representations of home primarily by engaging in dialogue with one another, and (2) call on all decent members of the society to pursue *justice* by whatever means are available?

Lu supplies an initial response to this question when she points out that engaging in the process of reconciliation that she describes can be a means of promoting justice. More precisely, achieving reconciliation can "provide or strengthen the motivational bases for agents to do justice, or redress injustice, at all," and it can help determine "how they pursue justice, or how they conceive of justice."[31] But this response invites further questions. First, to what extent and under what conditions do marginalized agents' interpretive struggles with their privileged counterparts promote justice in the kinds of cases I am now discussing? Second, is the value of this process of reconciliation purely instrumental in these cases? In other words, does this value simply fade away when reconciliation's usefulness for promoting justice has been exhausted?

Shame, Love, and the Burdens of Reconciliation

Suppose we provide a satisfactory response to the first challenge, which concerns the grounds for engaging in Lu's process of reconciliation at all. This leads us to a second challenge, which concerns the psychological burdens that marginalized agents may have to endure when they engage in this process; and this second challenge, like the first, is grounded in privileged agents' aversion to struggles over representations of home. Recall that Lu criticizes some conceptions of reconciliation on the grounds that they make excessive psychological demands on people who are victimized or oppressed. Such a conception might, for example, call on the survivors of genocide to forgive the perpetrators for the sake of achieving some form of social unity, or some form of individual psychic healing. As an alternative to these approaches, Lu develops an account on which reconciliation aims not at some highly demanding form of social unity or at individual agents' psychological transformation, but rather at addressing agents' alienation from the unjust institutions and practices that structure their lives. On this view, reconciliation proceeds by way of the kind of interpretive struggle that I have been discussing. The problem that I now want to consider is that, in virtue of privileged agents' aversion to such struggles, marginalized agents' successful participation in the process of reconciliation, as Lu describes it, may sometimes require the same kinds of psychological burdens that Lu wishes to avoid.

Baldwin's work offers an exceptionally clear characterization of the psychic forces that tend to render privileged agents unwilling to examine their society with clear eyes, and it offers an illuminating discussion of the burdens that marginalized agents must bear if they wish to subdue those forces and remedy their devastating effects. Consider Baldwin's early characterizations, which I discussed in the previous section, of the shame and fear that White Americans are apt to feel when they confront honest narratives of their society's treatment of Black people. Baldwin insists that it is possible for Americans to prevent White racism from undoing the country and to create a racially just community. But White Americans' shame and fear, which dispose them to avoid clear-eyed appraisals of their society's racial injustice, threaten to derail this transformation of American society. So, Baldwin claims, resisting and overcoming White racial domination involves coping somehow with this shame and fear. He argues that, in order to cope with these attitudes and curtail their devastating effects, Black Americans must take on a radical burden: They must exhibit a certain form of *love* for their White compatriots.

Baldwin describes this love in the opening section of *The Fire Next Time*, which takes the form of an open letter to his nephew. He writes that

> There is no reason for you to try to become like white people and there is no basis whatever for their impertinent assumption that *they* must accept *you*. The really terrible thing, old buddy, is that *you* must accept *them*. And I mean that very seriously. You must accept them and accept them with love. For these innocent people have no other hope. They are, in effect, trapped in a history which they do not understand; and until they understand it, they cannot be released from it.[32]

Later, he adds that those White Americans who deny "with brutal clarity" their Black compatriots' humanity "are your brothers—your lost younger brothers. And if the word *integration* means anything, this is what it means: that we, with love, shall force our brothers to see themselves as they are, to cease fleeing reality and begin to change it."[33]

Put all too briefly, Baldwin calls on Black Americans both to bear witness to the devastating impact of White racism *and* to accept White Americans as their brothers and sisters—as dangerously deluded members of a kind of American family. Regarding their White compatriots in this way can enable Black Americans to withhold hatred and contempt and to cling to a kind of faith in the possibility of creating a better world. And—crucially—when White Americans recognize that their Black compatriots view them with clear eyes, and nevertheless accept them as brothers and sisters, this may ease White Americans' psychic pressure to avoid honest appraisals of their society, and of their own positions within that society. It might enable them, in other words, to begin to face their social reality and, together with their Black compatriots, to work to change it.

Now return to Lu's account of reconciliation. In order to engage successfully, in the face of America's racial injustice, in the process of reconciliation that Lu describes—that is, in order to engage with White Americans in the kinds of interpretive struggles that I have discussed—Black Americans would have to cope with the very same manifestations of White shame and fear that Baldwin describes. If Baldwin is right that coping with this shame and fear would require Black Americans to love their White compatriots—that is, to regard them as brothers and sisters, to withhold hatred and contempt, and to hold onto faith in the possibility of creating a better social world with them—then, in this important instance, Lu's account of reconciliation also calls on marginalized agents to bear radical psychological burdens. Indeed, it calls on these agents to bear the kinds of psychological burdens that the account is designed to avoid.

To be clear, I am not claiming that Lu's account should be rejected on these grounds. I cannot discuss Baldwin's views in detail here, but I believe that his call for Black Americans to bear witness to the truth and exhibit love for their White compatriots in the course of pursuing racial justice can be justified, despite the associated burdens. It may be that a call for marginalized agents to exhibit such love for their privileged counterparts in the course of pursuing Lu's reconciliation can be justified as well. I will not try to settle that question here. Rather, my claim is that the distance between the conception of reconciliation that Lu develops and the conceptions that she criticizes and rejects because they demand too much from those who are victimized and oppressed may be much narrower than it initially appears.[34]

Notes

1 Lu discusses each of these examples in "Reconciliation as Non-Alienation," chapter 1 of this book.

2 Catherine Lu, *Justice and Reconciliation in World Politics* (Cambridge: Cambridge University Press, 2017).

3 Lu, "Reconciliation as Non-Alienation."

4 Lu, *Justice and Reconciliation*, p. 212.

5 Lu, *Justice and Reconciliation*, p. 186.

6 Lu, *Justice and Reconciliation*, p. 186.

7 Lu, *Justice and Reconciliation*, p. 186.

8 Lu, "Reconciliation as Non-Alienation."

9 Lu, "Reconciliation as Non-Alienation."

10 Lu, "Reconciliation as Non-Alienation."

11 Lu, "Reconciliation as Non-Alienation."

12 Lu, *Justice and Reconciliation*, p. 189.

13 Lu, *Justice and Reconciliation*, p. 193.

14 Lu, "Reconciliation as Non-Alienation."

15 James Baldwin, "A Talk to Teachers," in *James Baldwin: Collected Essays*, ed. Toni Morrison (New York: Literary Classics of the United States, 1998), 681.

16 James Baldwin, *The Fire Next Time*, in *James Baldwin: Collected Essays*, ed. Toni Morrison (New York: Literary Classics of the United States, 1998), 294.

17 Ralph Ellison, *Shadow and Act*, in *The Collected Essays of Ralph Ellison*, ed. John F. Callahan (New York: Random House, 1995), 49–55.

18 Ellison, *Shadow and Act*, 53.

19 Ellison, *Shadow and Act*, 52.

20 Ellison, *Shadow and Act*, 54.

21 See Malcolm X, *The Autobiography of Malcolm X* (New York: Ballantine Books, 1973), 155–168.

22 Malcolm X, *Autobiography*, 155–168.

23 Malcolm X, *Autobiography*, 155–168.

24 Baldwin, *The Fire Next Time*, 316.

25 Robyn C. Spencer, *The Revolution Has Come: Black Power, Gender, and the Black Panther Party in Oakland* (Durham, NC: Duke University Press, 2016), 14.

26 Spencer, *The Revolution Has Come,* 72.

27 *Eyes on the Prize,* episode 9, "Power! (1966–68)," directed by Louis J. Massiah and Terry Kay Rockefeller, written by Steve Fayer, Louis J. Massiah, and Terry Kay Rockefeller, aired January 29, 1990. PBS, 2006, DVD.

28 *Eyes on the Prize,* episode 9, "Power! (1966–68)."

29 See Scott Ellsworth, *Death in a Promised Land: The Tulsa Race Riot of 1921* (Baton Rouge: Louisiana State University Press, 1982).

30 Spencer, *The Revolution Has Come.*

31 Lu, "Reconciliation as Non-Alienation."

32 Baldwin, *The Fire Next Time,* 293 and 294.

33 Baldwin, *The Fire Next Time,* 294.

34 I am grateful to Catherine Lu and Saira Mohamed for helpful discussion.

PART II

REPARATIONS FOR RACIAL INJUSTICE

4

FRAMING REDRESS DISCOURSE

ROY L. BROOKS

We gather here today to right a grave wrong.
—President Ronald Reagan at the signing of legislation atoning for
the internment of Japanese Americans, August 10, 1981

My ambition here is to bring together for the first time two of the various projects that I have given considerable attention in the last twenty-five years. The first is a construction of models for redressing past atrocities such as the Holocaust, Apartheid, the Comfort Women, and Japanese American internment. The second is a clarification and synthesis of major theories, strategies, or norms for advancing racial justice in post–civil rights America. My argument is that, taken together, these frameworks—redress models and post–civil rights theories—provide a coherent and constructive means of framing our discourse on how best to redress slavery and Jim Crow (collectively referred to as "slave redress"). This chapter is a demonstration of that proposition. Before getting into the weeds, it might be useful to highlight important pieces in my argument.

Starting with redress models, I draw upon two basic approaches for redressing past atrocities, including slavery, that I have posited in the past: *tort model* and *atonement model.* Backward-looking, victim-focused, and compensatory (sometimes punitive), the tort model's primary concern is to recover damages for loss or harm suffered by the victims; in other words, recompense. Forward-looking, perpetrator-focused, and restorative, the atonement model stresses the importance of the perpetrator's demonstration of a sincere effort to make amends; in other words, redemption.

The perpetrator's redemptive act lays the foundation for the victim's forgiveness.[1]

I join that analysis with post–civil rights theories I have in the past synthesized from the diverse thinking of civil rights scholars, commentators, and pundits expressed in the decades since the death of Jim Crow. I have organized these ideas into four core beliefs regarding the best way to achieve racial progress in our post–civil rights society. These post–civil rights theories, or norms, are: *traditionalism* (racial neutrality); *reformism* (racial integration); *critical race theory* (social transformation—integration on steroids); and *limited separation* (Black solidarity or identity without excluding Whites).[2] This juxtaposition of non-nefarious (i.e., nonracist) perspectives generates a dynamic consideration of the race problem very much in the spirit of the diverse positions on civil rights taken by my classmates at Yale Law School sitting night after night around the "Black Table" some fifty years ago.[3]

Whether the nation should proceed with slave redress under the tort model or atonement model intersects with the larger question of which post–civil rights norm—traditionalism, reformism, critical race theory, or limited separation—generates the best strategy for maximizing racial progress in the coming years. The redress question, in other words, should be determined in a manner that is congruent with our collective strategy for achieving racial justice in this post–Jim Crow, post–civil rights period. We must know in which direction we are going before we begin the journey. That is my main argument.

The intersection of these frameworks also unavoidably adds complexity to the analysis of slave redress. Devoid of any formal grounding in the foundational question of "in which direction are we going," the current debate on "reparations," it could be argued, is undertheorized or perhaps even misdirected. Using the post–civil rights theories as touchstone for proposing slave redress (my main argument), I come to the following conclusions in this chapter.

- Traditionalism favors partial atonement; specifically redress in the form of a government apology but, in deference to the racial-neutrality norm, no government reparations. Private reparations are acceptable, however.
- Reformism favors full atonement; specifically, a "genu-

ine" government apology and solidifying reparations. The apology is made believable by a regime of reparations that collectively effectuate racial integration across society. This entails reparations at both the group or institutional level ("rehabilitative reparations") and the individual level ("compensatory reparations"). Rehabilitative reparations might include a constitutional precommitment for racially integrated schools and colleges created through a regime of racial preferences. Compensatory reparations might entail cash reparations distributed to individuals directly as supplemental income.

- Critical race theory also suggests full atonement. But for race crits, the apology must be solidified by reparations calculated toward social transformation (equity rather than equality). This vision of equity might include rehabilitative reparations in the form of a constitutional precommitment for racially integrated schools and colleges implemented through racial quotas to ensure diversity and inclusion, and compensatory reparations in the form of cash reparations distributed on a conditional basis for wealth accumulation.

- Limited separation's core belief in racial identity suggests that it is not interested in pursuing an apology or atonement from the government, which has a White identity. It is only interested in compensatory justice, which is at the heart of the tort model. This might mean a redress scheme consisting of rehabilitative reparations in the form of a constitutional precommitment for the legality of Black schools and Historically Black Colleges and Universities (HBCUs) that receive public funds, public funding of schools and colleges controlled by Blacks, and cash payments to established Black institutions that could support a range of community services and business developments.

Thus, all post–civil rights theories (even conservative traditionalists) support slave redress in one fashion or another but offer different paths to redress. It goes without saying that this internal conflict must be reconciled before any specific plan for slave redress is presented in final form to the US Congress and the American people.

This chapter is written in three parts. The first part briefly sets forth the reasons I believe the nation must move forward with slave redress. It gives content to President Reagan's entreaty of "right[ing] a grave wrong." The second part explains in greater detail the competing redress models and the competing post–civil rights theories. The third part intersects these frameworks, applying the post–civil rights perspectives to the slave-redress models, suggesting the outcomes just sketched. This is my fair estimation as to how the frameworks match up. In conclusion, I offer my personal assessment of the juxtapositions that, it is hoped, moves the ball down the field. The complexity of the analysis, to be sure, is matched by its importance.

A GRAVE WRONG TO RIGHT

I begin with an allegory of a poker game that I have used many times in the past. It goes as follows:

> Two persons—one White, the other Black—are playing a game of poker. The game has been in progress for almost four hundred years. One player—the White one—has been cheating during much of this time, but now announces: "From this day forward, there will be a new game with new players and no more cheating." Hopeful but somewhat suspicious, the Black player responds, "That's great. I've been waiting to hear you say that for some four hundred years. Let me ask you, what are you going to do with all those poker chips that you have stacked up on your side of the table all these years?" "Well," says the White player, somewhat bewildered by the question, "I'm going to keep them for the next generation of White players, of course."[4]

The allegory speaks to the lingering effects of slavery. When slavery ended in 1865, it was not replaced with a system of racial equality. Except for a brief period of Reconstruction, slavery folded into a system of racial oppression commonly referred to as "Jim Crow." This regime of separate-but-equal was in effect a system of racial preferences for Whites that lasted until 1972 when Congress passed the Equal Employment Opportunity Act of that year. This Act, inter alia, made it illegal for state and local governments to discriminate on the basis of race in employment.[5]

Slavery had two lasting impacts on Black lives that remain with us today. If these conditions never materialized, we would not have a race problem today. The first lingering effect of slavery is the race-specific rhetoric of racism the slaveholders and their supporters conjured up to justify the economic exploitation of Blacks. Attitudes associated with racist rhetoric are still with us today. They manifest as overt forms of racism—racial antipathy and the belief in White supremacy (old-fashioned racism)—and covert forms of racism—White privilege and implicit bias. Covert forms of racism are less motivational than cognitive and, therefore, are more difficult for the person harboring this mindset to detect.[6]

Second, slavery produced capital deficiencies in Black communities, enslaved and freed. These include basic capital (life and liberty) and deficiencies in financial capital (income and family wealth), human capital (formal education and skill sets), and social capital (social esteem and the ability to get things done).[7] These capital deficiencies followed Blacks into the Jim Crow period, and when African Americans emerged from Jim Crow circa 1972, they were burdened by the worse schools, housing, jobs, and social esteem. While some immigrants, White or minority, came to the United States with nothing (zero), African Americans had minus zero. Some five decades into the post–civil rights period, African Americans still have the worse schools, housing, jobs, and social esteem. In fact, the racial differentials are little changed from the end of Jim Crow in 1972, and in some instances they have gotten worse.[8]

The distance between slavery and today is even closer than the Civil War. For hundreds of thousands of African Americans, slavery did not end in 1865. It ended after World War II, into the 1950s. This is within the lifetime of many Americans today. In total, about 800,000 African Americans were forced into systems of convict leasing and debt bondage under state or municipal laws, often dying before their sentences could be completed.[9] They were convicted on such trumped-up charges as burglary or grand larceny, or on even more minor charges such as vagrancy. For example, "Black men and women were arrested and found guilty of vagrancies violations for not having jobs, for being unable to show documents proving that they were employed, or for having jobs that did not serve the interest of whites. . . . [V]agrancy laws exploited Black adults and their children."[10]

This form of slavery was outlawed in 1941 when the US Attorney General signed an order, called Circular No. 3591, which for the first time created federal law enforcing the Thirteenth Amendment's prohibition against involuntary servitude. The Attorney General signed the directive on December 12, 1941, just five days after the bombing of Pearl Harbor.[11] But it took time for the government to enforce the new law. So, for many Blacks, slavery did not end until after World War II. Born into this system of "slavery by another name," Ben Jobe reports:

> When we came off the plantation, 1945, I was around 11 years old. . . . [S]lavery ended in 1945, let me make that clear. Most people think it was 1865. Oh no, [it was] 1945, when the federal government finally put some teeth into [Circular No. 3591] . . . and arrested some of the slave owners.[12]

Whether ending in 1865 or 1945, slavery casts a long shadow over African Americans' chances for worldly success and personal happiness today. The capital deficiencies slavery created in Black communities have had an intergenerational impact on Black lives today. Economists estimate that for the vast majority of Americans, "up to 80% of lifetime wealth accumulation results from gifts from earlier generations, ranging from the down payment on a home to a bequest by a parent."[13]

The intergenerational aspect of wealth is dramatically illustrated in federal housing laws. From the 1940s to the 1960s, federal, state, and local governments passed housing laws that not only segregated the races, but also prevented African Americans from buying and owning homes throughout the country. For example, the Federal Housing Administration required developers like the Levitt Company to place restricted covenants in every deed which prohibited White homeowners from selling their homes to African Americans. The Fair Housing Act was passed in 1968 to put an end to this and other discriminatory laws. This legislation did not, however, provide a remedy for the considerable damage prior discrimination had visited upon African Americans. All the Fair Housing Act did was to prohibit discrimination prospectively. It did nothing to undo or compensate Blacks for the decades of housing segregation they had suffered.[14]

When suburbs like Levittown were built in the 1940s and 1950s, houses sold for about $8,000 each (the equivalent of about $70,000 in 2020 dollars). Most African American families could have afforded those homes. In 2020, those homes sold for roughly $500,000 and are no longer affordable to most African American (and many other) families. More significantly, two to three generations of White families who moved into those homes benefited from the tremendous equity appreciation in the value of those homes. In contrast, African Americans, who were forced to live in rented apartments, gain none of that family wealth. The result is that today, although Black income is on average 60 percent of White income, "43% of African Americans are homeowners, compared with 73% of whites," and "the median white household owns 86 times the assets of the median black household."[15] Scholars like Richard Rothstein argue that this enormous wealth gap is almost entirely attributable to government discriminatory housing policies practiced in the mid-twentieth century.[16]

Thus, long after the end of slavery, it still means something in our society today to be a Black person. Black and White Americans are still not at equal risk. Indeed, Orlando Patterson reminds us that Black lives are even very different from the lives of other racial minorities. He observes that "African Americans are the least assimilated racial or ethnic group, that although Asians and Latinos are disengaging their national origins from racial identity, similar to European immigrants of the past, African Americans (including multiracial blacks) are perceived as being 'black,' and choose to identify as 'black.' These identities are abetted by the fact that African Americans intermarry at a rate that is significantly lower than the rates for Asians and Latinos."[17] Hence, Blacks and other racial minorities have broadly similar experiences of racial subordination but with strong group variations in form, intensity, and duration.

African Americans at the top of the socioeconomic ladder are not immune from the lingering effects of slavery. "Unlike Oprah Winfrey, Donald Trump has not had to deal with racism in his life. Nor has he ever had to admonish his sons, 'it's unlikely but possible that you could get killed today. Or any day. I'm sorry, but that's the truth. Black maleness is a potentially fatal condition.'"[18] Indeed, Timothy Eugene "Tim" Scott, a Black Republican senator from South Carolina, reports his encounters with racial profiling by the police. He was stopped and released seven times in his first year serving in the Senate. He said that "the vast majority of the time, I was pulled over for driving a new car in the wrong neighborhood or something else just as trivial."[19]

Slavery's lingering effects can be summarized in two words: *systemic racism*. In other words, slavery's presence today is most tellingly felt in patterns of racial degradation embedded in the fabric of our society. Systemic racism occurs when it is deemed acceptable for White feelings to trump Black experiences. It manifests, inter alia, as: tremendous racial disparity in net family wealth in which White wealth is ten times greater than Black wealth; the racial wage gap for college-educated men, which is getting larger rather than smaller; racial disparities in our criminal justice system, particularly police killings of unarmed African Americans and disproportionately longer prison sentences; voter suppression laws enacted by dozens of states that, as a federal appeals court said of one of these laws, targets African Americans "with almost surgical precision"; the parade of major civil rights defeats at the Supreme Court, often by split decisions which indicate the outcomes were not preordained by law; the record of "deep-rooted racism in the military"; the denial of equal educational opportunity when racist teachers, whose victims are unlikely to attend office hours or take advantage of other educational opportunities associated with the teacher, are protected by academic freedom.[20]

So much of what White Americans may have thought was behind them and finished about slavery is present and unfinished. The old atrocity cries out for redress. Though the case for slave redress is undeniable in my view, the form of redress is very much open to debate.

Redress Models and Post–Civil Rights Theories

Competing approaches to redressing slavery have been broached over the years. These models of redress have never been cross-fertilized with core beliefs about the "best" way to achieve racial progress in our post–Jim Crow society. The connection between redress models and post–civil rights norms is suggested later in the chapter after they are briefly explained here.

Redress Models

Since the initial introduction of HR 40 in 1989,[21] scholars have fashioned two competing redress models. The first is the "settlement model," also called the "tort model."[22] Chiefly, it is backward-looking, victim-focused, and compensatory or sometimes punitive. Redress schemes produced through the tort model are designed to financially compensate victims for their demonstrable loss (most especially stolen labor), and on occasion to deliver punitive justice. The government or even a private beneficiary of slavery writes a check for X amount of dollars to settle the matter. Proponents of the tort model, in short, believe that the victims of wrongs as mortal as slavery and Jim Crow should not go without relief.[23]

Litigation is a major vehicle for effectuating the tort model.[24] Yet, litigation is, for the most part, a nonstarter as lawsuits for past atrocities face myriad procedural hurdles. Expiration of the statute of limitations and the lack of subject matter jurisdiction (the authority of a court to render a judgment in a case) are some of the legal obstacles these lawsuits face.[25] I have, however, argued that Congress and the courts ought to change the law to allow slave-redress litigation to go forward:

> If the slave descendants' claims are morally compelling, then they must be cognizable under U.S. law. Otherwise, the extant law stands as the "present embodiment" of America's worst atrocity and the corrupt laws that made it possible. This is a credibility check no less important than the Supreme Court's landmark 1954 school desegregation case of *Brown v. Board of Education*.[26]

Notwithstanding my own argument, I consider litigation under the tort model to be fundamentally deficient. My argument is that this type of litigation essentially presents a legal claim, not a moral claim, in which the quotidian language of tort litigation—including the calculation of individual damages for millions of people—takes center stage. This approach, in my view, exaggerates the complexity and contentiousness of what ought to be a mutual movement toward racial reconciliation.[27] Even if the tort model were pursued through the conciliatory channels of bipartisan legislation rather than within the adversary process that defines our legal system, it would still be deficient in my view. Personal accountability is not expected under the tort model. The parties merely effectuate a settlement, meaning that the perpetrator pays up without having to admit liability. The perpetrator is allowed to declare victory and go home. Neoconservative Charles Krauthammer would gladly have the government write a check as a means of closing the books on the American race problem.[28] In my view, this is a kind of justice on the cheap. No matter how large the check, this type of redress does not do well by the victims, especially the millions of deceased enslaved Blacks. There is a better approach to redress—the atonement model.

Unlike the tort model, the atonement model is forward-looking, perpetrator-focused, and restorative. Its primary objective is reconciliation between the perpetrator and victims in an ongoing relationship. Largely shaped by Germany's redress program for victims of the Holocaust as well as other post–World War II redress campaigns, the atonement model applied to American slavery and Jim Crow posits that racial reconciliation is possible only when the perpetrator comes to identify with the victims' collective humanity. The atonement model, then, imbibes a post-Holocaust vision of heightened morality, egalitarianism, identity, and restorative justice. There is much to unpack here.[29]

Under the atonement model, redress comes in two stages. First and foremost, the perpetrator issues an apology and tenders reparations to make the apology believable. Apology is an acknowledgment of guilt rather than a punishment for guilt. When the perpetrator of an atrocity apologizes, it confesses the deed, admits the deed was an injustice, repents, asks for forgiveness. The victims then calculate the sincerity of the apology by the weight of the reparations. Meager reparations undercut the sincerity of the apology. Hence, reparations give substance to the perpetrator's apology and help to repair the damage to the victim and society caused by the atrocity.

Reparations come in many forms. They can be paid at the individual level ("compensatory reparations") in the form of cash payments or nonmonetary outlays (e.g., family recognition or a scholarship) to the victims or their families. Reparations can also be paid at the group or community level ("rehabilitative reparations"). They can be in the form of cash payments to the victims' institutions (e.g., support for HBCUs) or nonmonetary measures that benefit the victims' community (e.g., new laws, expanded services, commemorations, or museums).[30] The distinction between compensatory and rehabilitative reparations is not a hard one. It serves the purposes of reminding the public that cash payments to the victims is not the only (or even the best) way to redress slavery. Whether in the form of reparations, apology, or something else (e.g., truth trials which are established to determine the truth about the atrocity), redress is limited only by the imagination.

Forgiveness is the second step under the atonement model. This is the victims' side of the equation. It is responsive to the perpetrator's atonement. Once an appropriate apology and sufficient reparations are provided by the perpetrator, the question of forgiveness arrives on each victim's desk like a subpoena; it necessitates a response. Forgiveness is not, however, immediately forthcoming; nor is it inevitable. It all depends on the quality of the reparations, which evolve over time through negotiations. As I have stated on another occasion:

> With the government's genuine apology for slavery and Jim Crow, with the construction of the museum of slavery, and with the creation of the atonement trust fund, slave descendants will have good reason to embrace America as a country that is worthy of their respect—a country that does not ignore its discriminatory past or the consequences that flow therefrom. Atonement should convince disaffected blacks that it is time to change their behaviors and attitudes toward America. After atonement, it will be difficult to justify the racial chip so many slave descendants wear on their shoulder, in some instances as a badge of honor. . . .
>
> It would, however, be Pollyannaish to expect disaffected slave descendants to adopt, at least initially, the star-spangled view of America that is held by so many immigrants of color, such as the Somali refugee working as a police officer in an inner-city neighborhood who gushes: "I go to work every day, put my life on the line—and it is a pleasure to do that, . . . because this country I owe

a lot. I owe my life and my family's life. So the most precious thing
I can offer to this country is not money, not time, but my life. That
is my intent—to . . . be a good citizen. There is no place like the
United States, when it comes to immigrants." . . . Slave descendants
are casualties of America's history of race relations; new immigrants
of color are not. . . .

* * *

. . . [T]he government's apology and reparations will give slave
descendants a much greater investment in America than they now
have. With a genuine sense of belonging to the American family,
slave descendants should begin to see themselves not as limited by
skin color as they once were, and even less limited by [their own
justified] racial anger preatonement. The atonement trust fund
will give them the financial and human capital needed to overcome
many of the lingering effects of slavery and Jim Crow, including low-
performing public schools and meager family resources to sustain
a college education. . . . In a postatonement America, slave descendants should feel secure enough in their investment as citizens
to overlook everyday sources of racial friction—such as the sales
clerk's dirty look or the carload of whites who yell racial slurs as they
speed by.

None of this means slave descendants will be free from all racism in postatonement America. Atonement will not obviate the
need for on-going civil rights reforms. Slave descendants will have
to continue to use our civil rights laws to fight racial discrimination
wherever it occurs. Atonement only means that slave descendants
now have reason to begin to trust the government's commitment to
racial justice.[31]

My deployment of the atonement model in this chapter focuses
less on the victims' civic responsibility—forgiveness—than on the
perpetrator's moral responsibilities—apology and reparations.

The atonement model as well as the tort model must be con-
textualized within the victims' community. In the context of slave
redress, this means paying attention to the strategies for achieving racial justice African Americans have been pondering since the
death of Jim Crow circa 1972.

Post–Civil Rights Theories

Over the years, I have clarified, synthesized, organized, and critiqued major positions regarding racial progress put forth by scholars and pundits since the end of the Civil Rights Movement. I have distilled these thoughts into four major post–civil rights theories: traditionalism; reformism; critical race theory; and limited separation. Each of these theories stakes out a position regarding what African Americans (and by extension women, Latinx, Asians, LGBTQ, and other outsiders) should do to achieve socioeconomic, sociolegal, and sociocultural progress in twenty-first-century America. What follows is a short summary of these theories with emphasis on socioeconomic progress.[32]

TRADITIONALISM
Traditionalism's basic belief is that race no longer matters in the African American quest for racial equality today.[33] Traditionalists are not saying that racism no longer exists. They in fact acknowledge the existence of racism today, but maintain that racism is not as "potent" in twenty-first-century America as it was during Jim Crow. Lingering racism does not prevent African Americans from achieving worldly success and personal happiness in our post–civil rights society. Systemic racism, whether in law enforcement or society as a whole, is fake news.

Traditionalists do acknowledge that African Americans continue to face socioeconomic problems. But these problems, they argue, are self-inflicted and, hence, are beyond the control of the ministrations of government. Teenage pregnancy, Black-on-Black crime, lack of educational achievement, and hyper–racial sensitivity are internal rather than external problems. They are behavioral rather than structural, traditionalists insist. And, as such, Blacks and only Blacks can resolve these problems.

These are the reasons traditionalists believe race no longer matters. From this predicate they argue that the government should be neutral regarding matters of race. It should not make the mistake it made in the past by mandating or sanctioning race-conscious laws or policies. Racial omission (the color-blind norm) was a sound strategy for the government and racial progress during the days of Martin Luther King, and it remains so today. The government, then, ought not to pollute the social environment by attempting to engineer racial outcomes or by otherwise making too much fuss about race. Race-conscious laws or policies are racially divisive, pure and simple. This thinking certainly provides the subtext for most of a conservative Supreme Court's decision-making in civil rights cases that impact the socioeconomic environment. The Court simply does not want to make too much about the problem of race in our society. Chief Justice Roberts, a steadfast traditionalist, referenced this point in one of his opinions, writing, "Simply because the school districts may seek a worthy objective does not mean they are free to discriminate on the basis of race to achieve it."[34] Whether invidious or benign, "negative" or "positive," race-conscious governmental action is discriminatory and, hence, ipso facto, "racist." Justice Thomas, a traditionalist and, as I shall explain in due course, an occasional limited separatist, argues that race-conscious governmental action is "racist" because it signals to society that Blacks are hapless victims in need of special treatment. Blacks are depicted as a people less than equal to Whites. Justice Thomas asserts with no dearth of passion:

> [T]here can be no doubt that racial paternalism and its unintended consequences can be as poisonous and pernicious as any other form of discrimination. So-called "benign" discrimination teaches many that because of chronic and apparently immutable handicaps, minorities cannot compete with them without their patronizing indulgence. Inevitably, such programs engender attitudes of superiority or, alternatively, provoke resentment among those who believe that they have been wronged by the government's use of race. These programs stamp minorities with a badge of inferiority and may cause them to develop dependencies or to adopt an attitude that they are "entitled" to preferences. . . . In my mind, government-sponsored racial discrimination based on benign prejudice is just as noxious as discrimination inspired by malicious prejudice. In each instance, it is racial discrimination, plain and simple.[35]

Racial charity, in short, undermines racial equality.

REFORMISM

Reformism embraces a different normative stance than traditionalism.[36] Glenn Loury, a onetime traditionalist who has made a dramatic move to reformism, argues that traditionalism's thrust—"it's time to move on"—is "simplistic social ethics and sophomoric social psychology."[37] Though reformism acknowledges behavioral issues among the lowest socioeconomic class in Black America, it posits that the race problem is less an internal problem than a structural one. Ergo, race still matters.

Reformists accuse traditionalists of cherry-picking the facts to fit their predetermined conclusion that race no longer matters. For example, in response to frequent attempts by traditionalists to use President Obama's election as evidence that race no longer matters, reformists point out that they conveniently ignore the fact that the most powerful person in the world lacked the power to raise racial issues with a strong voice in his own administration. President Obama's cultural weakness was on full display when he was severely rebuked by the media and public for seeing racism in the arrest of a renowned Black Harvard professor, Henry Louis Gates, by a White police officer, Sgt. James Crowley of the Cambridge Police Department. To be sure, Blacks commit way too much crime against other Blacks, as traditionalists constantly remind us. But FBI statistics show that the rates of Black-on-Black crime and White-on-White crime are virtually identical.[38]

Though they believe race still matters, reformists are not revolutionaries. "With due humility," Glenn Loury asserts, "I am a reformer, not an 'abolitionist.'"[39] Hence, reformists, like traditionalists, embrace the race-neutrality norm (racial omission) in our post–civil rights, post–Jim Crow society. The difference lies in the fact that reformists value racial integration more than do traditionalists and, therefore, are willing to use race-conscious means in pursuit of that goal. Racial integration is the best way to achieve racial equality, reformists believe, because the mainstream is where the best of everything is—the best schools, jobs, and so on. Thus, the difference between reformists and traditionalists lies in the relative emphasis given to the racial-omission and racial-integration norms. For traditionalists, the racial-omission norm trumps the racial-integration norm. For reformists, the racial-integration norm trumps the racial-omission norm.[40]

Justice Sotomayor begins one of her dissenting opinions by referencing reformist Cornel West's seminal work, *Race Matters*. In addition, she writes in her memoir that racial preferences are the strongest way to implement the racial-integration norm. In fact, her defense of racial preferences is just as passionate as Justice Thomas's renunciation of them, discussed earlier. She writes in her memoir:

> I had no need to apologize that the look-wider, search-more affirmative action that Princeton and Yale practiced had opened doors for me. That was its purpose: to create the conditions whereby students from disadvantaged backgrounds could be brought to the starting line of a race many were unaware was even being run. I had been admitted to the Ivy League through a special door, and I had more ground than most to make up before I was competing with my classmates on an equal footing. But I worked relentlessly to reach that point, and distinctions such as the Pyne Prize, Phi Beta Kappa, summa cum laude, and a spot on *The Yale Law Journal* were not given out like so many pats on the back to encourage mediocre students. These were achievements as real as those of anyone around me.[41]

Reformists see affirmative action as the gateway to integrating mainstream American institutions, which in turn is the best strategy for racial advancement in our post–civil rights society.

CRITICAL RACE THEORY
Critical race theory's central post–civil rights message is that White hegemony matters most in the struggle for racial advancement.[42] The antidote for White privilege is social transformation. Not unlike the racial-identity norm under limited separation discussed in due course, critical race theory's social-transformation norm is outside-of-the-box thinking about racial progress. Critical race theorists and limited separatists argue that racial omission and racial integration are not the only (and certainly not the best) ways to pursue racial advancement post–Jim Crow.

The core message of critical race theory—White hegemony matters most—is planted in the writings of the late Harvard law professor Derrick Bell. It is a message that goes to the very structure of our society. As Richard Delgado and Jean Stefancic, two pioneering critical race theorists, assert, "critical race theory questions the very foundations of the liberal order, including equality theory, legal reasoning, Enlightenment rationalism, and neutral principles of constitutional law."[43] Critical race theorists believe that appearances can be deceiving. Hence, reminiscent of *The Wizard of Oz*, they seek to "understand what is going on behind the curtain."[44] And looking behind the curtain, critical race theorists see a post–civil rights social order that is racially corrupt and has been from the very beginning. Look around, and what does one see?—Whites on top, people of color on the bottom. Everything important in our society *slants* in favor of insiders who are overwhelmingly straight White males. This racialized social order means but one thing: Ours is a racist society. Racism—whether at the individual or systemic level—is coextensive with racial disadvantage. Our society is not organically neutral or objective when it comes to matters of race. Instead, it is "non-neutral" or "anti-objective," all of which is socially constructive. In this context, color-blindness is a myth. When people think color-blind, they do not see monochrome; they see White. That's racism.[45]

Some Whites, known as "critical white theorists," acknowledge the privilege they have in the social order: "[W]hen . . . I apply for a job or hunt for an apartment, I don't look threatening. Almost all of the people evaluating me for those things look like me—they are white. They see in me a reflection of themselves, and in a racist world that is an advantage. I smile. I am white. I am one of them. I am not dangerous. Even when I voice critical opinions, I am cut some slack. After all, I'm white."[46] The deck is thus stacked in favor of insiders.

Critical race theorists maintain that the norms on which traditionalism (racial omission) and reformism (racial integration) operate do nothing to unstack the deck, to disassemble the constructed racial hierarchy embedded in our society. Racial omission and racial integration are "calculated to remedy at most the more extreme and shocking forms of racial treatment; . . . [they] can do little about the business-as-usual types of [racialized conditions] that people of color confront every day and that account for much of our subordination, poverty, and despair."[47] Racial omission and racial integration, in short, do not dig deep enough to redress systemic racism. And, as a result, these norms—collectively referred to as "formal equal opportunity" in legal theory[48]—legitimize the fundamental relationship between race and power in the social order.

Although critical race theorists are not reformists, they are at bottom integrationists. They want in, but on better terms than what reformists would settle for. For example, reformists generally support affirmative action but only to the extent of racial preferences, not racial quotas. In addition, they mainly justify such affirmative action on the ground that it promotes diversity. Critical race theorists believe racial preferences do not go far enough in changing the relationship between race and power in mainstream institutions, because they operate at the discretion of insiders.[49] In addition, critical race theorists take issue with the use of the diversity rationale to support affirmative action. Derrick Bell, in an article titled "Diversity's Distractions," summarizes the critical race theorist's critique of the diversity rationale:

> For at least four reasons, the concept of diversity, far from a viable means of ensuring affirmative action in the admissions policies of colleges and graduate schools, is a serious distraction in the ongoing efforts to achieve racial justice: 1) Diversity enables courts and policymakers to avoid addressing directly the barriers of race and class that adversely affect so many applicants; 2) Diversity invites further litigation by offering a distinction without a real difference between those uses of race approved in college admissions programs, and those in other far more important affirmative action policies that the Court has rejected; 3) Diversity serves to give undeserved legitimacy to the heavy reliance on grades and test scores that privilege well-to-do, mainly white applicants; and 4) The tremendous attention directed at diversity programs diverts concern and resources from the serious barriers of poverty that exclude far more students from entering college than are likely to gain admission under an affirmative action program.[50]

Critical race theorists, then, believe that the diversity rationale upholds affirmative action on grounds acceptable to White elites rather than on grounds most beneficial to outsiders, which are grounds that explicitly acknowledge and challenge the extant relationship between race and power in the social order; in other words, White hegemony. The diversity rationale prevents society from dealing with the real problem outsiders face. It does nothing to reset White control over the social order. Critical race theorists offer that affirmative action would not even be a topic of discussion if it were not for the history of racial oppression in this country. Reformists ignore this connection. They do not explain why affirmative action makes sense to outsiders. "While increasing diversity enriches the academic environment and enhances the curricular aims of education, the legal and rhetorical emphasis on diversity sidesteps the more challenging social issues of race and class inequality."[51] Unlike reformists, critical race theorists reject White hegemonic narratives and legitimize counterhegemonic narratives.

LIMITED SEPARATION

Far less preoccupied with fighting White racism or changing White institutions than either reformists or critical race theorists, limited separatists have a clear post–civil rights orientation.[52] They have a clear understanding of what matters most in moving forward with racial progress in today's society—to wit, racial identity or solidarity. Limited separatists are imbued with a strong sense that racial self-consciousness and self-sufficiency are positive features of Black identity. This type of Black identity is not only psychologically healing, but also the sine qua non of racial advancement for African Americans. Unfortunately, Blacks suffer from a dearth of positive racial identity, a paucity of racial pride and unity, limited separatists believe. Blacks are too preoccupied with gaining acceptance from Whites or making their fame and fortune in White institutions. Limited separatists want more Black pride, Black heritage, Black solidarity, and self-reliance. *The best place to find a helping hand is at the end of your own arm.*

Given this posture, one can safely surmise that limited separatists have an unfavorable opinion of formal equal opportunity. Both the racial-omission and racial-integration norms are conceptually incompatible with limited separatists' core message of racial solidarity, a message that is both race-conscious and (limitedly) separatist. Limited separatists would argue that, taken together, racial omission and racial integration are at best inchoate norms and at worst dangerous norms in the context of today's post–civil rights society.

Even during the Civil Rights Movement, many African Americans viewed the racial-omission and racial-integration norms with suspicion. While African Americans in general initially greeted the Supreme Court's decision in *Brown* with exuberance, a fair amount of apprehension set in among many Blacks, especially in the South, upon sober reflection. The fear was that formal equal opportunity might mean the closure of Black institutions or the end to public funding of such institutions. NAACP lawyers who argued *Brown* were certainly aware of these concerns. Judges Robert Carter and Constance Baker Motely, for example, mentioned these concerns in their memoirs, but dismissed them as unfounded. These fears have, by and large, proven to be true.[53]

Reflecting the dominant social attitude, the Supreme Court places little value in maintaining or creating Black institutions. During most of the post–civil rights period, the Court has, in fact, waged a sustained war against publicly funded Black institutions on the ground that they make a mockery of *Brown*. For example, the Court has placed Historically Black Colleges and Universities (HBCUs), which are quintessentially Black institutions, under a constitutional duty to dismantle their racial identity in deference to the racial-omission norm. In *United States v. Fordice*, the Supreme Court held that current policies traceable to de jure segregation that have a discriminatory effect "must be reformed to the extent practicable and consistent with sound educational practices."[54] Understanding the threat that this standard—"racial identifiability" attributable to de jure segregation—poses to the existence of HBCUs, Justice Thomas, who, if nothing else, is proudly Black and a limited separatist in the context of education, attempted to spin the majority's opinion in such a way as to save HBCUs. The Court, he opined in a concurring opinion, "do[es] not foreclose the possibility that there exists 'sound educational justification' for maintaining historically black colleges as such."[55]

Despite Justice Thomas's attempt to spin the holding in *Fordice*, HBCUs remain under attack. Indeed, on remand in *Fordice*, the lower court mandated color-blind admission standards at HBCUs in the state of Mississippi. This ruling was made over the vehement objection of Blacks who argued that the new standards would cut Black enrollment in half at Mississippi's three HBCUs. The Supreme Court denied an appeal in the case and, hence, refused to block the lower court's ruling.[56] There has, in fact, been a shift in the racial demographics of HBCUs since *Fordice.* This has cause many, especially HBCU alumni, to voice concerns about the storied identity and impact of HBCUs on the Black community, their constituency. "They point, for instance, to institutions like Bluefield State in West Virginia, which was founded to educate the children of Black coal miners but now has a campus that is 85 percent white."[57] Limited separatists have attacked Justice Harlan's famous defense of the racial-omission norm authored in his dissenting opinion in *Plessy v. Ferguson.* They point out that as Justice Harlan set about defending the ideal of a color-blind Constitution, this justice so lionized by traditionalists assured the nation that America's racial hierarchy would *not* change. The very same paragraph in which he embraced the color-blind Constitution opens with Justice Harlan avowing, "The white race deems itself to be the dominant race in this country. And so it is, in prestige, in achievements, in education, in wealth and in power. So, I doubt not, it will continue to be for *all time*, if it remains true to its great heritage and holds fast to the principles of constitutional liberty" (emphasis supplied).[58] Limited separatists ask, rhetorically, how could anyone who truly believes in racial progress embrace the racial-omission norm to the exclusion of all else?

In addition to attacking *Plessy*, limited separatists have targeted *Brown v. Board of Education*, which, of course, sits at the opposite end of the post-slavery spectrum of racial relations. Limited separatists see implicit racism in *Brown*'s assertion that "separate is inherently unequal."[59] Yet, some have had second thoughts about *Brown*. Professor Kevin Brown writes:

> I am one who firmly believes that what allowed Chief Justice Earl Warren to produce an opinion that all the justices of the Supreme Court could agree upon was the notion that segregation damaged only black people. Thus, I think the social science evidence was necessary because it allowed Warren to garner unanimous support for his opinion striking down segregation. As insulting to blacks as I find Warren's opinion in *Brown* fifty years later, my deep and long reflections of twenty years as a law professor assures me that striking down segregation, even at this cost, was a tremendous bargain for black people.[60]

Finally, it is important to emphasize that limited separation is not total separation. Whites and non-Blacks are not excluded under limited separation. In fact, a degree of racial integration exists in Black churches and HBCUs just as sexual integration exists in single-sex colleges. Exclusion occurs only when a limited separatist institution is in jeopardy of losing its identity with the addition of another non-member of the group. Limited separation, in fact, mandates a three-pronged test to determine not only the conditions under which a non-member can be excluded, but also the legitimacy of establishing limited separation in the first place. The three-pronged test is: (1) a compensatory need for establishing the institution; (2) general non-exclusion of non-members of the group; (3) exclusion of non-members is allowed only if the institution is in jeopardy of losing its identity with the addition of more non-members, as in the case of Bluefield State in West Virginia discussed earlier.[61]

Each of the post–civil rights theories is concerned with racial progress in a society that no longer legalizes discrimination against Blacks. Each has a strategy for proceeding based upon well-defined core beliefs: racial omission (traditionalism); racial integration (reformism); social transformation (critical race theory); and racial solidarity or identity (limited separation). The question I consider next is, how do these theories play out in the continuing debate over slave redress?

THEORETICAL APPROACHES TO SLAVE REDRESS

The public debate on the justification for redressing slavery assumes a binary debate between African Americans and Whites. I wish to proffer that the redress question is also (and more interestingly) a contested matter within the community of Black intellectuals and, more recently, the Black community as a whole. Traditionalists, reformists, critical race theorists, and limited separatists have something important to say about slave redress. Though each group desires racial progress, each suggests different approaches to the redress question based on their core beliefs about such progress. This internal debate reminds us, once again, that well-informed and well-intended African Americans are not monolithic in their thinking.

Traditionalism

Traditionalism posits the core belief that race no longer matters to Blacks achieving worldly success and personal happiness in our post–civil rights society. With the eradication of government-mandated or -sanctioned racial discrimination and segregation, the descendants of the enslaved must now work on their own culture—internal values and behaviors—to achieve the type of socioeconomic success other minority groups have achieved. The government's part in promoting racial progress post–Jim Crow is twofold: Acknowledge its own past failure to support the race-neutrality norm during slavery and Jim Crow; and remain neutral to the races and racial matters now and in the future. Thus, the best (and only) way to redress slavery and Jim Crow within the constraints of traditionalism is for the government to issue a public apology for slavery and Jim Crow and then deal with the lingering effects of these atrocities by remaining staunchly committed to the race-neutrality norm.

Accordingly, reparations per se are ill-advised.[62] They violate the race-neutrality principle. Even assuming, *arguendo*, that slavery and Jim Crow have lingering effects (including systemic racism), we ought not attempt to redress them with race-conscious governmental policies, the very thing that got us in trouble in the first place. Traditionalists would apply to the redress question the central message of *Brown v. Board of Education* as understood by Chief Justice Roberts: "Before *Brown*, school children were told where they could and could not go to school based on the color of their skin. . . . The way to stop discrimination on the basis of race is to stop discriminating on the basis of race."[63] In other words, two wrongs do not make a right. In addition, reparations are divisive and would not otherwise be helpful, as the impediments to socioeconomic success the descendants of the enslaved face today are largely self-inflected. Out-of-wedlock children, failure to take advantage of educational opportunities, crimes committed against neighbors, and other bad values and behaviors are internal problems and, therefore, within the control of the enslaved descendants. There is nothing government can do about the internal problems of any group except to stay true to principle—in this case racial omission. Finally, reparations, like all race-conscious policies, ultimately hurt the intended beneficiaries. They portray all African Americans as hapless victims incapable of going toe-to-toe with Whites.

Resurrecting an old variant of traditionalism does not change the outlook. This style of traditionalism, what can be called "radical traditionalism," has a Marxist flavor. It holds that focusing on race is particularly unhelpful to the Black worker. The main problem facing the Black worker is cyclical capitalism. Racism is epiphenomenal. Furthermore, race-conscious measures only exacerbate conflict between natural allies of the working class—Blacks and Whites. What Blacks should do, then, is take the government's apology and work with Whites to dismantle capitalism. Given the fact that racism has a major presence within the White-working-class culture, it could be argued, on the one hand, that radical traditionalism makes a valid point (it pays not to stoke the passions of these Whites) or, on the other hand, radical traditionalism makes no sense (it is a waste of time worrying about this so-called basket of deplorables).[64]

What would a government apology look like? That question was answered in 2009 when both Houses of Congress passed a Concurrent Resolution apologizing for slavery and Jim Crow. This extraordinary act of Congress, which many redress scholars thought would never happen, is faithful to the tenets of traditionalism. It is, however, a watered-down version of the House Bill in which a provision suggesting that Congress would pay reparations was omitted from the Concurrent Resolution by Republicans in the Senate.[65] The Concurrent Resolution is presented here in its entirety for two reasons: to make it easy for the reader to find its contents, and because it is very likely that this is all that African Americans will get in the way of redress from a Congress that will probably be dominated by traditionalists, mainly Republicans, for the foreseeable future.

S. CON. RES. 26
IN THE HOUSE OF REPRESENTATIVES

June 18, 2009
Referred to the Committee on the Judiciary

CONCURRENT RESOLUTION

Apologizing for the enslavement and racial
segregation of African-Americans.

Whereas during the history of the Nation, the United States has grown into a symbol of democracy and freedom around the world;

Whereas the legacy of African-Americans is interwoven with the very fabric of the democracy and freedom of the United States;

Whereas millions of Africans and their descendants were enslaved in the United States and the 13 American colonies from 1619 through 1865;

Whereas Africans forced into slavery were brutalized, humiliated, dehumanized, and subjected to the indignity of being stripped of their names and heritage;

Whereas many enslaved families were torn apart after family members were sold separately;

Whereas the system of slavery and the visceral racism against people of African descent upon which it depended became enmeshed in the social fabric of the United States;

Whereas slavery was not officially abolished until the ratification of the 13th amendment to the Constitution of the United States in 1865, after the end of the Civil War;

Whereas after emancipation from 246 years of slavery, African-Americans soon saw the fleeting political, social, and economic gains they made during Reconstruction eviscerated by virulent racism, lynchings, disenfranchisement, Black Codes, and racial segregation laws that imposed a rigid system of officially sanctioned racial segregation in virtually all areas of life;

Whereas the system of de jure racial segregation known as Jim Crow, which arose in certain parts of the United States after the Civil War to create separate and unequal societies for Whites and African-Americans, was a direct result of the racism against people of African descent that was engendered by slavery;

Whereas the system of Jim Crow laws officially existed until the 1960s—a century after the official end of slavery in the United States—until Congress took action to end it, but the vestiges of Jim Crow continue to this day;

Whereas African-Americans continue to suffer from the consequences of slavery and Jim Crow laws—long after both systems were formally abolished—through enormous damage and loss, both tangible and intangible, including the loss of human dignity and liberty;

Whereas the story of the enslavement and de jure segregation of African-Americans and the dehumanizing atrocities committed against them should not be purged from or minimized in the telling of the history of the United States;

Whereas those African-Americans who suffered under slavery and Jim Crow laws, and their descendants, exemplify the strength of the human character and provide a model of courage, commitment, and perseverance;

Whereas on July 8, 2003, during a trip to Goree Island, Senegal, a former slave port, President George W. Bush acknowledged the continuing legacy of slavery in life in the United States and the need to confront that legacy, when he stated that slavery was . . . one of the greatest crimes of history . . . The racial bigotry fed by slavery did not end with slavery or with segregation. And many of the issues that still trouble America have roots in the bitter experience of other times. But however long the journey, our destiny is set: liberty and justice for all.;

Whereas President Bill Clinton also acknowledged the deep-seated problems caused by the continuing legacy of racism against African-Americans that began with slavery, when he initiated a national dialogue about race;

Whereas an apology for centuries of brutal dehumanization and injustices cannot erase the past, but confession of the wrongs committed and a formal apology to African-Americans will help bind the wounds of the Nation that are rooted in slavery and can speed racial healing and reconciliation and help the people of the United States understand the past and honor the history of all people of the United States;

Whereas the legislatures of the Commonwealth of Virginia and the States of Alabama, Florida, Maryland, and North Carolina have taken the lead in adopting resolutions officially expressing appropriate remorse for slavery, and other State legislatures are considering similar resolutions; and

Whereas it is important for the people of the United States, who legally recognized slavery through the Constitution and the laws of the United States, to make a formal apology for slavery and for its successor, Jim Crow, so they can move forward and seek reconciliation, justice, and harmony for all people of the United States: Now, therefore, be it

That the sense of the Congress is the following:

    (1) Apology for the enslavement and segregation of African-Americans

The Congress—

    (A) acknowledges the fundamental injustice, cruelty, brutality, and inhumanity of slavery and Jim Crow laws;

    (B) apologizes to African-Americans on behalf of the people of the United States, for the wrongs committed against them and their ancestors who suffered under slavery and Jim Crow laws; and

    (C) expresses its recommitment to the principle that all people are created equal and endowed with inalienable rights to life, liberty, and the pursuit of happiness, and calls on all people of the United States to work toward eliminating racial prejudices, injustices, and discrimination from our society.

    (2) Disclaimer

Nothing in this resolution—

    (A) authorizes or supports any claim against the United States; or

    (B) serves as a settlement of any claim against the United States.

Passed the Senate June 18, 2009.[66]

The Concurrent Resolution may well resonate with most White Americans who, in my view, are ignorant or complacent about slavery. They are not necessarily racist in the conventional sense of the word (racial antipathy or White supremacy), but they deny the force and effect of slavery. They fail to see "racial slavery and its consequences as the basic reality, the grim and irrepressible theme governing both the settlement of the Western hemisphere and the emergence of a government and society in the United States that White people have regarded as 'free.'"[67] David Blight makes the important argument that one needs to go back to the end of the Civil War to understand this White mindset: "White Americans North and South were able to come together in the aftermath of that sectional struggle by celebrating the bravery of

white soldiers in both the Union and the Confederacy, all the
while minimizing the importance of slavery and the significance
of its destruction."[68]

The legendary David Brion Davis, Blight's mentor at Yale, argued
that White indifference about slavery is an indication that, though
the North won a military victory, the South won an ideological victory in the Civil War. In other words, the South convinced the rest
of the nation "that the role of slavery in American history [should]
be thoroughly diminished, even somehow as a cause of the [Civil
War]. . . . [T]he country gradually came to accept—or at least
not challenge—the Southern version of history in the years after
Reconstruction. 'The terrible price of reconciliation and reunion
was marginalizing slavery and race.'"[69]

That most Whites saw slavery as an event that had little regional
or national impact is not hard to understand. Ulrich Bonnell
("U.B.") Phillips's *American Negro Slavery* (1918) was the standard
work on slavery for generations. It was written from an unapologetically racist southern perspective. "[S]outhern slavery [was por-
trayed] as a benign and paternalistic institution, 'a training school'
and 'civilizing agency' 'for the untutored savage.'"[70] The book
appeared on course syllabi at Harvard University and other leading universities well into the 1950s. Phillips also painted Reconstruction as a failure. Like other White scholars, he ignored the
works of Black scholars, such as W.E.B. Du Bois's *The Suppression
of the African Slave Trade to the United States of America, 1638–1870*
(1896) and *Black Reconstruction* (1935), as well as important primary
sources, such as Frederick Douglass's autobiography, *The Life and
Times of Frederick Douglass* (1845; revised 1892).[71] Davis writes, "The
writings of Ulrich B. Phillips on slavery and of William S. Dunning
on Reconstruction were so rich in scholarly documentation and
so closely tuned to the nation's ideological needs—exemplified by
popular films from *Birth of a Nation* to *Gone with the Wind*—that
their influence on textbooks, fiction, journalism, and other historians would be difficult to exaggerate."[72]

By the mid- to late 1950s, an "anti-Phillips reaction" took root
among historians. Kenneth Stampp's seminal work on slavery, *The
Peculiar Institution: Slavery in the Ante-Bellum South* (1956), depicted
slavery as harsh, violent, and inhumane. This book along with

Stanley Elkins's *Slavery* (1959) and Eric McKitrick's *Andrew Johnson and Reconstruction* (1960) were the first of many attacks on Phillip's southern perspective.

Scholarship attacking the southern perspective came out more than a half-century ago. One would think that it rendered that perspective null and void. Why, then, do nonracist White Americans today continue to possess a collective amnesia regarding slavery's impact on current conditions in our society? Why do they not understand slavery's importance to the nation's development as a world power or its debilitating impact on the descendants of the enslaved, including systemic racism?

The answer may be that it is far easier to agree with principles than to live up to principles. As Ike Balbus asserts: *"Arguments about what should be are rarely a match for the needs that negate them"* [emphasis added].[73] Thus, "white Americans are unlikely to be moved by principled arguments in favor of reparations . . . [because] they have a deep psychological stake in resisting them." Continuing, Balbus explains that there is in Whites a "powerful unconscious resistance" to slave reparations because of "[t]he 'depressive' anxiety and guilt that inevitably accompany the awareness that we have harmed . . . [an innocent people]." The effort to reach Whites is, therefore, *"a work of mourning whose importance is matched only by its difficulty"* [emphasis in original].[74] Balbus and other psychologists maintain that a psychoanalytic case for depressive anxiety and guilt "does not require that any given individual white has actually harmed blacks but rather only that they have . . . harbored demonizing racial [beliefs]," or in other words, "that they have thought about doing so."[75]

If this analysis is correct, then, one can see a rational basis for traditionalism's approach to redress even if one would otherwise disagree with it. The government will not move without the support of White Americans. White Americans will have to cross a significant psychological barrier before accepting more than a government apology—reparations. Waiting for that to happen is wasted time; so why focus so much on reparations. Take the apology and declare victory. Reformists disagree. Their approach includes an attempt to educate non-racist White Americans along the lines presented in Part 1 above.

Reformism

Reformism's core belief is just the opposite of traditionalism's; namely, race still matters in our post–civil rights society. Nefarious—racial discrimination[76]—and non-nefarious—racial subordination[77]—sources of racial inequality in today's society sustain capital deficiencies (financial, human, and social) in Black society wrought by slavery and Jim Crow. The death of Jim Crow ended an atrocity, but it did not repair the racial damage caused by that atrocity or by the other atrocity, slavery. As a matter of morality, the primary perpetrator of these atrocities, the US government, has an obligation to repair this racial damage. It cannot just walk away from its dirty deeds. And as a practical matter, it is only the federal government that has the power to make the repair. Thus, reformism calls for a more activist government in redressing slavery than traditionalism.

Both traditionalism (with its apology) and reformism suggest that racial reconciliation is the main reason for going forward with slave redress. But whereas traditionalism envisions a minimalist governmental response to past atrocities, reformism imagines a maximalist governmental role, one that goes beyond apology. Specifically, reformism would prescribe atonement—apology plus reparations—as the only way to move the country toward racial healing in any meaningful way.

The atonement apology would look very different from traditionalism's apology. In addition to confessing the deed and admitting that the deed constituted an atrocity or grave injustice, the former would also indicate the government's remorse by explicitly asking for forgiveness. Even if the victims are not prepared to forgive, asking for forgiveness adds to the sincerity of the apology. The importance of asking for forgiveness was eloquently expressed by Elie Wiesel in remarks he gave at the dedication of a Holocaust Remembrance site at the Brandenburg Gate in Berlin. He urged Parliament to:

> [P]ass a resolution formally requesting, in the name of Germany, the forgiveness of the Jewish people for the crimes of Hitler. Do it publicly. . . . Ask the Jewish people to forgive Germany for what the Third Reich had done in Germany's name. Do it, and the

significance of this day will acquire a higher level. Do it, for we desperately want to have hope for this new century.[78]

Unlike the traditionalist apology, the reformist apology would also follow an extensive statement clarifying the historical record. "Clarification is desperately needed regarding the historical record on American slavery. The telling of this story has been the mother's milk of White misunderstanding about the peculiar institution and White complacency about its lingering effects."[79] My earlier discussion of analysis offered by David Bright and David Brion Davis certainly underscore this fact.

But simply saying "I'm sorry" is not enough. Reparations are needed to solidify the apology. Reformists would seem to prefer reparations in the form of system-wide reforms responsive to capital deficiencies in Black America. These reparations would target inequalities in education, employment, housing, voting, health, and policing, and would use a combination of rehabilitative (or institutional) and compensatory (or individual) reparations in this effort. Both sets of reparations could be monetary or nonmonetary. Although it may not be possible to completely redress these inequalities through reparations, I believe reformists would certainly want the government to try.

In education, for example, reformists would certainly want to use institutional reparations. "More than half of the nation's schoolchildren are in racially concentrated districts, where over 75 percent of students are either white or nonwhite. In addition, school districts are often segregated by income. The nexus of racial and economic segregation has intensified educational gaps between rich and poor students, and between white students and students of color."[80] Though there has been pushback based on the argument that the country has become less White, allegedly making it more difficult to integrate public schools, I believe reformists would not be deterred from moving forward with institutional reparations. They would likely be motivated by two facts in particular. First, "The predominant narrative among education activists is that school segregation has gotten worse in the past several decades."[81] Second, minority school districts annually receive $23 billion less in K-12 funding than similarly sized White school districts.[82]

Against this backdrop, reformists would at the very least call for a rehabilitative reparation in the form of a constitutional precommitment for racially integrated public schools. A constitutional amendment is necessary to prevent the Supreme Court from striking down local efforts designed to promote integrated schools. The Court could no longer strike down, as it did in *Parents Involved*, race-conscious student assignment plans voluntarily adopted by school boards to integrate de facto segregated schools.[83] Nor could the Court block inter-district remedies that integrate racially isolated school districts within a state as it did in *Milliken I*.[84] Most important, the amendment would nullify the untenable distinction between de jure and de facto segregation. That distinction makes no sense if the constitutional command as expressed in *Brown v. Board of Education* is equal educational opportunity. A constitutional precommitment for racially integrated schools would obviate the need for progressive school boards to try to act against de facto segregation by making the difficult claim that its schools were de jure segregated in the past even though they were not formally segregated by law.[85] The amendment, in short, would cut a clear path to integrated schools.

In addition to this rehabilitative reparation, reformists would support a compensatory reparation. The latter would likely be in the form of cash payments to each descendant of the enslaved. Compensatory cash reparations are income supplements. Assume that the payment is $30,000 per year per household member and that payment is to last one or two generations. This is all negotiable. A family of four would receive $120,000 per year per household. This money could be used to finance booster clubs that contribute extra money to public schools attended by enslaved descendants, to pay for private tutors, or to pay tuition at private schools. It can also be used to make a down payment on a home in a better school district. Beyond education, the compensatory reparation could also be used for such items as investments in financial instruments or to provide seed money to start a business. Determining the precise amount of each cash payment and how they are to be financed are issues that can be addressed at another time.[86] For now, it is sufficient to simply posit the idea of compensatory cash reparations and to consider, as I do later in this chapter, the merits of those reparations along with reformism's rehabilitative reparations in juxtaposition with the other post–civil rights strategies. Critical race theorists certainly challenge both forms of reformist reparations.

Critical Race Theory

The core post–civil rights belief of critical race theorists is that White hegemony matters most. Look around and what do you see: Whites on top and Blacks on the bottom. None of that is the natural order of things. It is entirely constructed, straight out of Anthropology 101: Elites construct their societies in their own image; straight White men are the elites in American society; ergo, American society is constructed in the image (and hence interest) of straight White men. While there is nothing necessarily nefarious about this development played out on a global stage, the social order in our country certainly came about for nefarious reasons—the subordination of Black Americans—as explained at the start of the chapter.

To effectively transition from a social order that is not objective and that unjustly slants in favor of insiders, reparations must pursue reconstruction rather than reform, equity rather than equality, critical race theorists believe. This is nothing less than a wholesale change in the relationship between race and power in our society. Redressing slavery is a matter of transitional justice.[87]

This way of thinking about slave redress certainly favors the atonement model, but not in the same way as reformists embrace the model. Critical race theorists would likely agree with the reformists' framing of the apology, but not with their framing of reparations. Race crits would probably solidify the apology with reparations in the form of system-wide transformation responsive to capital deficiencies in Black society. They would, in other words, seek social transformation across the board—education, employment, housing, voting, health, and policing—calling upon both rehabilitative and compensatory reparations. A few examples of institutional and individual reparations follow.

In education, critical race theorists would push not simply for school integration, but for *transformative integration*; integration that would bring about structural changes in educational systems. Transformative integration might include a rehabilitative reparation in the form of a constitutional precommitment for attendance quotas at wealthy White schools. Each school would be required to maintain a ratio of Black-to-White students K-12. A constitutional amendment removes the legal constraints of anti-progressive cases like *Parents Involved* and *Milliken I*, and reaffirms the authority of district courts to issue *Swann* remedies (including ratio quotas) even in the absence of a judicial finding of de jure segregation. Racial imbalance alone would now constitute a prima facie violation of the Constitution, a presumptive constitutional violation until proven otherwise.[88]

Critical race theorists would likely argue that racial quotas are necessary to ensure that Black and White students will attend the same schools. What is at stake is too important to leave to the discretion of local politicians or to the prejudices of parents, White or Black. Attending school with White students will give Black students equal access to quality instruction and adequate resources. In our society, green follows White. Not only government funds but private money from parent-created booster clubs and PTAs used to fund afterschool activities will also inure to the benefit of Black students attending these schools.

Racial quotas are transformative in yet another way, race crits might argue. The future of a racially healthy society depends on racial mixing starting in the lower grades. Young children of both races will learn "human nature in all its phases, with all its emotions, passions and feelings, loves and hates, its hopes and fears, its impulses and sensibilities."[89] What Justice Harlan said at a thoughtful moment in his lone dissent in *Plessy v. Ferguson* applies with perhaps greater force today: "The destinies of the two races, in this country, are indissolubly linked together."[90]

Turning to compensatory reparations, critical race theory would seem to be more interested in wealth accumulation than in income enhancement. There is no doubt that income disparity is a serious problem—"the median black household earn[s] just 59 cents for every dollar of income the median white household earned"[91]—but wealth disparity is the larger problem. All the data, including data presented in the beginning of the chapter, provide evidence of a huge disparity in wealth between Black and White Americans. For example, "Today, Black Americans constitute approximately 13 to

14 percent of the nation's population, yet possess less than 3 percent of the nation's wealth."[92] Also, the median White household owns 86 times the assets of the median Black household.[93] Measuring household wealth differently, "[f]or every $100 in wealth held by a white family, a Black family has just $10."[94] Redressing wealth disparity portends more social transformation than redressing income disparity, race crits would probably argue.

To create substantially more wealth within Black America, compensatory reparations in the form of cash payments to individuals would have to be conditional rather than direct. For example, rather than providing yearly payments of $120,000 of supplemental income for a family of four ($30,000 per person per year) which allows the family to do whatever it wishes with the additional disposable income (the reformist plan), critical race theorists would want to sink this money into wealth accumulation. Money would be used for limited purposes, such as property (home ownership or rental payments, freeing up other money for investments), direct investments (financial or business), or education (private grade schools, college tuition, or training programs). These reparations can also pay for homework supervision after school, coding classes, and other enrichment programs.[95]

I suspect critical race theorists would not want the government to determine the permissibility of expenditures for cash reparations, compensatory or rehabilitative. These expenditures could easily fall victim to partisan politics. Instead, redress funds could be held in trust with experienced private citizens acting as trustees. As I have stated on another occasion:

> A board of commissioners, consisting of reputable citizens selected by blacks, would oversee operation of the trust fund in their respective regions of the country. Commissioners and their staff would, for example, help fund recipients make the right choices in schools and business opportunities. All payments from the trust fund would be by electronic transfer. Recipients would never really see or handle the funds.[96]

An atonement trust fund may have some merit, even for limited separatists.

Limited Separation

The core belief of limited separatists is that racial solidarity or identity matters most in the pursuit of racial progress. Rather than placing all their eggs in the racial-integration basket, Blacks must have
the *option* of embracing their own identity—"things Black." Blacks
should be allowed to be unapologetically Black. Racial integration
has not been a vehicle for racial progress on which most Blacks
have been able to ride. Orlando Patterson and others report that
"African Americans are the least assimilated racial or ethnic group,
that although Asians and Latinos are disengaging their national
origins from racial identity, similar to European immigrants of the
past, African Americans (including multiracial blacks) are perceived as being 'black,' and choose to identify as 'black.' These
identities are abetted by the fact that African Americans intermarry
at a rate that is significantly lower than the rates for Asians and
Latinos."[97] Blacks and other racial minorities have broadly similar
experiences but with strong group variations in form, intensity, and
duration.

   Not unlike the other post–civil rights theorists, limited separatists would probably support slave redress on grounds of racial reconciliation. And, like the other theorists, they would view this social
goal through the prism of their core belief. Limited separatists'
fundamental belief in racial identity does not, however, appear to
create the need or desire for an apology from the government,
which sets it apart from the other theorists. Demanding an apology
might be too much of an investment in White acceptance. Limited
separatists just don't care. For them, racial reconciliation would
seem to only require a government program of reparations targeting Black institutions and individuals. This approach to redress
leans less toward the atonement model than the tort model.

   Starting with education for comparative purposes, limited separatists would likely prefer rehabilitative monetary and nonmonetary
reparations. The latter might take the form of a constitutional precommitment for public schools that opt for a Black identity and for
HBCUs. This constitutional amendment would soften *Brown*'s ruling that, "Separate educational facilities are inherently unequal."[98]
Black institutions would be constitutional under the amendment
if they pass muster under limited separation's three-pronged

test discussed earlier. The strict scrutiny test would no longer be applicable. Having passed constitutional scrutiny, these institutions (public and private K-12 schools and HBCUs) would then be eligible to receive reparations (public funds) without violating the Constitution. Other requirements set by the Black community would dictate the actual distribution of these funds, but the critical point is that the Constitution would no longer be an impediment in using public monies to fund Black educational institutions.

Black identity very much informs a limited separatist's understanding of what counts as a quality education. Thus, an integrated classroom is not a prerequisite. Blacks do not need to sit next to a White child to obtain a quality education. And rather than making Black schools "desegregative attractive" to White suburban students by updating programs and facilities or increasing teacher salaries,[99] limited separatists would want to pour these resources into Black schools for the sole purpose of improving the quality of education for Black students.

Scholars do not, in fact, agree on the extent to which integrated schools yield educational benefits. Some have concluded that Black students receive genuine educational benefits in this environment, while others have concluded that there are no demonstrable educational benefits.[100] Citing several scholars, Justice Clarence Thomas, an enthusiastic limited separatist when it comes to education— *"It never ceases to amaze me that the courts are so willing to assume that anything that is predominantly black must be inferior"* (emphasis added)[101]—makes the case that Black under-achievement in racially isolated schools is a myth:

> Before *Brown*, the most prominent example of an exemplary black school was Dunbar High School. . . . "Dunbar graduates earned fifteen degrees from Ivy League colleges, and ten degrees from Amherst, Williams, and Wesleyan." Dunbar is by no means an isolated example. . . . Even after *Brown*, some schools with predominantly black enrollments have achieved outstanding educational results. . . . There is also evidence that black students attending historically black colleges achieve better academic results than those attending predominantly white colleges. . . .
> The Seattle School Board itself must believe that racial mixing is not necessary to black achievement. Seattle operates a K-8

"African-American Academy," which has a "nonwhite" enrollment
of 99%. . . . That school was founded in 1990 as part of the school
board's effort to "*increase academic achievement.*" . . . According to
the school's most recent annual report, "[a]cademic excellence" is
its "primary goal." . . . This racially imbalanced environment has
reportedly produced test scores "higher across all grade levels in
reading, writing and math." . . . [T]he children in Seattle's African
American Academy have shown gains when placed in a "highly segregated environment."[102]

   Rehabilitative cash reparations go to Black institutions. Representing African Americans collectively, these institutions operate
at the heart of the Black ethos. They are physical manifestations
of Black identity and the facilitator of Black solidarity. Not only
Black schools (e.g., K-12 and HBCUs), but also Black social justice
organizations (e.g., NAACP and Urban League) and Black businesses of all types primarily servicing Black communities or Black
interests would be recipients of cash reparations. Schools and colleges are not the only organizations that educate African Americans. The Black News Channel, for example, endeavors to educate Black audiences with stories that offer a broader perspective
about their community than is currently provided by other news
networks. Health issues unique to African Americans, discussions
about HBCUs and federal housing policies affecting Blacks, and
the many positive accomplishments of African Americans are some
of the items covered by the Black News Channel in its effort to educate and entertain the Black community.

   I do not believe limited separatists would reject compensatory
reparations in the form of conditional cash payments to individual
Black families or individuals similar to what critical race theorists
would propose. Wealth accumulation seems more important to
limited separatists than income supplementation. Limited separatists would, however, prioritize individual spending and investing
in "things Black" such as Black schools, colleges, and businesses.
Reparations for home mortgages could be restricted to homes in
Black communities that could be part of a larger plan to revitalize
these communities along with public schools in these communities.
The revitalization plan could include a homeowner's association
(HOA) that would set and enforce living standards throughout the

community, including expulsion from the community. Like institutional reparations, individual reparations under limited separation would be designed to promote racial solidarity and identity. For limited separatists, this is the best way to maximize racial healing in today's post–civil rights society.

COMMENTARY

Each post–civil rights theory—traditionalism, reformism, critical race theory, and limited separation—conforms the discourse on slave redress—the tort and atonement models—to a particular post–civil rights norm. Each theory views slave redress through its own vision of what is needed to advance racial progress, and, hence, racial reconciliation, in our post–Jim Crow society. There is no dearth of considerations that add complexity to this analysis,[103] not the least of which is the fact that these core beliefs about racial advancement remain contested nearly a half-century after Jim Crow. Though legitimate and deserving of our time and attention, these norms of preference are not of equal merit in my opinion.

Traditionalism's approach to slave redress consists entirely of an apology from the perpetrator government. This strategy would back African Americans into a cul-de-sac. Reparations may not be a politically viable form of redress, as traditionalists argue, but that is not reason enough to abandon an otherwise sound social-justice measure. I believe in what I have called "practical idealism,"[104] meaning social justice theory should be idealistic yet practical. In other words, it should be, at least as initially articulated, morally defensible rather than politically viable; it must be within the reach of morally motivated individuals and institutions rather than politically popular. On that basis, I disagree with traditionalism's underlying message, shared by other scholars, which is that civil rights theory "must not be utopian—applicable only in an ideal world—but must be politically viable given the sociohistorical circumstances of contemporary black Americans."[105] I find this to be a most troubling notion. Ending slavery and Jim Crow were certainly pipedreams for a long time; but that did not prevent Frederick Douglass, Thurgood Marshall, Martin Luther King, and many other civil rights advocates from demanding change. These pioneers were quite willing to complicate the lives of White Americans, even make them feel uncomfortable. They set the moral compass for society and worked like hell to move society in the right direction. That has also been the way many civil rights scholars have conducted their scholarship, challenging received traditions. This type of moral clarity and resolve is needed today if the push for racial reconciliation is to have some semblance of integrity.

The argument that reparations are a form of racial paternalism is a familiar one. It arises in opposition to any asymmetrical civil rights measure and was certainly expressed quite often at the Black Table at Yale Law School of which I spoke in the chapter's introduction. If such measures make Blacks look like racial losers, then the problem lies with Whites, not with Blacks. Taking a page from limitation separation, I would argue that Blacks should never forgo an opportunity based on how they are viewed by Whites. Racial progress should never be held hostage to White prejudice or ignorance or inconvenience, or to what Cornel West calls "the white gaze." An individual's worldly success and personal happiness should never be sequestered to the views of others.

Traditionalism does, however, raise an important point about White needs that negate principled arguments. Rather than concede defeat, however, I would argue that redress discourse should endeavor to address legitimate White concerns. For example, the concern that public attention given to the problem of White privilege disadvantages the White working class must not be dismissed outright as racism. This claim comes up so often in the discussion of slave redress that it behooves us to give it serious attention here. My students often make the point that progressives are too quick to dismiss the concerns of the White working class, the group that feels most threatened when attention turns to White privilege. Here are the points that need to be made as one defends slave redress.

The lives of Whites living in struggling communities must be acknowledged. These communities suffer from deindustrialization and are often devastated by the opioid crisis. Those in favor of slave redress must answer this concern. It must first be pointed out that addressing the problem of White privilege is not meant to devalue the deep suffering of families in these communities. People who have worked thirty years for a company and are suddenly laid off can no longer take care of their families. These families are not privileged in a socioeconomic sense. This is a real concern that must not be ignored. But it must also be pointed out that the discussion about White privilege or systemic racism or diversity and inclusion deals with a *different* problem the solution of which does not undercut any attempt to address White-working-class concerns, let alone acknowledge the legitimacy of these concerns.

White privilege speaks to the plight of the other; in other words, intergenerational disadvantage based on one's race or the color of one's skin. It is about being denied a quality education, a good-paying job, a decent home, and decent medical service on a continuous and systematic basis. In his book, *Black Man in a White Coat: A Doctor's Reflection on Race and Medicine* (2015), Dr. Damon Tweedy exposes the myriad and systemic instances of discriminatory treatment African Americans receive in emergency rooms and hospitals. Other African Americans have made similar observations. One first-hand account is particularly disturbing:

"A few seconds in I said, 'I can feel this.'

"The doctor said, 'No, you don't, that's just pressure.'

"'No, I can feel you cutting me,' I told her.

"She didn't believe me. She kept going," says Ayana Moore, 43, a mother of two in Durham, NC. She is a scientist with several advanced educational degrees, including a master's in science and a PhD in physiology and biophysics. She is a by-choice mom with a solid health insurance plan that covered her insemination. She could afford the fertility medications and regular doctor's appointments.

She was considered advanced maternal age and had one run-in with a pesky uterine fibroid, but overall, she had an uncomplicated pregnancy.

None of this inoculated her from the problem plaguing Black women in the delivery room: Their pain is often ignored and dismissed by doctors.

"I could feel her cutting across and it got to the middle, I just started screaming," she says. One of the nurses finally yelled Stop! and in a blink Moore was out.

"I went from a room full of nurses and doctors to the room being empty except for custodians cleaning up. My mom was sitting there, and I was like, 'Oh, my God, what happened to the

baby?' I thought the worst," she said. Both mom and baby recov-
ered from the Caesarean section, but she said the birth of her son
was extremely traumatic.[106]

A Black woman is three to four times more likely to die in childbirth because the medical staff, whether males or females, do not
believe her when she says something does not feel right.[107]

The White working class does not face these problems or the
more general problem of systemic racism discussed earlier. They
suffer class subordination but not racial subordination. In contrast,
the Black working class suffers both class and racial subordination.
White privilege means that a member of the White working class
is much more likely to escape arrest than a Black member of the
same class for the same crime. As a result, the working-class White
is not placed in the position of having to post bail. The working-
class Black suspect, in contrast, having no assets to post bail, will
have to serve time in jail and probably lose his job for not showing
up for work. If a White family falls into poverty, it is less likely than
a Black family to arrive there as a consequence of an arrest and failure to post bail. Working-class Whites, in short, suffer disadvantage
in spite of their race. Working-class Blacks suffer disadvantage *because
of* their race.

Traditionalists also raise the issue of identity politics. In my
view, paying attention to the problem of White privilege or systemic racism is no more identity politics than giving attention to
the problems of the White working class. The basic concern is the
common good. Focusing on racial difference or class difference
is necessary to arrive at the common good, which is to say the
binary between unity and difference is a false binary. *In a racially
diverse society, the only way to achieve unity is through difference.* By
paying attention to the unique obstacles African Americans and
the White working class (or other groups) face in acquiring the
things all Americans want—fair access to quality education, quality jobs, quality housing, quality medical care, and fair treatment
in the criminal justice system—society as a whole benefits. The
American Dream becomes a reality for more Americans. Singling
out the special obstacles that groups face in achieving the American Dream serves the common good just as much as singling out
the things that unite us as Americans. Plato stated the guiding

principle: "When equality is given to unequal things, the resultant will be unequal."[108] Not only is traditionalism's don't-rock-the-boat approach to slave redress tepid, so too is its idea of an apology. The government apology contemplated by traditionalism fails as an apology and, therefore, lacks credibility. It is not a genuine apology, the elements of which I enumerated earlier in my discussion of the atonement model. Although the government's so-called apology confesses the deed and admits the deed was an injustice, there is no expression of remorse and no request for forgiveness. Even if the victims are unlikely to express their forgiveness, asking for forgiveness adds to the sincerity of the perpetrator's apology as also discussed previously.

Traditionalism's apology also lacks believability for another reason; namely, it explicitly forecloses the possibility of the government solidifying the apology with a redemptive act—to wit, a reparation. The failure to leave open the possibility of reparations of any kind means that damages visited upon enslaved descendants wrought by slavery and Jim Crow, which Congress itself acknowledges in its failed apology, will never be repaired. A halfhearted apology with no solidifying reparation offers little redress for slavery. White Americans may not be ready psychologically for more than an apology, as traditionalism tell us, but both the enslaved and their descendants deserve better than that if society is to achieve any semblance of racial reconciliation.

In addition to the argument that reparations are politically unpopular, traditionalism justifies avoiding reparations on the basis of a normative position expressed by Chief Justice Roberts's interpretation of *Brown v. Board of Education* and by the two-wrongs-don't-make-a-right maxim. The Chief Justice, as I mentioned earlier, reads the racial-omission norm into *Brown* based on the fact that, "Before *Brown*, school children were told where they could and could not go to school based on the color of their skin." But it was only *Black children* who were negatively affected by segregation laws. There is no evidence that White children struggled to attend Black schools. What a cruel irony that the Chief Justice of the United States would attempt to rewrite what is arguably the Supreme Court's most important case, certainly its most important civil rights case.

The argument that reparations collide with the anti-discrimination principle or the multiple-wrongs injunction is rather weak. There is a difference between Jim Crow discrimination and asymmetrical remedies like reparations. The former is designed to exclude and stigmatize, the latter is intended to include and validate; the former is negative, the latter is positive. Similarly, assuming, *arguendo*, that reparations constitute a "wrong," to argue that it breaches the multiple-wrongs injunction misses the point of the command. "Two wrongs don't make a right" presupposes the second wrong is of equal or greater evil than the first wrong.[109] The state's execution of a serial killer invokes a lesser wrong than the fifty killings for which the murderer was executed.[110] Gunning down Hitler in cold blood is a lesser wrong than exterminating six million Jews. Likewise, reparations that are calculated toward racial healing entail a lesser wrong (again, assuming, for the sake of argument, that a wrong has been committed) than race-conscious decisions designed to exclude, subordinate, or stigmatize. Wrongs cannot be judged in a vacuum. The purpose for which the action is taken cannot be ignored when assessing an action's justice or injustice; otherwise, how could we ever explain justifiable wrongs, such as wrongs committed in self-defense?

It is less that traditionalism is unwilling to challenge White thinking about race than that it is burdened by the strictures of its core conviction that race no longer matters. But still, the failure to challenge Whites robs Blacks of the power that comes from simply understanding the racialized conditions under which we live. I say, again, redress theory, like all civil rights theory, should be utopian rather than political in the early stages. The proper path forward must be moral, debated, respectful of all legitimate views, and garner a consensus before the horse trading, or ox-goring, begins.

I have spent a number of pages on traditionalism only because I reject almost everything it has to offer about slave redress, including the assumptions on which it operates. Not unlike a court that gives due process to the party it ultimately rules against, I felt it important to give traditionalism its due before rejecting it. I need not be so generous with reformism, critical race theory, or limited separation because I accept each one in part.

Reformism and critical race theory are broadly symmetrical in their approach to slave redress. Both posit that atonement—apology plus reparations—is the best path to racial reconciliation. Each calls for a genuine apology solidified by meaningful reparations. To that extent, I agree with both approaches. Reformism's norm of racial integration and critical racial theory's norm of social transformation dictate different reparative strategies for concretizing the apology and, thereby, moving toward racial reconciliation. In my view, critical race theory offers the superior approach, although I do not find anything objectionable in reformism.

Rehabilitative reparations in the form of a constitutional precommitment for racial preferences (reformism) or racial quotas (critical race theory) have similar redress benefits. Both overturn Supreme Court rulings that have allowed public schools to remain separate and unequal throughout the post–civil rights period. Most important, the legal significance of the distinction between de jure and de facto segregation is gone. Racial imbalance by itself would now be sufficient to establish a constitutional violation. It no longer has to be tied to traceable de jure segregation or intentional discrimination.[111] As Justice Marshall said in his dissent in *Milliken I*, the distinction between de jure and de facto segregation is "superficial," one not found in the Constitution but merely created by the justices themselves.[112] Also gone is *Milliken I*'s limitation on the use of interdistrict remedies for de facto school segregation.[113] Many civil rights scholars consider *Milliken I* to be the most tragic decision for racial progress since *Plessy v. Ferguson*.[114]

In agreeing with reformism and critical race theory, I am not suggesting that the issue regarding de jure and de facto segregation is easy to resolve. Holding a school district responsible for correcting racial imbalance caused by changing housing patterns within the school district seems unfair at some level. This is especially so when the school board implemented measures that created a unitary school system thirty years ago, and, thus, was in compliance with *Brown* at that time. On the other hand, I believe racial inequality should be viewed as a chronic condition that must be treated constantly. Society collectively must stay on its meds.

The real difference between reformism and critical race theory lies in the choice between racial preferences and racial quotas. Racial quotas are taboo in our society and have been since at least the time of *Bakke*.[115] But if school administrators, together with local politicians, White teachers, and White parents are predisposed to view Black students as a "problem," if they doubt the qualifications of these students, they will find ways to limit school integration. Simply taking account of race will not guarantee educational opportunities for Black students when the ultimate decision rests on the judgment and goodwill of those who assume Black students are a "problem." More than racial preferences, racial quotas change the relationship between race and power in the context of public education. This type of effort is necessary for racial reconciliation, and for that reason I favor a constitutional precommitment for racial quotas in the context of K-12 education. Racial quotas in this context makes the most sense to me as a rehabilitative reparation.

It also makes sense, in my view, for the government to issue compensatory cash reparations in the form of conditional payments rather than direct payments as a means of wealth accumulation. The pushback is that direct payments allow for the exercise of agency. If Blacks want to blow their reparative funds gambling in Las Vegas, that is quite alright. After all, it is their money. The legacy of slavery gives the victims the right to do whatever they want with reparative money. We do not place constraints on White control over their money. Treating slave descendants differently is a form of racism. I beg to differ.

Reparative funds are responsive not to an individual injury but to a collective injury. Slavery operated at the group level; it was directed toward Black identity rather than individual behavior. Collective wrongs call for collective remedies. It would be different if reparations had been provided by slaveholders to their former enslaved *in personam* at the end of the Civil War. Direct payment would seem more appropriate under such circumstances. But in dealing with the descendants of the enslaved, I believe conditioning cash payments on wealth accumulation is most responsive to the atrocity of slavery and a more effective path to racial reconciliation.

But I do, indeed, share the distrust of government implicit in the call for direct payments. For that reason, I favor the atonement trust fund. It is a superior alternative to government control over cash payments, whether direct or conditional. Also, conditional payments funneled through an atonement trust fund avoid the problem of predatory inclusion. This problem occurs when unscrupulous vendors (e.g., insurance companies or investment schemers) or greedy relatives take advantage of unsophisticated recipients of reparative income. Trustees of an atonement trust will stand in a fiduciary relationship with the beneficiaries of the trust, the descendants of the enslaved. They will protect the funds and the recipients of the funds.

Limited separatists maintain that racial identity is essential to racial advancement and, hence, racial reconciliation. For that reason, limited separatists call for a constitutional precommitment legitimizing Black public schools and HBCUs as well as cash payments made directly to these and other Black institutions. In terms of individual reparations, they favor payments conditioned on fortifying Black solidarity; such as tuition limited to Black educational institutions, mortgaging restricted to revitalizing Black communities, and investments in Black businesses. These institutional and individual reparations undercut the racial omission norm favored by traditionalism, the racial integration norm favored by reformism, and the social transformation norm—specifically transforming White, mainstream institutions—favored by critical race theory.

Although, as I have indicated earlier, scholars differ on whether integrated schools generate important educational benefits, both reformists and critical race theorists suggest that racially isolated education is not quality education. In other words, quality education in a culturally diverse society, they seem to believe, must be defined, ipso facto, as education that takes place within a diverse or integrated student population. Students need to learn how to relate to "the other" in addition to learning the Three Rs. To be sure, both Black and White students can be educated in the Three Rs in racially isolated schools, as Justice Thomas argues. I fear, however, that students in racially isolated schools will emerge therefrom as educated fools. I fear that they will not be able to "relate to our national life in all its facets," they will not "know[] the wellspring— the aspirations and fears, the affections and indifferences—from which particular kinds of thought and behavior flow."[116] Racially isolated education my be comfortable but it is not as enriching as racially integrated education.

The pushback is that there is no dearth of evidence suggesting that Black children who are encouraged to explore and embrace their racial identity at school and who are taught in schools surrounded by peers and faculty members who share their racial identity grow up with better self-esteem and racial-esteem and, consequently, have better learning outcomes.[117] This finding is replicated at the university level. Adequately funded HBCUs are widely recognized for the value they bring to African Americans and the nation as a whole. As Michael Lomax, president of the United Negro College Fund, states, "HBCUs are, like our Black churches, cornerstone institutions in the Black community. Like the lives of Black men and women, our HBCUs are constantly undervalued, disparaged, under assault, and put at risk. And just as we unequivocally declare that 'Black Lives Matter,' so too we affirm that HBCUs' continued existence matters."[118]

Limited separatists merely want White- and Black-identified schools to be treated *pari passu*. They see the choice as an individual one. The decision is based on what works best for the student.

In the end, the country will have to debate the merits of each of the approaches to slave redress outlined in this chapter. In my view, all the proposals have merit with the exception of two: the absence of reparations (traditionalism) and the absence of an apology (limited separation), including a genuine apology (traditionalism). Thus, I totally reject traditionalism and partially reject limited separation, which is to say I totally reject the tort model. These are the parameters I believe are necessary for a productive discussion of the redress issue.

CONCLUSION

Post–civil rights theories provide interesting and important perspectives in our thinking about slave redress. I have suggested some of the ways in which they might frame our understanding of the redress issue. My analysis focuses on the perpetrator's side of the issue, not the victim's forgiveness. The latter can be incorporated in the framework at another time. Necessarily, my discussion has been illustrative rather than comprehensive of the types of redress proposals each post–civil rights theory might advance. In addition, I have not attempted to decide which of these proposals offers the "best" path to racial reconciliation, which I think is the social goal of each of the theorists. I merely wish to stimulate discussion of a subject whose importance may be little understood and whose complexity is certainly underestimated.

NOTES

1 The competing redress models were first published in the form of a book, Roy L. Brooks, *When Sorry Isn't Enough: The Controversy Over Apologies and Reparations for Human Injustice* (New York: NYU Press, 1999), and subsequently refined in another book, Roy L. Brooks, *Atonement and Forgiveness: A New Model for Black Reparations* (Berkeley: University of California Press, 2004, 2019).

2 The project began with the publication of my book, *Integration or Separation? A Strategy for Racial Equality* (Cambridge, MA: Harvard University Press, 1996). It was further developed with a socioeconomic emphasis in *Racial Justice in the Age of Obama* (Princeton, NJ: Princeton University Press, 2009) and then with sociolegal and sociocultural emphases in Roy L. Brooks, *The Racial Glass Ceiling: Subordination in American Law and Culture* (New Haven, CT: Yale University Press, 2017). Post–civil rights theories also shape the presentation of cases in one of my casebooks, *The Law of Discrimination: Cases and Perspectives* (New Providence, NJ: LexisNexis, 2011).

3 Not limited to African Americans, the law students who sat at the Black Table in the Yale Law School cafeteria after dinner held diverse viewpoints, which we all respected. In addition to myself, students who sat at the table included Lani Guiner on the left, Clarence Thomas on the right, on occasion Hillary Rodham and Bill Clinton in the middle. Sam Alito, now a Supreme Court justice, never sat at the table but sometimes sat within earshot of its discussions. His analysis of the Black experience in one case in particular, *Fisher v. University of Texas (Fisher II)*, 136 S. Ct. 2198, 2216 (2016) (arguing that the university's affirmative action program exacerbates intra-racial class conflicts between middle-class and working-class Black students), indicates that he was listening to the discussions. Our discussions were in the tradition of the founding generation's debates about republican government and the philosophers' arguments about justice in Plato's *Republic*. For a more detailed discussion about the "Black Table," see Brooks, *Racial Justice in the Age of Obama*, ix.

4 Brooks, *Racial Justice in the Age of Obama*, 10.

5 42 U.S.C. 20003 to 2000e-17 (Supp. V 1972). On the idea of affirmative action for Whites, see Ira Katznelson, *When Affirmative Action Was White: An Untold History of Racial Inequality in Twentieth-Century America* (New York: W.W. Norton, 2005), arguing that twentieth-century programs that help to define the welfare state, such as the New Deal and Fair Deal of the 1930s and 1940s, purposefully discriminated in favor of Whites. However, there was nothing racially remedial about these programs, which dis-

tinguishes them from the affirmative action programs designed for racial minorities starting in the 1960s and 1970s.

6 These socio-psychological conditions are manifestations of systemic racism discussed at the end of this part of the chapter. The rise in White supremacy, particularly within Donald Trump's Republican Party, has been documented by the FBI and noted by many observers. Max Boot, "Think Republicans in Washington Are Bad? They're Far Worse at the State Level," *Washington Post*, May 10, 2021, www.washingtonpost.com. See also Brooks, *The Racial Glass Ceiling*, 92–93. Robert C. Smith defines White privilege as "an implicit sense of group position." Robert C. Smith, *Racism in the Post–Civil Rights Era* (New York: SUNY Press, 1995), 42, and Peggy McIntosh famously described it as "an invisible weightless knapsack of special provisions, assurances, tools, maps, guides, codebooks, passports, visas, clothes, compass, emergency gear, and blank checks." Peggy McIntosh, "White Privilege and Male Privilege: A Personal Account of Coming to See Correspondences Through Work in Women's Studies," in *Critical White Studies: Looking Behind the Mirror*, ed. Richard Delgado and Jean Stefancic (Philadelphia: Temple University Press, 1997), 291. See ibid. at 297. Implicit bias reflects the way one looks at the world, how one organizes the social environment in which we all live. It consists of mental shortcuts or schema people naturally employ to make sense of their world. Implicit bias occurs when, for example, a supervisor, who does not consciously think about race when making an employment decision, operates on the basis of certain "gut feelings," such as a belief that the White candidate would "fit in more comfortably" than the Black candidate. The Implicit Association Test (IAT) measures implicit bias. See, e.g., Christine Jolls and Cass R. Sunstein, "The Law of Implicit Bias," *California Law Review* 94 (2006): 969, 971 (sources cited therein).

7 See Brooks, *Atonement and Forgiveness*, 42–43 (discussing the work of Glenn Loury and others). I discuss other ways of articulating the lasting impact of slavery, including Stuart Henry and Dragan Milovanovic's "harms of repression" and "harms of reduction." See ibid.

8 I discuss later in this part of the chapter the wage differential between Black and White college-educated males.

9 See "Slavery, Race, and Inequality in America," *Bill Moyers Journal*, Broadcast Date: June 6, 2008, interviewing Douglas Blackmon. See also Douglas A. Blackmon, *Slavery by Another Name: The Re-Enslavement of Black Americans from the Civil War to World War II* (New York: Anchor Books, 2008). "As many as 200,000 black Americans were forced into back-breaking labor in coal mines, turpentine factories and lumber camps [alone]. They lived in squalid conditions, chained, starved, beaten, flogged and sexually violated. They died by the thousands from injury, disease and torture."

Kathy Roberts Forde and Bryan Bowman, "Exploiting Black Labor After the Abolition of Slavery," *U.S. News & World Report*, February 7, 2017, www. usnews.com. "In some Alabama prison camps, convicts died at a rate of 30–40% a year." "Slavery by Another Name," *PBS*, Episode 1, Broadcast Date: February 12, 2012, at 29:35 minutes.

10 Steven S. Rogers, *A Letter to My White Friends and Colleagues: What You Can Do Right Now to Help the Black Community* (New York: Wiley, 2021), 61.

11 See Blackmon, *Slavery by Another Name*, 377.

12 Jackie MacMullan, Rafe Bartholomew, and Dan Klores, *Basketball: A Love Story* (New York: Crown Publishing, 2018), 132–133. Enforcement of Circular No. 3591 by Attorney General Francis Biddle is discussed in Blackmon, *Slavery by Another Name*, 377–382. Biddle, who held racist views of Blacks in line with his contemporaries, was no hero. He was simply doing his duty, which was to enforce the compact of freedom forged in the Civil War. In 1951, "Congress passed even more explicit statutes, making any form of slavery in the United States indisputably a crime. Reports of involuntary servitude continued to trickle in to federal investigators well into the 1950s." Ibid., 381.

13 Dalton Conley, "The Cost of Slavery," *New York Times*, February 13, 2003, www.nytimes.com.

14 See Richard Rothstein, *The Color of Law: The Forgotten History of How Our Government Segregated America* (New York: W. W. Norton, 2017).

15 Roy L. Brooks, "Op-Ed: Reparations Are an Opportunity to Turn a Corner on Race Relations," April 23, 2019, *Los Angeles Times*, www.latimes. com.

16 See Rothstein, *The Color of Law*.

17 Brooks, *The Racial Glass Ceiling*, 7 (sources cited therein). Other social scientists have come to a similar conclusion. See ibid.

18 Ibid. at 8.

19 Ibid. at 6–7.

20 "At $171,000, the net worth of a typical white family is nearly ten times greater than that of a Black family ($17,150) in 2016. Gaps in wealth between Black and white households reveal the effects of accumulated inequality and discrimination, as well as differences in power and opportunity that can be traced back to this nation's inception." Kriston McIntosh, Emily Moss, Ryan Nunn, and Jay Shambaugh, "Examining the Black-White Wealth Gap," February 27, 2020, *Brookings*, www.brookings.edu . The wage differential between college-educated Black and White males of similar experience is larger today than it was in 1972. And the former are doing everything conservatives say Blacks should be doing to get ahead. See Brooks, *Racial Justice in the Age of Obama*, 148, fig. 38 (1975–2003). A study using similar data (both male and female college graduates) pub-

lished in 2019 reports that "young black college graduates are paid, on average, 12.2 percent less than their white counterparts." Elise Gould, Zane Mokhiber, and Julia Wolfe, "Class of 2019," College Edition, *Economic Policy Institute*, May 14, 2019, www.epi.org. To the extent that these wage disparities are largely due to grades, that would suggest that the racial gap in the quality of K-12 education has *grown* since the end of Jim Crow. Yet grades do not tell the whole story. Two researchers report that though "a higher proportion of Asians than whites graduate from the top half of law schools, . . . [w]hite law graduates get a median annual boost to earnings that is substantially higher than minority law grads." Debra Cassens Weiss, "A Law Degree Provides a Larger Earnings Boost to Whites than Minorities," Lawyer Pay, October 2, 2017, *ABA Journal*, www.abajournal.com. The *Washington Post* has created a database of every known deadly police shooting in America since 2015. As of May 17, 2021, the paper reports that: "Although half of the people shot and killed by police are White, Black Americans are shot at a disproportionate rate. They account for less than 13 percent of the U.S. population, but are killed by police at more than twice the rate of White Americans. Hispanic Americans are also killed by police at a disproportionate rate." "Fatal Force," *Washington Post*, May 17, 2021, www.washingtonpost.com. Ben Crump, arguably the leading civil rights lawyer in the country today, has witnessed systemic racial disadvantage in the criminal justice system firsthand. He has represented numerous unarmed Black individuals, including George Floyd and Michael Brown, killed by police officers. In addition to police killings of unarmed Black Americans, Crump points to the fact that African Americans receive disproportionately longer prison sentences. Most Black encounters with the criminal justice system do not make headlines, Crump observes. He also notes that these acts are all committed one person at a time rather than all at once; yet the result is the same—systemic racism manifested as "racial genocide." See Ben Crump, *Open Season: Legalized Genocide of Colored People* (New York: HarperCollins, 2019). In *N.C. State Conf. of the NAACP v. McCrory*, 831 F.3d 204, 215 (4th Cir. 2016) *cert. den. North Carolina v. N.C. State Conf. of the NAACP*, 137 S. Ct. 1399 (2017), the appellate court enjoined implementation of several voter restrictions enacted in the state's 2013 Omnibus Law. This law followed a similar pattern of voting restrictions found in other states which, as of this writing, have yet to be reviewed by the courts. These restrictions included: (1) the elimination of preregistration; (2) the elimination of out-of-precinct provisional voting; (3) the elimination of same-day registration; (4) the reduction of the time for early voting; and (5) the requirement of a photo ID to vote. Ibid. at p. 242. In reversing the district court's judgment, the appellate court found that each of these restrictions had been enacted with racially discriminatory intent. Ibid. at 215. These restrictions "unmistakably" reflected the General Assembly's motivation to "entrench itself . . . by targeting voters who, based on race, were unlikely to vote for the majority party," ibid. at 233, and did so with "*almost surgical precision*" using the data on voting practices, ibid. at 214 (emphasis added). The Brennan Center for Justice reports on systemic racism in voting, specifically the pattern of voter suppression laws that has taken shape just since the 2020 presidential election. "As of March 24, [2021], legislators have introduced 361 bills with restrictive provisions in 47 states." "State Voting Bills Tracker 2021," April 1, 2021, *The Brennan Center for Justice*, www.brennancenter.org. The Supreme Court's inglorious racial history is discussed in Brooks, *The Racial Glass Ceiling*, chs. 1 and 2. Educational institutions are not off the hook if the teacher targets all students, Black and White; in other words, if the teacher is an equal opportunity offender. The teacher's rants adversely affect Black students more than White students because Black and White Americans are not at equal risk in our society. "Even blacks who have 'made it' . . . have a sense that they are not equal in social status in spite of their socioeconomic success and the election and reelection of a black president." Brooks, *The Racial Glass Ceiling*, 6.

21 HR 40 was introduced by Rep. John Conyers (D-Mich.) in 1989 and reintroduced every year thereafter until 2017. See Commission to Study and Develop Reparation Proposals for African-Americans Act, H.R. 40, 115th Cong. (2017). The bill never made it out of committee. Rep. Sheila Jackson Lee (D-TX) and Sen. Cory Booker (D-NJ) picked up the crusade in 2019, introducing parallel legislation in the House and Senate that same year. See Commission to Study and Develop Reparation Proposals for African-Americans Act, S. 1083, 116th Cong. (2019).

22 See Brooks, *Atonement and Forgiveness*, ch. 4.

23 See ibid.

24 See ibid.

25 See ibid. at 138.

26 Ibid. at 137–138.

27 For a more detailed criticism of the tort model, see ibid. at 138–140.

28 See Charles Krauthammer, "Reparations for Black Americans," *Time*, Dec. 31, 1990, 18.

29 See Brooks, *Atonement and Forgiveness*, ch. 5.

30 See ibid. at 155–156.

31 Ibid. at 202–206.

32 The theories were broached in the socioeconomic context in Brooks, *Racial Justice in the Age of Obama*, and later applied to the sociolegal and sociocultural race contexts in Brooks, *The Racial Glass Ceiling*.

33 See Brooks, *Racial Justice in the Age of Obama*, ch. 2.

34 *Parents Involved in Community Schools v. Seattle School District No. 1*, 551 U.S. 701, 747–748 (2007) (Roberts, CJ).

35 *Adarand Constructors, Inc. v. Pena*, 515 U.S. 200, 241 (1995) (Thomas, J., concurring).

36 See Brooks, *Racial Justice in the Age of Obama*, ch. 3.

37 Glenn C. Loury, *The Anatomy of Racial Inequality* (Cambridge, MA: Harvard University Press, 2004), 144.

38 See Helene Cooper, "Obama Criticizes Arrest of Harvard Professor," *New York Times*, July 22, 2009, www.nytimes.com; Toby Harnden, "Barack Obama's Support Falls Among White Voters," *Telegraph*, August 2, 2009, www.telegraph.co.uk; Michael A. Fletcher and Michael D. Shear, "Obama Voices Regret to Policeman," *Washington Post*, July 25, 2009, www.washingtonpost.com; Krissah Thompson and Cheryl W. Thompson, "Officer Tells His Side of the Story in Arrest of Harvard Scholar," *Washington Post*, July 24, 2009, www.washingtonpost.com. On the matter of Black-on-Black crime versus White-on-White crime, see Brooks, *Racial Justice in the Age of Obama*, 32–33 ("In 2002, for example, 74.5% of violent crimes perpetrated against African Americans were committed by other African Americans. In that same year, however, 72.6% of violent crimes perpetrated against whites were committed by other whites."). For further discussion of how race still matters, see ibid. at 37–53.

39 Loury, *The Anatomy of Racial Inequality*, 121.

40 Historically, de facto segregated schools on average are "inferior in terms of the quality of their teachers, the character of the curriculum, the level of competition, average test scores, and graduation rates." Brenna Lermon Hill, "A Call to Congress: Amend Education Legislation and Ensure That President Obama's 'Race to the Top' Leaves No Child Behind," *Houston Law Review* 51 (2014): 1177, 1184 (quoting Gary Orfield and Chungmei Lee, "The Civil Rights Project, Historic Reversals, Accelerating Resegregation, and the Need for New Integration Strategies," Civil Rights Project, UCLA, August 2007, http://civilrightsproject.ucla.edu). It is important to note that de facto segregated schools are not the type of racially isolated schools that limited separation envisions. Rather, they seek schools that are adequately funded and controlled by Blacks. See Brooks, *Racial Justice in the Age of Obama*, 71–73. For a more detailed yet older discussion, see Roy L. Brooks, *Integration or Separation? A Strategy for Racial Equality* (Cambridge, MA: Harvard University Press, 1996), 214–234.

41 Sonia Sotomayor, *My Beloved World* (New York: Alfred A. Knopf, 2013), 191. Justice Sotomayor quotes Cornel West, *Race Matters* (Boston: Beacon Press, 1993), in her dissenting opinion in *Schuette v. Coalition to Defend Affirmative Action, Integration & Immigration Rights & Fight for Equality by Any Means Necessary* (BAMN), 134 S. Ct. 1623, 1676 (2014) (Sotomayor,

J., dissenting). The 25th anniversary edition of *Race Matters* was published in 2018 with a new introduction.

42 See Brooks, *Racial Justice in the Age of Obama*, ch. 5.

43 Richard Delgado and Jean Stefancic, *Critical Race Theory: An Introduction* (New York: New York University Press, 2001), 3.

44 Jerry L. Anderson, "Law School Enters the Matrix: Teaching Critical Legal Studies," *Journal of Legal Education*, 54 (June 2004): 201, 210.

45 See, e.g., Derrick Bell, *Race, Racism, and American Law*, 2nd ed. (Boston: Little, Brown, 1980); *And We Are Not Saved: The Elusive Quest for Racial Justice* (New York: Basic Books, 1987); *Faces at the Bottom of the Well: The Permanence of Racism* (New York: Basic Books, 1992); "Who's Afraid of Critical Race Theory," *University of Illinois Law Review* (1995): 893. See also Brooks, *Racial Justice in the Age of Obama*, 89–101.

46 Robert Jensen, "White Privilege Shapes the U.S.: Affirmative Action for Whites Is a Fact of Life," *Baltimore Sun*, July 19, 1998, www.baltimoresun.com.

47 Richard Delgado, "Recasting the American Race Problem," *California Law Review* 79 (1991): 1389, 1394 (reviewing Roy L. Brooks, *Rethinking the American Race Problem* [Berkeley: University of California Press, 1992]).

48 See, e.g., Brooks, *The Racial Glass Ceiling*, 38–39, 41–43, 46, 62–63, 170n21 (sources cited therein).

49 See ibid. at 63, 66–67.

50 Derrick Bell, "Diversity's Distractions," *Columbia Law Review* 103 (2003): 1622, 1622. The critical race theory position on affirmative action was famously stated in Charles Lawrence and Mari J. Matsuda, *We Won't Go Back: Making the Case for Affirmative Action* (New York: Houghton Mifflin, 1997).

51 Maurice C. Daniels and Cameron Van Patterson, "(Re)considering Race in the Desegregation of Higher Education," *Georgia Law Review* 46 (Spring 2012): 521.

52 See Brooks, *Racial Justice in the Age of Obama*, ch. 4.

53 See Robert L. Carter, *A Matter of Law: A Memoir of Struggle in the Cause of Equal Rights* (New York: New Press, 2005), 156–157, 172; Baker Motley, *Equal Justice Under the Law: An Autobiography* (New York: Farrar, Straus and Giroux, 1998), 119. Testimony before the US Senate indicated that perhaps a majority of African American principals and teachers did lose their jobs. See Kevin D. Brown, "Review: Robert L. Carter, *A Matter of Law: A Memoir of Struggle in the Cause of Equal Rights*," *Vermont Law Review* 31 (2007): 925, 939. See also Roy L. Brooks, *Structures of Judicial Decision Making from Legal Formalism to Critical Theory*, 2nd ed. (Durham, NC: Carolina Academic Press, 2005), 285n13 (sources cited therein); Alvis V. Adair, *Desegregation: The Illusion of Black Progress* (Lanham, MD: University

Press of America, 1984); Harrell R. Rogers Jr. and Charles S. Bullock III, *Law and Social Change: Civil Rights Laws and Their Consequences* (New York: McGraw-Hill, 1972), 94–97; David G. Carter, "Second-Generation School Integration Problems for Blacks," *Journal of Black Studies* 13 (1982): 175, 175–188; Derrick Bell, *And We Are Not Saved: The Elusive Quest for Racial Justice* (New York: Basic Books, 1987), 102, 109 (citing *Brief of Amicus Curiae Nat'l. Educ. Assoc., United States v. Georgia*, 445 F.2d 303 (5th Cir. 1971) (No. 30–338) which provides empirical data on burden borne by Black teachers, administrators, and students in integrating public schools); James E. Blackwell, *The Black Community: Diversity and Unity*, 2nd ed. (New York: Harper & Row, 1985), 158–160; Harold Cruse, *Plural but Equal: A Critical Study of Blacks and Minorities and America's Plural Society* (New York: William Morrow, 1987), 22. In addition to school closings, many integrated schools experienced "second generation resegregation"—i.e., segregation within these schools—with the over-placement of Black students in slow-learner, such as "educable mentally retarded," classes and White students in advanced classes. See Brooks, *Rethinking the American Race Problem*, 77.

54 *United States v. Fordice*, 505 U.S. 717, 729 (1992).

55 Ibid. at p. 748 (Thomas, J., concurring).

56 The Court's decision denying certiorari in the case is reported in an article written by Peter Applebone. Applebone, "Equal Entry Standards May Hurt Black Students in Mississippi," *San Diego Union-Tribune*, April 24, 1996, p. A10.

57 "The Feed," Georgetown University, September 27, 2019, https://feed.georgetown.edu.

58 *Plessy v. Ferguson*, 163 U.S. 537, 559 (1896) (Harlan, J., dissenting).

59 See, e.g., Kevin Brown, "Has the Supreme Court Allowed the Cure for De Jure Segregation to Replicate the Disease?," *Cornell Law Review* 78 (1992): 1, 4–6.

60 Kevin Brown, "Review: Robert L. Carter, A Matter of Law: A Memoir of Struggle in the Cause of Equal Rights," *Vermont Law Review* 31 (2007): 925, 948. This article was written years after Professor Brown's original criticism of *Brown* mentioned a moment ago.

61 See Brooks, *Racial Justice in the Age of Obama*, 76–77.

62 The Concurrent Resolution apologizing for slavery and Jim Crow, discussed shortly, deleted language from the reformist House Resolution that suggested Congress would issue reparations. The House Resolution, passed on July 29, 2008, stated that the House of Representatives "expresses its commitment to rectify the lingering consequences of the misdeeds committed against African Americans under slavery and Jim Crow," H. Res. 194 (110th): "Apologizing for the enslavement and racial segregation of African-Americans," Govtrack, July 29, 2008, www.govtrack.us.

63 *Parents Involved*, 551 U.S. at 747–748 (Roberts, CJ).

64 Radical traditionalism traces back to the writings of young professors at Howard University in the 1930s. See, e.g., Sterling Denhard Spero and Abram Lincoln Harris, *The Black Worker: The Negro and the Labor Movement* (New York: Columbia University Press, 1931). On the prevalence of racism in the White working-class culture, see Brooks, *The Racial Glass Ceiling*, 92–93.

65 The House Resolution, passed on July 29, 2008, stated that the House of Representatives "expresses its commitment to rectify the lingering consequences of the misdeeds committed against African Americans under slavery and Jim Crow," H. Res. 194 (110th): "Apologizing for the enslavement and racial segregation of African-Americans," Govtrack, July 29, 2008, www.govtrack.us/congress/bills/110/hres194/text.

66 S. Con. Res. 26 (111th): "A concurrent resolution apologizing for the enslavement and racial segregation of African Americans," Govtrack, June 18, 2009, www.govtrack.us.

67 Brooks, *Atonement and Forgiveness*, 148–149.

68 Ibid. at 149.

69 Ibid. (sources cited therein).

70 Ibid. (sources cited therein).

71 David Blight's exquisite biography of Frederick Douglass, *Frederick Douglass: Prophet of Freedom* (New York: Simon & Schuster, 2018), won a Pulitzer Prize for History.

72 Brooks, *Atonement and Forgiveness*, p. 150. One indication of the extent of the South's ideological victory—of its gaslighting—is the fact that Frederick Douglass's autobiography was out of print from the end of the nineteenth century to 1960. Ibid.

73 Ibid. at 150 (sources cited therein).

74 Ibid. at 151 (sources cited therein).

75 Ibid.

76 See Brooks, *Racial Justice in the Age of Obama*.

77 See Brooks, *The Racial Glass Ceiling*.

78 Brooks, *Atonement and Forgiveness*, pp. 145–146 (citing Roger Cohen, "Wiesel Urges Germany to Ask Forgiveness," *New York Times*, January 28, 2000, A3).

79 Ibid. at 148.

80 Keith Meatto, "Still Separate, Still Unequal: Teaching about School Segregation and Educational Inequality," *New York Times*, May 2, 2019, www.nytimes.com.

81 Alvin Chang, "The Data Proves That School Segregation Is Getting Worse," *Vox*, May 5, 2018, www.vox.com. See also Gary Orfield, Jongyeon Ee, Erica Frankenberg, and Genevieve Siegel-Hawley, "*Brown* at 62: School

Segregation by Race, Poverty and State," Civil Rights Project/Proyecto Derechos Civiles, May 16, 2016 (revised May 23, 2016). For the dissenting view, see, e.g., Robert VerBruggen, "The NYT Is Wrong: Schools Aren't Resegregating," The Corner, May 2, 2018, *National Review*, www.national-review.com.

82 Lauren Camera, "White Students Get More K-12 Funding Than Students of Color," *U.S. News & World Report*, February 26, 2019, www.usnews.com.

83 *Parents Involved in Community Schools v. Seattle School District No. 1*, 551 U.S. 701 (2007).

84 *Milliken v. Bradley*, 418 U.S. 717 (1974).

85 See *Parents Involved*, 418 U.S. at 819 (Breyer, J. dissenting). Citing *Yick Wo v. Hopkins*, 118 U.S. 356, 373–374 (1886), Justice Breyer states that "our precedent has recognized that de jure discrimination can be present even in the absence of racially explicit laws." Ibid.

86 The total amount of reparations could be equivalent to a desired increase in the percentage of the national wealth owned by Blacks. "Today, Black Americans constitute approximately 13 to 14 percent of the nation's population, yet possess less than 3 percent of the nation's wealth." William Darity Jr., Testimony concerning HR40, The Commission to Study and Develop Reparations Proposals for African-Americans, June 19, 2019 (116th Congress 2019–2020), http://spotlight.duke.edu. Alternatively, the reparations amount could be determined by multiplying the average racial earnings gap by the number of enslaved descendants each year the program is in existence. See Brooks, *Atonement and Forgiveness*, 162–163.

87 Transitional justice consists of a wide range of social measures, judicial and non-judicial, designed to redress legacies or structures of human rights abuses. As regards slavery, it is what should have happened during Reconstruction. The South African government's movement from Apartheid to democratic government and racial reconciliation in the 1990s is an example of transitional justice, albeit one that has yet to be fully successful. See Brooks, *When Sorry Isn't Enough*, part 8. In my view, Ruti Teitel's *Transitional Justice* (New York: Oxford University Press, 2000) remains the best scholarship on the subject of transitional justice.

88 In *Swann v. Charlotte-Mecklenburg Board of Education*, 402 U.S. 1 (1971), a unanimous Supreme Court held that a district court has broad equitable powers to remedy a finding of de jure segregation, including ordering the use of racial quotas in the assignment of students and teachers as well as changing attendance zones. The validity of this holding is in serious doubt today given more recent decisions like *Parents Involved* and *Milliken I* plus the Court's general indisposition toward the use of race in government decision-making. However, *Swann* is an indication that racial

quotas are not a far-fetched legal proposition. See, e.g., Brooks, *Atonement and Forgiveness*, 174–176.

89 *Board of Education of the City of Ottawa v. Tinnon*, 26 Kan. 1, 19 (1881).

90 *Plessy v. Ferguson*, 163 U.S. 537, 560 (1896) (Harlan, J., dissenting).

91 Wilson and Williams, "Racial and Ethnic Income Gaps Persist Amid Uneven Growth in Household Incomes," Economics Policy Institute, Working Economics Blog, September 11, 2019, https://www.epi.org/blog/racial-and-ethnic-income-gaps-persist-amid-uneven-growth-in-household-incomes/. These are 2018 figures, which were the same for 2017. The racial gap has actually widened since 1975. See Roy L. Brooks, *Racial Justice in the Age of Obama*, 140–41 (figs. 22–25).

92 Darity Jr., Testimony concerning HR40, The Commission to Study and Develop Reparations Proposals for African-Americans. Professor Darity, it is worth noting, is the Samuel DuBois Cook Professor of Public Policy, African and African American Studies, and Economics and Director of the Samuel DuBois Cook Center on Social Equity, Duke University.

93 Brian Thompson, "The Racial Wealth Gap: Addressing America's Most Pressing Epidemic," *Forbes*, February 18, 2018, www.forbes.com.

94 Michael W. Kraus and Jennifer Richeson, "The Wealth Gap Facing Black Americans Is Vast—and Vastly Underestimated," *Yale Insights*/Ideas from the Yale School of Management, July 15, 2020, https://insights.com.yale.edu.

95 Should redress funds be used for charter school vouchers? If, as the research seems to suggest, charter schools drain limited taxpayer funds from public schools, see Brian Washington, "How to Prevent Charter Schools from Draining Away Public School Funding in Your Community," National Education Association, May 27, 2018, https://educationvotes.nea.org "(It has been long recognized that the growth of charter schools creates costs for local school districts)," then redress funds should not be used to support such schools. The money should, instead, be used to help turn around public schools, which are the schools most Black children attend.

96 Brooks, *Atonement and Forgiveness*, 161.

97 Brooks, *The Racial Glass Ceiling*, 7 (sources cited therein).

98 *Brown*, 347 U.S. at 495. Cf. *United States v. Fordice*, 505 U.S. 717 (1992) (higher education).

99 The Supreme Court has struck down a court-approved "desegregative attractive" plan. See *Missouri v. Jenkins* (Jenkins III), 515 U.S. 70 (1995).

100   See *Parents Involved*, 551 U.S. at 761.

101   *Missouri v. Jenkins* (Jenkins III), 515 U.S. at 114 (Thomas, J., concurring).

102   See *Parents Involved*, 551 U.S. at 761–765. Emphasis added.

103   Beyond such mundane questions as eligibility, see Brooks, *Atonement and Forgiveness*, 197, and costs, see ibid. at 162–163 (questions that cannot be resolved until the larger question of post–civil rights strategy is resolved), more challenging questions of a conceptual nature include whether lingering effects of an atrocity which can be addressed through extant laws should be part of the discussion. For example, mass incarceration is a lingering effect of both slavery and Jim Crow. See, e.g., Blackmon, *Slavery by Another Name*, discussed earlier. Aspects of mass incarceration may be amenable to extant civil rights laws such as class action Section 1983 lawsuits. Typically, redress discourse is unique from a legal perspective in that atrocities, such as slavery, Jim Crow, and South African Apartheid, were legal under domestic law when they took place and, hence, are not amenable to extant law. In addition, they are *past* atrocities, meaning that the question for consideration concerns post-conflict justice—compensatory, retributive, or restorative justice. None of the reparative schemes discussed in this chapter can be effectuated through extant law. All require changes in the law. I would argue, preliminarily, that mass incarceration should be included in the reparative discussion to the extent that the problem cannot be fixed by existing law. However, questions of this nature require additional reflection and, thus, are beyond the scope of this chapter.

104   Brooks, *Racial Justice in the Age of Obama*, 110–111.

105   Tommie Shelby, *We Who Are Dark: The Philosophical Foundations of Black Solidarity* (Cambridge, MA: Harvard University Press, 2005), 250.

106   Sarah Hosseini, "Black Women Are Facing a Childbirth Mortality Crisis. These Doulas Are Trying to Help," February 28, 2019, On Parenting, *Washington Post*, www.washingtonpost.com.

107   Ibid.

108   Plato, "Laws," *Plato in Twelve Volumes*, R. G. Bury, trans. (Cambridge, MA: Harvard University Press, 1968), 757. Apparently borrowing from Plato, Justice Felix Frankfurter wrote: "There is no greater inequality than equal treatment of unequals." *Dennis v. United States*, 339 U.S. 162, 184 (Frankfurter, dissenting).

109   See Kenneth W. Simons, "The Logic of Equality Norms," *Boston University Law Review* 80 (2000): 693, 763. "If I am forgetful and permit one child to stay up a few minutes past her bedtime, I might permit the other child to do the same." Ibid., 763–764.

110   There might be other grounds for eliminating state executions, such as racial bias and wrongful convictions.

111   See, e.g., *Pasadena City Board of Education v. Spangler*, 427 U.S. 424 (1976).

112   See *Milliken v. Bradley*, 418 U.S. 717, 783 (1974) (*Milliken I*) (Marshall, J., dissenting). Justice Breyer argues that "nothing in our equal protection law suggests that a State may right only those wrongs it committed." *Parents Involved in Community Schools v. Seattle School District* No. 1, 551 U.S. 701, 844 (2007) (Breyer, J., dissenting).

113   See *Milliken v. Bradley*, 418 U.S. 717 (1974). *Milliken v. Bradley*, 433 U.S. 267 (1977) (*Milliken II*), which is the appeal of *Milliken I* on remand, is a much more progressive opinion in that it permits a district court to order a wide array of remedies, including tax increases, upon a finding of an intra-district violation of *Brown I*'s desegregation mandate.

114   163 U.S. 537 (1896).

115   *Regents of the University of California v. Bakke*, 438 U.S. 265 (1978), is a landmark decision in which the Supreme Court upheld affirmative action in the form of racial preferences but not racial quotas.

116   Roy L. Brooks, "What About Souter's Human Resume?" Op-ed opinion, *New York Times*, August 1, 1990, www.nytimes.com.

117   See, e.g., Sheretta T. Butler-Barnes, Seanna Leath, Amber Williams, Christy Byrd Rona Carter, and Tabbye M. Chavous, "Promoting Resilience Among African American Girls: Racial Identity as a Protective Factor," Empirical Article, *Child Development*, November 20, 2017, https://doi.org/10.1111/cdev.12995; Kim Eckart, "Promoting Self-Esteem Among African-American Girls Through Racial, Cultural Connections," *University of Washington News*, December 21, 2017, www.washington.edu. See also "Study Shows Strong Racial Identity Improves Academic Performance of Young Black Women," Weekly Bulletin, January 2, 2018, *Journal of Blacks in Higher Education*, www.jbhe.com.

118   "Statement from UNCF President Dr. Michael Lomax on Murder of George Floyd and Renewed Anti-Black Violence," UNCF, *Intrado GlobeNewswire*, June 7, 2020, www.globenewswire.com. See "Quote of the Week," Weekly Bulletin, June 11, 2020, *Journal of Blacks in Higher Education*, https://mailchi.mp.

5

REPARATIONS WITHOUT
RECONCILIATION

DESMOND JAGMOHAN

Do I really *want* to be integrated into a burning house? White Americans find it as difficult as white people elsewhere do to divest themselves of the notion that they are in possession of some intrinsic value that black people need, or want . . . The only thing white people have that black people need, or should want, is power.

—James Baldwin

Let me begin by laying my cards on the table. In what follows I do not directly address the scholarly and public debates over the justification of reparations. I do, however, share the moral intuition that we owe redress for past wrongs, and especially those of slavery and Jim Crow. I also think emphasizing corporate responsibility rather than personal liability will enable us to better fulfill this duty.[1] Grounding reparations on benefits unjustly accrued to individual wrongdoers invites tiresome empirical debates.[2] It is also morally diversionary. Slavery and Jim Crow were unjust because they contravened fundamental moral rights and political principles.[3] The duty of reparations, I assume, results from the nation's role in these institutions. In deeming millions of African Americans chattel property, US law sanctioned slavery and its unspeakable injuries. Yes, the country rejected its poisoned legacy by ending slavery. But soon justice lost its lure. The federal government steadied the hands of lynchers and provided constitutional cover for peonage, segregation, and disenfranchisement. After roughly a decade, the newly freed were once again subjected and degraded.

140

The generations directly responsible for creating these systems have passed on, but the nation remains and so do its debts.[4] If we have an obligation to repay the national debt, whether we incurred it or not, and future generations will have to shoulder the burdens we bestow, then we have a duty to redress the state's historical debts, especially those that shaped and structured the enduring injustices faced by African Americans.[5]

Agreement regarding the justification of reparations does not settle what counts as fair restitution. Scholars generally agree that a fair reparations program should be retrospective and progressive, providing victims compensation for past wrongs and offering wrongdoers the promise of moral repair.[6] The crucial aim, however, is reconciliation—restoring a healthy social and moral relationship between victims and wrongdoers.[7] To achieve reconciliation the state must atone, and the victims must forgive. I, too, welcome a way out of the past.

But I have concerns about this way forward. First, and by revisiting certain historical moments, I suggest the reconciliation view discounts the moral value of compensation. Earlier conceptions of reparations framed property as a lot more than monetary restitution. In addition to protecting victims from future harms, property ownership provides a material basis for independence and transformation. Second, the reconciliation view, which burdens redress with mending our threadbare civic bonds, can unknowingly shift the moral focus from victims to wrongdoers. In making this claim I don't mean to imply that supporters of reconciliation place salving the consciences of Whites above redressing wrongs suffered by African Americans. That would be a condescension that questions their moral sincerity. Third, the reconciliation view might be recklessly hopeful. Advancement by African Americans generally elicits a sense of hardship and heartache from Whites. Black progress has consistently been met with White backlash—lynching followed emancipation; conservative retaliation came on the heels of civil rights legislation. It is hard to say the present warrants greater optimism when the country still needs reminding that Black lives matter.

This chapter revisits an earlier view of reparations to question whether forgiveness and reconciliation should be considered necessary conditions of justice. In the 1860s, liberal egalitarians called

on the federal government to provide the freedpeople with land
and a home as recompense for slavery and a safeguard against
future domination. An undercurrent of realism, even of pessimism,
propelled this view, which assumed White supremacy would continue to overshadow Black lives. Radical Republicans and African
Americans who insisted on exit—say, Black nationalists like Martin R. Delany—expected that redressing racial wrongs would elicit
from Whites anger and vengeance, not remorse and reconciliation.
For that and other reasons both groups prioritized land ownership. It was commonly assumed that material independence helps
protect personal freedom and aids social mobility. Property can
shield people from dependency and degradation. Basically, reparations meant compensating past wrongs, not overcoming anger
and resentment or restoring friendly social relations. Its advocates
demanded neither forgiveness from those with scarred backs nor
atonement from those with stained hands. This more chastened
view of reparations, I argue, sought to secure Black lives above all.

My argument takes the following form. First, I outline a case for
reparations that is genuinely sensitive to the normative diversity
of African American politics. Still, I argue that this view undere-
stimates the moral value of compensation and inflates the ethical
meaning of atonement, forgiveness, and reconciliation. In the
end, fair reparations may require redistribution without reconciliation. Second, I revisit the argument Radical Republicans made
in the 1860s for property ownership as a means of redressing slavery, protecting against future domination, and spurring republican
renewal. Like many at the time, these liberal egalitarians viewed
property ownership as constitutive of freedom. Third, and to
emphasize the relationship many drew between earning and standing, I turn to the 1850s writings of Martin R. Delany, a seminal
figure in the Black nationalist tradition. Delany argued that racism in the North reduced free Blacks to nominal slaves. Therefore,
both enslaved and free African Americans merited reparations.
But he struck a far more pessimistic tone than Radical Republicans a decade later when he determined the United States would
always deny the material and social bases of self-respect and the
value of self-determination. Therefore, African Americans should
emigrate. His reparations claim was evocative at best. But he did
outline a set of ideals—self-determination, economic autonomy,

and self-respect—that became constituent features of Black nationalism. Fourth, and drawing on those ideals as normative sources, I offer one plausible account of why, in the 1960s, Black nationalists, though skeptical of the prospects of reparations, argued that if they ever materialized they should support the following ends: autonomy, power, and dignity.

ATONEMENT, FORGIVENESS, AND RECONCILIATION

Roy Brooks offers a fairly convincing defense of atonement, forgiveness, and reconciliation as essential for repairing the historical harms of anti-Black oppression in the United States.[8] He argues that a history of group-based oppression, social closure, and marginalization explains many of the disadvantages that plague the lives of African Americans, including discrimination in voting, education, employment, housing, health, and policing.[9] A mix of laws, norms, foot-dragging conservatism, and liberal indifference has shaped the long, strange career of White supremacy from playgrounds and pools to hospitals and graveyards.[10] For generations, federal housing policies and racial covenants worked in tandem to create and maintain a residential color line.[11] And there is a deadly underside to this color line. Separate and unequal communities undermine development of human and social capital.[12] A lack of good schools, decent jobs, and safe streets increases capital deficiencies, intensifies inequality, and menaces Black lives. This barrier makes it difficult to engage in cooperative projects, form mutual connections, and cultivate social networks with White and other non-Black citizens.[13] From Chattanooga to Chicago, the color line remains to this day. But instead of facing their grim racial history, Americans tend to comfort themselves with distortions and perversions.[14] Many Whites find it inconceivable that they should know more, or wish to know more, about the history of slavery and Jim Crow. As a result, their indelible scenes are expunged, daily, from public memory, which results in a hermeneutical injustice—occlusions and misrepresentations further sidelining the experiences of African Americans and weakening their case for reparations.[15]

Though Whites' racial amnesia has led many African Americans to further distrust the state, the state must recover its moral legitimacy for the good of all citizens. This theme above all others

seems to absorb Brooks.[16] Reparations provide the state an opportunity to regain its moral authority, but the state will have to choose
between two models. The *tort model* takes a backward-looking and
victim-focused view of redress; it emphasizes demonstrable historical injuries and monetary and nonmonetary restitution for individual victims or their heirs.[17] For Brooks, this model buys "justice on
the cheap."[18] It omits the moral side of reparations, which include
atonement, forgiveness, and reconciliation. On his view, the state
should instead endorse the *atonement model*, which takes a more
rehabilitative approach to reparations. It insists the state apologize
and pay sufficient restitution so that its victims can forgive and
the nation can heal.[19] "Forward-looking, perpetrator-focused, and
restorative," Brooks says, "the atonement model stresses the importance of the perpetrator manifesting a true desire to make amends;
in other words, redemption. The perpetrator's redemptive act lays
the foundation for forgiveness."[20]

The *atonement model* is sequential, with the first step being for
the state to apologize *and* provide sufficient compensation.[21] The
state must offer a genuine apology, which involves acknowledging,
admitting, repenting, and asking forgiveness for the atrocities. But
the apology's sincerity also depends on the sufficiency of the compensation the state provides.[22] Genuine repentance and adequate
restitution trigger the second step, which is a plea from the state
(representing the people) for forgiveness that "arrives on each
victim's desk like a subpoena" demanding a response.[23] Put differently, the state must offer an authentic apology and provide suitable
compensation to redeem its moral authority and mend frayed civic
bonds. It seems that for Brooks, the state's redemption and reconciliation between victims and wrongdoers are decisive goals of reparations. That is why he thinks the "*apology is as much for the perpetrator
as it is for the victim.*"[24] This commitment infiltrates every aspect of
his argument. The worry I have is that, on this view, compensation
seems to matter morally because it authenticates apology—which is
necessary for activating forgiveness and paving the way to redemption and reconciliation—rather than because it provides restitution
for rights violations. It is also worth asking whether the atonement
model simply demands too much of reparations. One advantage
of the tort model is that it views reparations as merely a vehicle for
making victims whole again and therefore does not treat it as an

instrument for fashioning what seems like an impossible future—a redeemed American state and restored civic culture.[25]

Those worries aside, Brooks is probably the first person to recognize that there is no mechanism for determining what counts as sufficient restitution. In "Framing Redress Discourse," Brooks argues that since African Americans comprise a normatively divided body, they will be internally split over what counts as fair reparations. Still, reparations must attain authorization from the group to rule out constraints on freedom and mitigate the expressive harms of top-down and paternalistic approaches. One solution is to assess reparations according to political visions African Americans already endorse. There are four post–civil rights sociopolitical visions, argues Brooks: (1) traditionalism, (2) reformism, (3) critical race theory, and (4) limited separatism. Each takes a distinct view of the nature of White supremacy, the means of dismantling it, and the meaning of racial justice.[26] Consequently, each outlook would conceive of fair reparations differently. There are many ways one can analytically describe the moral diversity of African American politics.[27] As a leading scholar of civil rights, constitutional, and antidiscrimination law, Brooks naturally views these broader visions through a narrower jurisprudential lens. Still, I accept his classification. Below, I consider the first three positions and explain why Brooks thinks *critical race theory*—rather than the others—ought to set the terms of reparations. In the chapter's final section, I examine his fourth view, *limited separatism.*

The first outlook Brooks presents is *traditionalism,* which can be illustrated by the political views expressed by Supreme Court Justice Clarence Thomas. Since, according to Brooks, viewing redress through a purely legal lens risks eliding the moral meaning and social promise of reparations, I extend each view to a political vision. If a reparations program requires normative authorization from below, then it should be evaluated in light of a far wider set of social perceptions, moral intuitions, and political ideals held by African American citizens rather than a legal doctrine or set of views held by lawyers and law professors. Traditionalism denotes Black conservatism, but the latter represents a larger set of commitments that correspond to views held by, say, Justice Thomas, the economist Thomas Sowell, and the social critic Shelby Steele. Basically, Black conservatives would endorse the tort model of reparations:

a partial apology and financial restitution for individual victims. However, they would strongly oppose explicitly race-conscious policies, which they see as morally unfair and consequentially harmful. It is unclear whether their principled objection to such policy would apply evenly to questions of distributive and compensatory justice.[28] But Brooks thinks it would.[29] Black conservatism views overtly race-conscious policy as discriminatory—legal prejudice parading as social justice. According to Black conservatives, programs like affirmative action and welfare also harm the dignity of African Americans because they encourage dependency, weaken people's sense of efficacy, and undermine self-respect.[30] Expressive injuries also follow. Affirmative action unintentionally bolsters racist views, including the malicious belief that African Americans are perpetual victims unable to compete in a meritocratic society.

For Brooks, the ideal of color-blindness leads to racial omission in law and life. That is precisely the point for Black conservatives, who simply want a reprieve from constant public discussion of race, little of which rises above liberal condescension, they think, and most of which drains the well of public sympathy. Moreover, their social assumptions and moral ends make them skeptical of the notion that restitution is owed for historical wrongs. This is because they view disparities in education, employment, and wealth as resulting from moral failures and aberrant norms rather than historical injustices or structural disadvantages.[31] For Black conservatives, the *self* is the source of disparity and holds the promise of emancipation: Instead of appealing to the state for assistance, African Americans should pull themselves up through virtues like hard work and personal responsibility. Essentially, traditionalists' consistent antipathy toward redistributive policy would limit their view of reparations to a platitude and a pittance.

Brooks considers *reformism* the next viable candidate for determining fair reparations. He argues that reformists would endorse the atonement model: a genuine apology and sufficient restitution (monetary and nonmonetary) for both individuals and the group. Such compensation may subsidize social reform. Income supplements for descendants of slavery could be used to reduce inequalities in education, housing, and employment.[32] The crucial point, however, is that a reparations program will involve far more than redressing past wrongs: It should aim to redeem the nation and repair long festering wounds. Brooks's reformists are liberal egalitarians who view integration as crucial to achieving racial justice as a moral end. They understand that the country began as a simultaneous experiment in democracy and tyranny.[33] Dr. King, for example, explained that America has long "been torn between selves—a self in which she proudly professed the great principles of democracy and a self in which she sadly practiced the antithesis of democracy."[34] While recognizing this contradiction has shaped the country's basic structure—its sociopolitical institutions, civic habits, and economic arrangements—reformists refuse to succumb to cynicism or despair.

They are conscripts of hope: men and women devoted to an eternal faith in the republic. That is why they struggle so admirably to eradicate White supremacy. At least since the writings of Frederick Douglass, they have considered White supremacy a perversion of the country's founding ideals and democratic promise.[35] Ralph Ellison, for example, insisted African Americans affirm the ideals on which the country was built and not the men and women who, for centuries, committed violence in the name of those ideas. The principle of America is greater than the "vicious power and all the methods used to corrupt its name."[36] For Ellison, the fate of America lay with those most brutalized and sacrificed in its name.

While Brooks finds nothing objectionable about reformism, he thinks *critical race theory* offers the "superior approach."[37] Because it posits the most demanding view of racial justice, according to Brooks, it should set the terms of reparations.[38] Critical race theorists are after more than reform. They want a transformation of American society. To convey the difference between them and reformists, and perhaps convince you that this difference really matters in the end, let me first note that critical race theorists also endorse the atonement model of reparations, which calls for a sincere apology and sufficient compensation. That is because critical race theorists are integrationists at heart. But they fear diversifying existing hierarchies while leaving those hierarchies in place fails to significantly advance racial justice. Black politics should counter White hegemony, the enduring relationship between race and power, rather than seek inclusion in a house of oppression.[39] It makes sense that as a member of this camp, Brooks would conclude that it offers the most attractive vision. Critical race theory does seem to offer a more egalitarian liberalism. It has an extensive list of reforms for structurally transforming society. However, the two groups differ in both means and ends. Reformists see racial preferences as sufficient for reducing racial disparities while critical race theorists think racial quotas are more effective for achieving racial equity.[40] The latter are also more willing to depart from liberal principles when doing so aids racial justice.

Critical race theorists know that financial capital is one of the simplest yet most consequential resources in life. That is why they attach a group-benefit condition to monetary compensation. Whereas a reformist would stress income for individual households, a critical race theorist wants to close the racial wealth gap and will therefore want to restrict reparations in the form of cash payments to purchasing property, investing in Black businesses, and funding education, all of which build equity that can be bequeathed from one generation to the next. This is important since future generations will no longer have a right to reparations. To this end, Brooks proposes an *atonement trust fund*:

> The federal government would finance, and reputable trust administrators selected by prominent black Americans would administer, a trust fund for every newborn black American child born within a certain period of time—five, ten, or more years . . . The purpose of the trust fund is to provide a core group of blacks with one of the most important resources slavery and Jim Crow have denied them—financial capital, family resources, or an estate, handed down from generation to generation . . . [Thus] each black child would receive the proceeds from the trust fund annually or upon reaching a certain age. He or she would then have the financial wherewithal to take a meaningful step toward a successful future, including enrolling in and graduating from college. The atonement estate would also be earmarked for elementary and secondary education, allowing parents to take their children out of inferior public schools.[41]

There is much to admire in this proposal: appropriate compensation of this sort could reduce the racial wealth gap and other race-based disparities. Add to it apology and nonmonetary compensation that set the historical record straight—museums, public programing, curriculum reforms—and we should, over time, see a decrease in African Americans' distrust of the state and a subsequent increase in the odds of reconciliation.[42]

If the state did these things, it could seek forgiveness, asking victims to withdraw their resentment and be willing to trust it and White Americans.[43] Brooks says if the state atones and provides fair restitution, it will generate an "unconditional obligation" on African Americans to seek reconciliation.[44] And it's in the best interests of African Americans to do so.[45] Brooks does not think African Americans should promise reconciliation merely as a strategy for attaining restitution.[46] It is, however, possible to repurpose Derrick Bell's interest convergence theory, which holds that Whites only take actions to improve the lives of Black people if doing so is in their self-interest, to view the atonement model as selling Whites reparations as something that ultimately benefits them—redemption and repair.[47] The unspeakable truth may be that many Whites care only about their moral salvation. Should this bother us? In our quieter moments, beyond the academic echo chamber, most of us hold out hope for reconciliation. A little voice whispers to us daily—though morally attenuated by a dreadful history, we can someday recover the abandoned ideals of America. Brooks's atonement model voices this latent hope in the face of public disappointment and racial pessimism. Yet the question remains whether we should share his faith in reconciliation.

SECURING FREEDOM IN SLAVERY'S SHADOW

Arguments for redressing slavery are quite old, some having emerged before the institution's demise.[48] On January 16, 1865, General William Tecumseh Sherman issued Special Field Order No. 15, which claimed roughly four hundred thousand acres of land in Confederate territory for settling nearly forty thousand emancipated slaves. Two months later, Congress founded the Bureau of Refugees, Freedmen, and Abandoned Land and authorized the agency to lease such land to freedpeople. The next year, it passed the Southern Homestead Act, providing freedpeople an opportunity to purchase eighty-acre plots. These efforts did not go far enough. The bureau leased plots rather than transferring ownership, and the homestead law sold unfertile land to penniless people. Yet, these policies implicitly expressed that reparations were due.[49] At any rate, the nation's commitment to freedom lasted a mere decade. In 1876, Congress repealed the homestead law and, a year later, the nation completely abandoned Reconstruction.

I suggested that contemporary scholars like Brooks view apology and reconciliation as essential features of meaningful reparations. Earlier Americans considered neither a constituent of justice. Liberal egalitarians like the radical wing of the Republican Party considered reparations to be a means of redressing past wrongs and protecting victims from future harms. They advocated land ownership as a reparative and preventive measure, fearing the material remnants of slavery would generate similar domination in the future and that restitution itself would invite reprisal. The contemporary emphasis on atonement and redemption, which are perpetrator-focused, may ask too much of victims, I believe. Tethered to hope, advocates of reconciliation and repair rarely consider what so many have known for so long: In America, racial progress consistently elicits bitterness and fury from many Whites, not contrition and understanding. After emancipation, White Southerners regained through the market what they had lost in war—dominion over Black lives.

In any case, the Radical Republicans tried to empower African Americans facing the vulnerabilities of freedom without force. Before Lincoln issued the Emancipation Proclamation, some in his party warned that freedom required more than breaking chains. "Mr. President," pleaded Senator Charles Sumner in May 1862, "if you seek Indemnity for the past and Security for the future; if you seek national unity under the Constitution of the United States, here is the way in which all these can be surely obtained. Strike down the leaders of the rebellion and lift up the slaves."[50] Indemnity meant compensation for past injuries and protection against future ones.[51] Future protection required the federal government to empower the emancipated men and women. Like most reparations programs, this conception was both backward- and forward-looking. Its advocates recognized the momentous nature of ending slavery but warned that the freedmen and women would enter freedom owning only their bodies. Their clothes, homes, and tools would remain the property of their masters. In the end, this destitution would become a constant and conspicuous feature of slavery's afterlife. The freedpeople "were sent away empty-handed,"

Frederick Douglass recalled, "without friends and without a foot of land upon which to stand. Old and young, sick and well, were turned loose to the open sky, naked to their enemies."[52] As the demands for uncompromising measures and calls for extended military occupation grew louder, popular conviction waned and the North moved gradually and anxiously toward expedience and away from justice.[53] The Union, which had just fought a war driven by a deep faith in freedom, searched for an easy answer to history's most difficult question. Knowing that the nation might soon default on its promises, leaving freedpeople unprotected from their previous owners, and now embittered enemies, Radical Republicans pleaded with Congress in the spring of 1867 to do more than extend negative liberties. The federal government should ensure freedpeople have a level playing field, they argued, and it would be unfeasible to think they might have a fair chance without military occupation, education, and the vote.[54] And even these forms of security did not square the nation's debt.

The Radical Republicans also believed that the state should provide emancipated families with forty acres of land and a home. This proposal can be read as an early conception of reparations for the harms of slavery. Its supporters considered property ownership both redress for slavery and a form of self-protection against future dependency and domination. Sumner implored Senate colleagues to guarantee "a piece of land" upon which to begin anew.[55] Thaddeus Stevens of Pennsylvania pressed his colleagues in the House of Representatives to deliver to each adult male and female head of a family "a homestead of forty acres of land" and "$100 to build a dwelling."[56] Stevens rhetorically asked the nation, "Have they not a right to it? I do not speak of their fidelity and services in this bloody war. I put it on the mere score of lawful earnings. They and their ancestors have toiled, not for years, but for ages, without one farthing of recompense. They have earned for their masters this very land and much more. Will not he who denies them compensation now be accursed, for he is an unjust man?"[57] Several decades later, W. E. B. Du Bois—moving seamlessly between Stevens, Locke, and Marx—observed that "for 250 years the Negroes had worked this land, and by every analogy in history, when they were emancipated the land ought to have belonged in large part to the workers."[58]

Stevens framed slavery as a rights violation in need of redress.[59] He identified the wrongful act (slavery), its victims (the enslaved), and its perpetrators (enslavers, including those who fought in its defense). Enslaved people had a moral right to the fruits of their labor, which enslavers had stolen, and this unjust enrichment necessitated recompense.[60] Governments have an obligation to protect their citizens and denizens from rights violations, he further reasoned, and when they fail to do so, as in this case, they must later endeavor to secure justice for the victims. Stevens thought the Union should confiscate Southern land and redistribute some of it as reparations to the freedpeople.[61] Land ownership would both establish independence and secure it for some time. To appreciate his bleak but correct sense of a future without reparations, one need only recall that most Americans saw material independence as a crucial basis of social power and personal freedom. For good or ill, they saw little distance between earning and standing.[62] Being landless in an agrarian economy meant destitution and exploitation.[63] Stevens thought having voting rights, access to public education, and owning land were essential for the freedmen to be truly independent.[64]

Radical Republicans also considered property ownership politically transformative. Sumner said, "indemnity and security are both means to an end, and that end is the National Unity under the Constitution."[65] Many believed access to free soil and free labor—a rallying cry of abolitionists and westward migrants—was necessary for maintaining both free men and free republics.[66] In 1865, Stevens told an audience in Lancaster, Pennsylvania, that a lasting freedom would require a revolution in Southern institutions, habits, and manners that would "startle feeble minds and shake weak nerves."[67] The "whole fabric of Southern society *must* be changed, and never can it be done if this opportunity is lost. Without this, this Government can never be, as it never has been, a true republic."[68] Stevens pressed on:

> It is impossible that any practical equality of rights can exist where a few thousand men monopolize the whole landed property. The larger the number of small proprietors the more safe and stable the government . . . If the South is ever to be made a safe republic, let her lands be cultivated by the toil of the owners or the free labor

of intelligent citizens . . . This subdivision of the land will yield ten bales of cotton to one that is made now, and he who produced it will own it and *feel himself a man.*[69]

Sumner argued that since the nation had enfranchised the freedman it should go further and economically empower him with a homestead.[70] Du Bois took a similar position on the issue. During a different crisis, he recalled the warning of Sumner and Stevens that "beneath all theoretical freedom and political right must lie the economic foundation."[71] Land ownership, which was the "absolutely fundamental and essential thing to any real emancipation of the slaves," was eventually denied.[72] The confiscation and reparation plan garnered little support, even among White Northerners, and ultimately failed.[73]

Owning land enabled a greater range of free choices and, consequently, allowed the development, exercise, and expression of moral agency. Owning a given space or territory accorded certain rights, powers, and privileges that, taken together, created a sphere in which freedpeople could reconstruct their lives, raise children, and better control their future. And the shadow of slavery likely made that right to exclude others from their persons, children, and things seem like the quintessence of freedom. Recall that according to law and custom, enslaved people were articles of property, not juridical persons. And, obviously, property cannot own property— only persons can own things. Allowing enslaved people to legally own property would have granted them rights, privileges, and powers incompatible with the institution of slavery. Their ownership rights would legally exclude others, including their owners, from their property. But according to the law, slave owners owned their slaves and all the things that came into their possession, including their children. Lest we forget, slavery was a distinct rather than merely extreme form of domination; unlike other forms of severe domination, it was alone in permitting one human being to legally own another.[74] Ownership, not coercion, grounded slave owners' right to possess (hold in captivity), use (exploit and assault), derive capital from (rent or work), and alienate (kill, sell, or bequeath) their human property. Being property, which barred enslaved people from owning property, made property ownership all the more formidable.

Property is also constitutive of personhood.[75] Indeed, some of our personal property gives our lives their individuality. The memories, narratives, and traditions that shape a person's sense of self are regularly tied to property—say, a home, an iron skillet, or a guitar. Property also grounds many of our long-term projects and therefore lends meaning to our lives.[76] In the agrarian South, land and tools were more than instruments for making a living. A parcel of ground, a mule, and a plow enabled one to realize one's long-term projects and, accordingly, one's normative self-conception. Many thought land ownership encouraged free labor, which, in turn, developed moral character: Being a farmer cultivated self-reliance, industriousness, and grit. And being an economically self-sufficient man signified the presence of those and other moral traits. Conversely, being a dependent farmhand conveyed more than having fallen on hard times; it was the result of moral failures. Ownership also placed Black people in a legally reciprocal relationship with others—including Whites—thus affording them a form of recognition as a property owner. In a context in which Blacks were denied recognition as social equals, this more limited form of recognition was all the more important and its denial all the more dreadful.

The freedpeople learned a piercing new truth—contracts can be as effective as chains, leases as potent as lashes. After emancipating the slaves, the nation refused to make freedom a reality. It threw them into competition with their angry rivals, and the result was Jim Crow. Douglass explained that in preserving their hold on the land, the former masters retained their grip on Black lives:

> They could not, of course, sell their former slaves, but they retained the power to starve them to death, and wherever this power is held there is the power of slavery. He who can say to his fellow man, "You shall serve me or starve," is a master and his subject is a slave. This was seen and felt by Thaddeus Stevens, Charles Sumner, and leading stalwart Republicans; and had their counsels prevailed the terrible evils from which we now suffer would have been averted. The negro to-day would not be on his knees, as he is, abjectly supplicating the old master class to give him leave to toil.[77]

In general, Whites owned the land that Black Southerners worked as sharecroppers and tenant farmers. They also owned the cabins they lived in and often compelled them to purchase on credit, at exorbitant rates of interest, tools, clothing, and rations. The result was a cycle of debt and dependency. Force, fraud, and prejudice were abundant, but necessity also obliged millions of Black Southerners to do this sort of work.[78] For those toiling the same fields they had worked as slaves, freedom must have seemed a cruel joke. Standing neck deep in debt, the freedman could not look his landlords in the eye, confront him on the street, or contest his power at the—at that time—open ballot box.[79]

At first glance, the Radical Republican conception of reparations may seem consistent with the modern view, especially given its emphasis on civic renewal. As I noted, it held that free institutions and markets would eventually reform the characters, norms, and habits of White Southerners. On closer scrutiny, though, its supporters never considered atonement, forgiveness, and reconciliation necessary ends of reparations. Their proximity to slavery might explain why. They knew that those who had routinely inscribed their power on the backs of enslaved people were not clamoring for forgiveness, much less craving reunion. More important, the earlier view of reparations envisioned reprisal rather than reconciliation.

INEQUALITY, RACISM, AND DIGNITY

Martin R. Delany (1812–1885) was one of the founders of Black nationalism, a political theory that responded to anti-Black oppression in the United States by advocating for an independent Black state.[80] In the twentieth century, Black nationalism emphasized intrastate means—territorial separation and community empowerment—of realizing self-determination. In what follows, I neither defend the values nor refute the prejudices of the Black nationalist tradition. I simply assume that it can nurture our moral imagination by keeping our enthusiasm for reconciliation from sliding into racial innocence. Reading Black nationalism or Afro-pessimism invites an unsettling realism: an encounter with blunt truths. Delany's writings, I argue, convey a complex, yet concrete, understanding of race-based disadvantages. He contended that the persistent inequalities in the lives of free Blacks harm not only individuals but also the entire race. And since it can be claimed that African

Americans continue to face durable inequalities, the next section
draws on my reading of Delany to help explain why Black nationalists in the 1960s emphasized autonomy, power, and dignity through
a limited form of political separatism.

Delany believed both enslaved and free Blacks were due reparations. According to him, a free Black person in the North was a
nominal slave, someone who occupies the "same position politically, religiously, civilly, and socially (with but few exceptions) as
the bondman occupies."[81] This is an overstatement since racism,
though morally awful, is not enslavement. Still, in contemplating
racial oppression from the perspective of a formally free but effectively subjugated person, Delany anticipated Jim Crow. He was possibly the first person to argue that reparations are due for those
conditions in the antebellum North that anticipated those of the
postbellum South. "Nothing less than a national indemnity, indelibly fixed by virtue of our own sovereign potency," Delany urged,
"will satisfy us as a redress of grievances for the unparalleled wrongs,
undisguised impositions, and unmitigated oppression, which
we have suffered at the hands of this American people."[82] While
Delany interwove compensatory justice and self-determination, he
also concluded that African Americans would never attain reparations or be permitted to realize the value of self-rule in the United
States. I am unable to develop or critique his conception of reparations because, having decided that the United States would never
make amends, Delany moved on to an argument for exit. He told
attendees at the 1854 National Emigration Convention of Colored
People in Cleveland that it was improbable that African Americans would realize their political desires and that emigration was
the only "sure, practicable and infallible remedy for the evils we
now endure."[83] Delany, like the Radical Republicans, emphasized a
sphere of freedom, but he extended it to sovereign territory.

Before delving into Delany's description of White supremacy,
which can reveal much about his, and perhaps our, time, we can
agree that he proposed a costly response to oppression. But we
can interpret his call for emigration as a philosophical rather than
purely practical response to White supremacy. The utopian contours of his writings, which conceal deep layers of pessimism, can
be read as involving a form of ideal theorizing. He sketched for
readers a world beyond the radically non-ideal conditions of White

supremacy, and for this vision to be an effective analytical or literary device it had to be located elsewhere. Two aspects of his argument will occupy me. The first is his social criticism or conception of racial oppression in the North—namely, his view of how White supremacy vitiated the autonomy, independence, and self-respect of African Americans. The second is what was to be gained from exiting: specifically, self-determination, economic independence, and dignity.

Delany stressed the value of self-determination when he described the political injustice faced by free Blacks. During the Jacksonian era, Americans witnessed significant democratic expansion. For the first time, non-landowning, and therefore non-taxpaying, White men could vote and seek public office. In the contemporary popular imagination, disenfranchisement means denying or frustrating voting rights. But historically, enfranchisement meant the ability to vote and hold office, the latter of which allowed for far greater representation of group interests. For example, urban workers, guilds, and rural farmers could elect members of their respective groups to represent their group's interests. Coming of age in this context, Delany said the nation was "unfaithful to her professed principles of equality."[84] As it expanded rights for White men, it further restricted those rights for Black men.

For Delany, and most Americans, a free republic is based in equal constitutional protections for all citizens.[85] Northern states that permitted African Americans to vote also barred them from office. To defend a more expansive view of enfranchisement that includes both voting and representation, Delany turned to the Romans, who considered the citizen someone exempt from arbitrary restraints.[86] He explained that there is a false impression that "*voting* constitutes, or necessarily embodies, the *rights of citizenship*."[87] This radical error, he added, was now obtaining "favor among an oppressed people."[88] Next, Delany argued that the Romans had at least four classes of "citizens," including the *Quiritium*, the wailing or supplicating citizen—one who could elect his superiors but never aspire to office.[89] This was precisely the condition of free Blacks in the North, he concluded, for they could "elevate their superiors" to public offices they could never aspire to or "even hope to attain."[90] They were permitted to choose who rules them but they could not rule.

Yet self-determination means having an opportunity to be part of the *"ruling element* of the country."[91] One can lose sight of this fact because suffrage is an ambiguous term. At first glance it seems to only denote "a vote, voice, approbation."[92] The wrong, as Delany saw it, lay in the fact that African Americans could only endorse Whites to rule them without having the right to exercise a right that should be *"inherent* and *inviolate.*"[93] As a result, they were politically akin to indentured servants or apprentices, those summoned to give their "approbation to an act which would be fully binding without [their] concurrence."[94] African Americans enjoyed only the arbitrary privileges "conceded by the common consent of their political superiors."[95] Sovereign citizens, on the contrary, are the ultimate source of authority in their country; they were not.[96] Delany further argued that there "can neither be *freedom* nor *safety* for the disenfranchised. And it is a futile hope to suppose that the agent of another's concerns will take a proper interest in the affairs of those to whom he is under no obligations."[97] To be self-determining, then, is to be allowed to compete for the highest honors and offices in the country or commonwealth, including public offices.[98]

In *Conditions,* Delany argued that racial ideology accompanies political injustice. Racism rationalizes and reinforces political oppression.[99] When the majority excludes a racial minority, it often appeals to that group's racial identity as justification for abrogating its rights.[100] Delany saw this as a widespread practice:

> Wherever the objects of oppression are the most easily distinguished by any peculiar or general characteristics, these people are the more easily oppressed, because the war of oppression is the more easily waged against them. This is the case with the modern Jews and many other people who have strongly-marked, peculiar, or distinguishing characteristics. This arises in this wise. The policy of all those who proscribe any people, induces them to select as the objects of proscription, those who differed as much as possible, in some particulars, from themselves. This is to insure greater success, because it engenders the greater prejudice, or in other words, elicits less interest on the part of the oppressing class, in their favor.[101]

If race determined who was exploited, then racial ideology delivered a post hoc justification for that mistreatment. "It is not enough, that these people are deprived of equal privileges by their rulers," Delany wrote, but "to succeed, the equality of these classes must be denied, and their inferiority by nature as distinct races, actually asserted."[102] Whites justified political inequality by insisting on African Americans' "incapacity for self-government."[103]

Delany observed a similar process in the market. There, poverty undermined social equality and self-respect. Most Americans viewed material independence as necessary for avoiding domination, but Delany also stressed collective consequences, arguing that extensive poverty among African Americans injured the group as a whole. Free Blacks were restricted to menial work and its socially subordinating effects. Recall that it was commonplace to assign moral meaning to economic fortune and failure. Achievements in the market bolstered public perception of Whites as productive, innovative, and intelligent. Large ships at the dock and massive buildings in cities were seen as living monuments of their "industry, enterprise, and intelligence."[104] It did not matter that slaves had built those vessels and towers. What counted is that others saw them as evidence of Whites' moral traits. Material accomplishment occupied the role honor held in aristocratic societies.[105] That meant a group without any such achievements led others to the opposite conclusion. The same was true of individuals. A poor man can appeal for equal respect but his plea will go unheard if he has no attainments to his name.[106] That Black Northerners were primarily menial workers—Black men were mainly drivers, cooks, and waiters, and Black women, sitters, maids, and laundresses—resulted in an expressive harm for the group as a whole.[107] They might, in the end, provoke "feelings of commiseration, sorrow, and contempt" but they could never win respect or admiration for the group.[108] For Delany this was a social fact, not a moral ideal.[109]

Delany did not condemn menial work as inherently degrading.[110] Such work subjected the individual to dependency and unfreedom. It is true that Delany shared many of the inegalitarian assumptions of his day. He had in mind appraisal respect—social respect based on the evaluation of one's attainments—rather than recognition respect, that is, equal moral respect due to all persons simply because they are persons.[111] Regardless, he thought the fact that the whole race did such work resulted in an additional and expressive harm: widespread perception of African Americans as incapable of performing non-menial work because they lack the necessary qualities of mind and character. The racialized economy resulted from social closure and opportunity hoarding by Whites, Delany explained by using a hypothetical case of two families, each with several children.[112] In one family, the children had access to schools, attained an education, and went on to work as a teacher, a farmer, and a merchant, among other professions. They fared well in the market and achieved respectability. In the other family, the children had no access to education, and thus training, and ended up working in menial jobs. Delany asked rhetorically: "Would there be an equality here between the children of these two families? Certainly not. This, then, is precisely the position of the colored people generally in the United States, compared with the whites."[113] Whites, using a mix of exclusion and marginalization, denied African Americans opportunities for economic independence and then pointed to the resulting poverty and subordination as justification for barring them from better jobs and schools.

Implicitly running through Delany's critique is a link between economic injustice, societal racism, and moral harm. Placing him in a more contemporary light, we might say he had a conception of the inner cost of stigma—a morally and socially discrediting quality assigned to a group.[114] Stigmas were often made to justify the wrongs that yielded them. The racist public discourse often rationalized the very disadvantages that produced the stigmas and stereotypes. Delany's main conclusion was that structural injustices undermined social equality and vitiated self-respect. In addition to inspiring and feeding racial ascriptions or stereotypes, they also infected the inner life of their victims. In time, life itself dimmed; self-respect fell prey to poverty. Many became resigned to their degradation, Delany observed.[115] Even the few born to better prospects sought out menial work rather than respectable and elevating jobs.[116] That is because their dignity and confidence were among the targets of White supremacy. They could no longer imagine themselves holding certain jobs or attaining certain positions. Though Delany's writings may trouble our moral sense, the broad imprint of what he described can perhaps reveal much about our present moment.

THE CURRENCY OF JUSTICE: BLACK POWER

Dr. Martin Luther King Jr., despite his irrepressible genius and supreme goodness, was quite unfair to Black nationalism when, in his final book, he cautioned that its present advocates were also prophets "of despair and disappointment"; Black Power, he said, "is a cry of daily hurt and persistent pain."[117] The movement, which emerged in the late 1960s, included many who had recently struggled alongside King in the South.[118] In taking aim at his faith in White allies and non-violence as an effective means of resistance, the new movement drew his wrath. For King, "a separate black road to power and fulfillment" was a deeply unrealistic idea.[119] "Disappointment produces despair and despair produces bitterness," he argued, "and the one thing certain about bitterness is its blindness."[120] Once certain political emotions take hold, they warp perception and impair judgment. In their grip, you see an enemy in every friend, an impasse in every barrier.

In King's political imaginary, pessimism leads to recklessness. He argued that, at its core, Black Power was "a nihilistic philosophy born of the conviction that the Negro can't win. It is, at bottom," King explained, "the view that American society is so hopelessly corrupt and enmeshed in evil that there is no possibility of salvation from within."[121] Having dispensed with any pretense of diplomacy, King went for the throat:

> But revolution, though born of despair, cannot long be sustained by despair. This is the ultimate contradiction of the Black Power movement. It claims to be the most revolutionary wing of the social revolution taking place in the United States. Yet it rejects the one thing that keeps the fire of revolutions burning: the ever-present flame of hope. When hope dies, a revolution degenerates into an undiscriminating catchall for evanescent and futile gestures. The Negro cannot entrust his destiny to a philosophy nourished solely on despair, to a slogan that cannot be implemented into a program.[122]

Like their forerunners, modern heirs of Black nationalism had no faith in American society. They accepted the premise that coalition with White allies might not effect meaningful change.[123] To draw attention to present forms of anti-Black oppression, Black nationalists did, at times, elide those gains made by interracial coalitions, from Emancipation to the Civil Rights Act.

Yet it does not follow that the political theory of Black nationalism is unceasing despair or that its personification in Black Power amounted to a slogan in search of an argument and program. Black Power prioritized the same ends as Delany—autonomy, self-sufficiency, and dignity—and outlined an agenda for their attainment. First, Black nationalist politics should aim to transform local communities into sources of belonging and empowerment so they offer greater opportunities for solidarity, which supports the aspiration for collective self-determination and encourages redistributive duties among Blacks.[124] Second, it should help create and sustain a Black economy by encouraging African Americans to support Black businesses and join Black cooperatives.[125] Third, it should emphasize the social good of self-respect. While frustration and anguish certainly motivated some to join the movement and pursue these ends, disappointment and despair are not essential features of the political theory of Black nationalism. For the rest of this section, I consider a single but seminal work in the tradition—*Black Power* by Kwame Ture (Stokely Carmichael) and Charles Hamilton.[126]

The authors argued for a sequential politics that gave self-rule lexical priority over strategic alliance. First, African Americans had to formulate, deliberate, and decide what their shared interests are, before forming coalitions with Whites and in pursuit of the ends they—meaning African Americans—had authored. Ture and Hamilton maintained that, politically, "decisions which affect black lives have always been made by white people."[127] Partially inspired by the pluralist turn in political science, they further reasoned that white Americans tend to behave like a single interest group, responding in "a particularly united, solidified way when confronted with blacks making demands which are seen as threatening to vested interests."[128] African Americans cannot breach the resulting citadels and should therefore turn inward. The concept of Black Power is simply "a call for black people to define their own goals, to lead their own organizations and to support those organizations. It is a call to reject the racist institutions and values of this society."[129] Bargaining from a position of weakness would mean appealing to the moral conscience or good graces of Whites, casting Blacks in "a beggar's role, hoping to strike a responsive chord."[130] So, while Black Power did not reject coalition politics, it did insist that African Americans first "consolidate behind their own, so that they can bargain from a position of strength."[131] And then only once they have found common ground—thus satisfying the self-rule condition—should they "see what kinds of allies are available."[132] The result would be a coalition politics consistent with the value of self-determination.

First, Black Power morally prioritized self-determination: the idea that members of a group ought to collectively decide their common concerns, shared interests, and collective ends. Historically, in most cases, a sovereign state has offered the ideal institutional mechanism for a people to realize the value of self-determination. Political oppression—and other reasons for not having a say in matters of public life—meant African Americans could not realize the *value* of self-determination through formal arenas of American politics. And yet participating in institutionalized political cooperation and coming to identify with and value that cooperation is the essence of self-rule.[133] The challenge, then, is for Black politics to make a normative reality of the "goal of black self-determination . . . full participation in the decision-making process affecting the lives of black people, and recognition of the virtues in themselves as black people."[134] Doing so would be morally rehabilitative. Local politics offered a path forward, Ture and Hamilton argued. Politically changing your community can be morally transformative. In addition to political experience and wisdom, participating in self-rule cultivates confidence in your ability to achieve your ends.[135] This view strikes me as a transformative communitarianism, not a politics of affliction leading to blindness, anguish, and disillusionment.[136]

Second, and despite its utopian tendencies, Black nationalism had often taken a materialist and realist view of politics. For example, Ture and Hamilton argued that "political relations are based on self-interest: benefits to be gained and losses to be avoided."[137] They thought that a "man's politics is determined by his evaluation of material good and evil. Politics result from a conflict of interests, not of conscience."[138] The tradition of Black nationalism emphasized economic empowerment by frequently drawing attention to the harms of poverty. African Americans must pursue material independence to secure greater social and political freedom. Without a trace of irony, Ture and Hamilton saw this promise in Booker T. Washington's old stomping ground. They said Tuskegee, Alabama offered fertile soil for a politics sensitive to the cost of economic dependency. The town's Black citizens were mostly self-employed or worked for federal institutions, and not being dependent on Whites for jobs meant they were largely immune to "economic reprisals" by Whites if they organized politically.[139] That meant they were able to use their economic power without fear.[140]

From these materialist premises, Ture and Hamilton drew the plausible, if depressing, inference that even liberal Whites would not endorse policies that threatened their wealth. Moral convergence on racism will not bridge diverging material interests.[141] That is why an economically secure group rarely forms a coalition with an economically insecure group.[142] And when it does it tends to use the alliance to advance its own interests. Whites, for example, "could be morally self-righteous about passing a law to desegregate southern lunch counters or even a law guaranteeing southern black people the right to vote," Ture and Hamilton observed, but "laws against employment and housing discrimination—which would affect the North as much as the South—are something else again."[143] For them, nostalgic agrarians and American socialists consistently pursued a politics "clearly not consistent with the long-term progress of blacks."[144] The Populist Movement of the late nineteenth century served as a cautionary tale.[145] Its visionaries were among the South's largest landowners and most vicious exploiters of Black tenant farmers.[146] In part, Populists like Tom Watson invoked interracial class interests to counter Northern banks and corporations because they threatened their monopoly on Black labor. It was therefore vital that African Americans formulate their shared long-term interests and use those interests as criteria for forming coalitions with Whites rather than have those interests defined by allies.

Third, Black nationalism has always emphasized the dignitary harms of White supremacy. The asymmetrical social power of

Whites limits more than African Americans' access to good jobs, schools, and neighborhoods. It also damages individuals' self-respect and the group's image. There are countless ways White supremacy can pierce one's soul, from television shows to school curricula. American public life targets the moral sense of African Americans, even leading some members of the group to conceive of themselves and their ends as contrary to their own well-being and the group's welfare.[147] To preserve their self-respect against such an onslaught they will have to reject the "assumption that the basic institutions of this society must be preserved. The goal of black people must *not* be to assimilate into middle-class America," Ture and Hamilton further warned, "for that class—as a whole—is without a viable conscience as regards humanity."[148] To recover and redefine themselves, African Americans will have to reconsider the terms of order: "We shall have to struggle for the right to create our own terms through which to define ourselves and our relationships to the society."[149] This moral realignment values dignity, not money. It views poverty and distress as socially repugnant, not evidence of "laziness or lack of initiative."[150] As noted earlier, Black nationalism views engaging in political struggle—from antipoverty initiatives to protesting voting rights—as morally transformative. Doing so cultivates a new consciousness, solidifies resolve, and refines political skills.

Black nationalism also draws attention to the ways systemic racism libels the group as a whole. The emphasis it places on Black pride connotes neither conceit nor chauvinism. For centuries, African Americans had been slurred and slandered, and this vilification also levied an inner cost. To repair the resulting injury, Ture and Hamilton argued for cultural preservation and racial pride as means of moral repair and valuable ends in themselves.

> The racial and cultural personality of the black community must be preserved and that community must win its freedom while preserving its cultural integrity. Integrity includes a pride—in the sense of self-acceptance, not chauvinism—in being black, in the historical attainments and contributions of black people. No person can be healthy, complete and mature if he must deny a part of himself; this

is what integration has required so far. This is the essential difference between integration as it is currently practiced and the concept of Black Power.[151]

Ture and Hamilton further argued that anti-Black oppression
undercuts personal efficacy—a sense of confidence in one's capacity to formulate and pursues one's own ends. Only by developing
a new and more efficacious sense of themselves to "deal effectively
with the problems of racism" will African Americans be able to
usher in a politics that is authored from within rather than imposed
from outside.[152]

Given its commitment to political autonomy, economic independence, and dignity, what would Black nationalism demand
from a reparations program? In Brooks's account, the terms of
redress increase as one moves from traditionalism to critical
race theory, but limited separatism occupies a peculiar place in
the model. The limited separatists ask less of the state than the
critical race theorists, but that is not because they think they are
owed less. Rather, they deny, on realist grounds, the possibility
of massive social transformations while also not caring whether
the state apologizes. They are likely to neither forgive nor reconcile. It seems that Brooks eliminates Black nationalism (limited separatism) because it rejects core features of the atonement
model: apology, forgiveness, and reconciliation. According to
this model, once African Americans experience significant structural changes, they should forgive and reconcile. But Brooks also
admits that neither forgiveness nor reconciliation may be morally
required for redressing slavery and Jim Crow,[153] in which case
they are merely postscripts to justice. Why, then, insist on reconciliation? Besides, tying it to restitution may deny citizens the
moral good of providing reparations simply because it is the right
thing to do.

In the 1960s, Black nationalists argued that compensatory
and rehabilitative reparations should go directly to Black communities, not individuals. The receiving organizations were to
use monetary and nonmonetary compensation to advance the
normative ends discussed above—self-determination, economic
independence, and the social bases of dignity and self-respect.

From barbershops to bookstores, Black businesses catered to the interests and desires of Black people, making life less alienating and more dignified.[154] Black nationalists insisted that reparations support housing, land, and business cooperatives to simultaneously further sociopolitical autonomy and collective economic empowerment. The Black Panther Party, for example, contended that reparations be paid to Black communities.[155] The civil rights activist James Forman proposed the "establishment of a Southern Land Bank to help brothers and sisters who have to leave their land because of racist pressure, and for people who want to establish cooperative farms but who have no funds."[156] And the founders of the Republic of New Afrika envisioned reparations supporting an "independent black nation"[157] in the "black belt" region of the American South.[158]

Furthermore, reparations should subsidize Black institutions dedicated to correcting epistemic injustice. However, Black nationalists envisioned far more than slavery museums or other means of setting the historical record straight and correcting White ignorance. For Black nationalists, nurturing self-respect and dignity required promoting positive Black identity.[159] Forman, for instance, called on the federal government to fund the establishment of the following institutions: (1) Black publishing and printing houses; (2) radio and television networks located in Black metropolitan areas; (3) research centers dedicated to studying the problems that most affect Black people; (4) job training for African Americans to address problems plaguing Black communities; and (5) education and other training programs that make African Americans more economically competitive. In general, Black nationalists supported the study of African American history, culture, and art. Essentially, they were far more concerned with fostering positive Black identity than educating Whites.

This view of reparations closely approximated the nineteenth-century conception of redress as recompense for past wrongs and security against future harms. After living some time under the conditions of more autonomous Black communities with greater resources, Black nationalists might decide sufficient reparations were paid and thus reassess their views of the state. Perhaps they had turned to separatism from desperation. But would they really forgive the state for slavery and Jim Crow? If King is right that White backlash is a persistent feature of American life,[160] then securing reparations would likely invite reprisals and therefore undermine the African Americans' willingness to forgive and Whites' inclination to seek reconciliation.

CONCLUSION

While the state owes restitution for slavery and Jim Crow, requiring African Americans to forgive adds retrospective insult to historical injustice. Viewing reconciliation as the final end of reparations suggests a moral condescension. The crucial injury is not alienation from the state and its White majority. James Baldwin is right. "The only thing white people have that black people need, or should want, is power."[161] And as victims of persistent injustice, they should be skeptical of the fraternal promise of reconciliation. The present hardly encourages optimism. The median African American family has $24,100 in wealth, which is 12.7 percent of the $189,100 in wealth owned by the average White family.[162] Black households also have the lowest homeownership rate, median price, down payments, and median household income.[163] Today Black men are 2.5 times more likely than White men to be killed by police, and those shot are twice as likely as White people to be unarmed.[164] And African Americans are incarcerated in state prisons at 5.1 times the rate of Whites, and in five states, ten times the rate.[165] Given the terrible past and awful present, it seems doubtful reparations are probable and patronizing to make it conditional on forgiveness, reconciliation, and redemption.

Reparations for slavery and White supremacy should not be a means of effecting a moral and structural transformation of American society. Stressing reconciliation and repair as the crucial aims of reparations unwittingly elevates moral concern for perpetrators above justice for victims. Redressing past atrocities should be an end in itself. To see why, we revisited arguments by liberal egalitarians in the 1860s and the Black nationalist tradition, namely, views of reparations that refused to bind restitution to the state's redemption or racial reconciliation. A fair reparations program should redress historical injustice and secure victims from similar wrongs in the future. According to the Black nationalist tradition, that requires shoring up the group's autonomy, independence, and dignity. The Black nationalist tradition should not lead us to reject, in principle, the desire to redeem the state or attain racial reconciliation, however, but it should prompt us to ask whether it is fair to burden the claimants of reparations with these broader and shared ends. Throughout I assumed providing restitution for slavery and Jim Crow is a moral imperative, and the state should do so regardless of whether such redress further frays or mends our civic bonds. A virtue of earlier views of reparations is that they separate the imperative of compensatory justice from the quite reasonable desire to emancipate the republic from its awful past. Yet we must confront the equally reasonable proposition that slavery and Jim Crow are unpardonable wrongs—unforgivable crimes that have permanently soiled the American state and its White majority. Even if reparations become policy, we should consider the possibility that this may undermine the state's standing among some, if not many, Whites, and therefore derail any hope for reconciliation.

TABLE 5.1. Tort vs. Atonement Model of Redress

Tort Model of Redress	Atonement Model of Redress
Backward-looking	Forward-looking
Victim-focused	Perpetrator-focused
Legal claim	Political and moral claim
Closes the book on race	Opens the path to reconciliation
No apology	Step 1: Apology (1a):
Reparations:	Sufficient reparations (1b):
–Compensatory: monetary restitution to individuals for demonstrable historical injuries	–Compensatory: monetary and nonmonetary restitution for specific group members
	–Rehabilitative: monetary (investments) and nonmonetary restitution (laws) aimed at empowering the group as a whole
	Step 2: Forgiveness (2)

Source: Based on models provided in Roy L. Brooks, "Framing Redress Discourse," this volume.

TABLE 5.2. Comparison of Theories

Theories	Traditionalism	Reformism	Critical Race Theory	Limited Separatism
1. Atonement	Partial	Full	Full	Partial
a. Apology	Partial Apology	Genuine Apology	Genuine Apology	No Apology
2. Reparation	Partial	Full	Full	Full
b. Redress Hermeneutical Injustice (Compensatory)	None	Nonmonetary: Correct Historical Record	Nonmonetary: Correct Historical Record	Nonmonetary: Fund Black Public Projects
c. Redress Capital Deceits (Compensatory)	Monetary: Restitution for Individual Injury	Monetary: Direct Income Supplements	Monetary: Wealth Investments; Atonement Fund	Monetary: Wealth Investments; Atonement Fund
d. Redress Capital Deceits (Rehabilitative)		Monetary: Racial Integration Nonmonetary: Racial Preferences	Monetary: Social Transformation Nonmonetary: Racial Quotas	Monetary: Black Empowerment Nonmonetary: Support Positive Identity
e. Forgiveness and Reconciliation: Redressing Relationship with the State	Significant Progress Toward a Color-Blind Society, Attained through Minimalist Policy	Significant Progress Toward Racial Integration, Attained through Maximalist Policy	Significant Progress Toward a Transformed Society in which Power No Longer Tracks Whiteness, Attained Through Maximalist Policy	Meaningful Progress Toward Group Autonomy, Power, and Dignity

Source: Based on models provided in Roy L. Brooks, "Framing Redress Discourse," this volume.

NOTES

1 On arguments regarding unjust enrichment, see Bernard Boxill, "The Morality of Reparations," *Social Theory and Practice* 2 (1972): 113–123; Howard McGary, "Justice and Reparations," *Philosophical Forum* 9 (1977–78): 250–263; and Randall Robinson, *The Debt: What America Owes to Blacks* (New York: Dutton, 2000). I share Roy L. Brooks's emphasis

on the nation as the source of liability and corrective agent in Roy L. Brooks, *Atonement and Forgiveness: A New Model for Black Reparations* (Chicago: University of Chicago Press, 2004), 141–179. These arguments try to counter those who grant that those who directly suffered enslavement or Jim Crow are due reparations, but their present-day heirs do not have the same rights to reparations the state owed their ancestors but never paid them. Bernard Boxill, "A Lockean Argument for Black Reparations," *Journal of Ethics* 7, no. 1 (2003): 63–91. Alfred L. Brophy argues that much of American history has, in fact, followed a legislative model of reparations in "Reconsidering Reparations." In *Indiana Law Journal* 81, no. 3 (Summer 2006): 812–849. Interestingly, no one makes the claim that Japanese Americans are due reparations for internment during the Second World War because Whites or any group accrued benefits unjustly. The nation owed restitution for taking away their freedoms—rights violations, not unjust enrichment. The same is true of slavery. But the difficulty arises, philosophically, in answering why their heirs inherited that right. It is well beyond this chapter's scope to answer these sorts of questions.

2 On this claim, see Robert Fullinwider, "The Case for Reparations," in *Redress for Historical Injustice in the United States: On Reparations for Slavery, Jim Crow, and their Legacies*, ed. Michael T. Martin and Marilyn Yaquinto (Durham, NC: Duke University Press, 2007), 121–133. It is difficult to identify the net benefits gained from slavery and who, specifically, are the recipients of those benefits. Obviously, we can say slaveholders were unjustly enriched. Since cotton was the most prized and traded commodity of the nineteenth century, almost anyone profiting from American finance and industrialization was indirectly engaged in slavery, including abolitionists. Still, descendants of millions of White and non-White immigrants after emancipation might object that they received no benefits from slavery. Even poor White Southerners might argue that slavery depressed wages and thus harmed rather than benefited them. There is also the counterfactual reasoning underlying compensatory justice claims. In cases of historical injustice such as slavery, can we really restore the status quo ante that compensatory justice seeks to do? Can we say slavery left subsequent generations worse off when those generations would not have existed without the injustice? Put differently, the problem of non-identity arises. See, for example, Christopher Morris, "Existential Limits to the Rectification of Past Wrongs," *American Philosophical Quarterly* 21 (1984): 175–182. For these and other reasons, some political philosophers opt for redistributive instead of compensatory justice. See chapters 1 through 7 of *Compensatory Justice, NOMOS XXXII*, ed. John W. Chapman (New York: New York University Press, 1991).

3 I am not sure it matters morally whether Whites benefited from slavery or not. Insisting on this claim as the basis for reparations can lead to unfortunate conclusions. There are all sorts of idiosyncratic cases from history that can allow even slaveholding families to evade moral responsibility. There are cases of those who owned no slaves but then inherited a disabled or elderly enslaved person. In some places, and according to law, they could not manumit that slave and thus had to care for them. Most Southern states legally prohibited slaveholders from manumitting their slaves without permission from the county. The act of manumission was bizarre, at best, for it allowed for a personal act to transform what the law deemed property into a juridical person; second, the act effected naturalization, which is the sole authority of the state. Barring personal manumission without state sanction prevented slaveholders from abandoning elderly and disabled slaves to the public funds. Obviously, many such arguments were made in bad faith. But disproving them is irrelevant for justifying reparations since the prohibition of manumission can serve to aid rather than hinder the case for reparations. It strengthens the claim of corporate liability—the active role of the state in shoring up slavery.

4 Focusing on the nation as the primary wrongdoer resolves the problem of *duration* and thus doubts about the persistence of the debt across time. We can therefore skirt questions that often sink reparations arguments. While there is agreement that the generations responsible for slavery and Jim Crow owed restitution, there is always the objection that subsequent generations fairly acquired those initially unfair benefits. Of course, unknowingly buying stolen property does not mean you get to keep it. We could also argue that all American citizens and denizens benefit from slavery because slave labor fueled the nation's economic development. It is easier to show what the nation gained from slavery. Still, I am disinclined to draw strong normative conclusions from such empirical premises.

5 The most controversial part of reparations is the claim that past injustice has harmed present-day African Americans, and that this harm should be compensated. My sense is that these past injustices also matter because they are structurally connected to the enduring injustices African Americans suffer from. Jeff Spinner-Halev, *Enduring Injustice* (Cambridge: Cambridge University Press, 2021), 56–84.

6 I use victims and their heirs interchangeably.

7 Desmond Tutu, *No Future Without Forgiveness* (New York: Doubleday, 1999), 255–283; Janna Thompson, *Taking Responsibility for the Past: Reparation and Historical Injustice* (Cambridge: Polity Press, 2002), 38–53 and 113–129; Margaret Urban Walker, *Moral Repair: Reconstructing Moral Relations after Wrongdoing* (Cambridge: Cambridge University Press, 2006), 1–

39 and 191–230; and Charles Griswold, *Forgiveness: A Philosophical Exploration* (Cambridge: Cambridge University Press, 2007), 59–71. For a critique of this view, see McGary, "Reconciliation and Reparations," 548.

8 Roy L. Brooks, *Atonement and Forgiveness*.

9 Roy L. Brooks, *Atonement and Forgiveness*, 36–97.

10 C. Vann Woodward, *The Strange Career of Jim Crow* (Oxford: Oxford University Press, 1955).

11 Richard Rothstein, *The Color of Law: The Forgotten History of How Our Government Segregated America* (New York: W. W. Norton, 2017); and Richard R. W. Brooks and Carol M. Rose, *Saving the Neighborhood: Racially Restrictive Covenants, Law, and Social Norms* (Cambridge, MA: Harvard University Press, 2013).

12 Elizabeth Anderson, *The Imperative of Integration* (Princeton, NJ: Princeton University Press, 2010), 1–66.

13 Elizabeth Anderson, *The Imperative of Integration*, 188.

14 The public outcry against critical race theory is really a revolt against including in elementary and high school curricula lessons on conquest, slavery, and White supremacy.

15 Although *hermeneutical injustice* speaks more directly to Brooks's argument for correcting the historical record, Miranda Fricker's emphasis on *testimonial injustice* sheds important light on how African Americans' claims regarding persistent injustice have been denied credibility based on racial prejudices about the speakers. Miranda Fricker, *Epistemic Injustice: Power and the Ethics of Knowing* (Oxford: Oxford University Press, 2007), 147–162.

16 Roy L. Brooks, "Framing Redress Discourse," in this volume.

17 Brooks, "Framing Redress Discourse," in this volume.

18 Brooks, "Framing Redress Discourse."

19 Roy L. Brooks, *Atonement and Forgiveness*, 156.

20 Brooks, "Framing Redress Discourse."

21 Brooks, "Framing Redress Discourse."

22 An apology "offers the perpetrator an opportunity to reclaim *its* moral character and initiate conditions that help repair *its* broken relationship with the victims." In this view, restoring moral *authority* or moral *standing* makes more sense than moral *character*. While I agree that the state is the appropriate agent owing redress for slavery and Jim Crow, I am not sure it makes sense to say the state has a moral character, though we do speak of national character. Maybe Brooks means the apology affords White citizens an opportunity to reclaim their moral character by affirming the apology. Brooks, "Framing Redress Discourse."

23 Brooks, "Framing Redress Discourse."

24 Brooks, *Atonement and Forgiveness*, 146.

25 For Brooks, the tort model's normative defect is that it is victim-focused, that it does not offer perpetrators a clear path to redemption. I am not sure why he thinks the tort model is restricted to individual victims and targets only individual firms. I am not sure its true that the tort model, by definition, can't sustain cases against states (corporate agents) on behalf of groups and demand, among the terms of fair restitution, a public recognition of the harms committed.

26 Brooks uses terms such as "racial advancement," "racial progress," "racial justice," and "racial reconciliation" interchangeably. But "racial progress" is too vague to do meaningful normative work. It makes more sense to view each body of thought and practice as an inchoate conception of what racial justice requires. I therefore refer to each as a normative vision or political vision.

27 It was once common to divide African American thought into integration versus separatism. See, for example, Bernard Boxill, "Two Traditions in African American Political Philosophy," in *African-American Perspectives and Philosophical Traditions*, ed. John P. Pittman (New York: Rutledge, 1997). In *Black Visions: The Roots of Contemporary African-American Ideology* (Chicago: University of Chicago Press, 2001), Michael Dawson identifies at least six different ideological commitments still animating African American politics.

28 There is some vagueness in Brooks's framing of the conservative position. A Black conservative would likely object to race-conscious distributive policies, but I am not sure why Brooks thinks all of his objections would apply to compensatory justice.

29 Brooks, "Framing Redress Discourse."

30 Clarence Thomas, *My Grandfather's Son: A Memoir* (New York: Perennial, 2007).

31 See, for example, Thomas Sowell, *Race and Culture: A World View* (New York: Basic Books, 1994); Thomas Sowell, *The Vision of the Anointed* (New York: Basic Books, 1996); Shelby Steele, *The Content of Our Character* (New York: Harper Perennial, 2001).

32 Brooks, "Framing Redress Discourse."

33 Judith Shklar, "Redeeming American Political Theory," *American Political Science Review* 85, no. 1 (March 1991): 3–15.

34 Dr. Martin Luther King Jr., *Where Do We Go From Here: Chaos or Community?* (Boston: Beacon Press, 1967), 72.

35 Frederick Douglass, "The Constitution of the United States: Is It Pro-Slavery or Anti-Slavery?" In *Frederick Douglass: Selected Speeches and Writings*, ed. Philip S. Foner and Yuval Taylor (Chicago: Lawrence Hill Books, 1999), 380–390.

36 Ralph Ellison, *Invisible Man* (New York: Vintage Books, 1952), 574.

37 Brooks, "Framing Redress Discourse."

38 Brooks, "Framing Redress Discourse."

39 Brooks, "Framing Redress Discourse."

40 Brooks, "Framing Redress Discourse."

41 Brooks, *Atonement and Forgiveness*, 159–160.

42 Brooks, *Atonement and Forgiveness*, 148.

43 Brooks, *Atonement and Forgiveness*, 165.

44 Brooks, *Atonement and Forgiveness*, 168.

45 Brooks, *Atonement and Forgiveness*, 169.

46 Interest convergence is a descriptive rather than normative claim about how civil rights reform has worked in American history. Brooks rightly argues that interest convergence cannot dismantle White hegemony, which requires socially transformative legal measures. See Roy L. Brooks, *The Racial Glass Ceiling: Subordination in American Law and Culture* (New Haven, CT: Yale University Press, 2017), 177, fn. 69.

47 Derrick A. Bell, Jr., "*Brown v. Board of Education* and the Interest-Convergence Dilemma," *Harvard Law Review* 93 (1980): 518.

48 Brooks, *Atonement and Forgiveness*, 1–19; Martha Biondi, "The Rise of the Reparations Movement," in *Redress for Historical Injustice in the United States*, 255–269; William A. Darity Jr. and A. Kirsten Mullen, *From Here to Equality: Reparations for Black Americans in the Twenty-First Century* (Chapel Hill: University of North Carolina Press, 2020), 1–26.

49 W. E. B. Du Bois did not frame Reconstruction's promise explicitly in terms of redress, but he did offer a compelling account of land reform as a means of securing freedom for the freedmen and women. *Black Reconstruction* (New Brunswick, NJ: Transaction Publishers, 2013 [1935]). For a political history of the era and its policies, see Eric Foner, *Reconstruction: America's Unfinished Revolution, 1863–1877* (New York: Harper & Row, 1988). On why forty acres amounted to a false promise , see Jeffrey R. Kerr-Ritchie, "Forty Acres, or, An Act of Bad Faith," in *Redress for Historical Injustice in the United States*, 222–237. We can agree that the state diluted the policy to the point of having little effect before abandoning it altogether, but that does not mean its advocates were sincere.

50 Charles Sumner, "Indemnity for the Past and Security for the Future," speech in the US Senate, May 19, 1862.

51 For the term's legal meaning at the time, see Edwin Baylies, "Bonds of Indemnity," *A Treatise on the Rights, Remedies and Liabilities of Securities and Guarantors* (New York: Baker and Godwin, 1881), 129–132.

52 Frederick Douglass, *Life and Times of Frederick Douglass* (Boston: Wolfe, Eiske and Co., 1895), 613.

53 C. Vann Woodward, "Equality: The Deferred Commitment," in *The Burden of Southern History* (Baton Rouge: Louisiana State University Press, 1968), 69–88.

54 Charles Sumner, "Further Guaranties in Reconstruction: Loyalty, Education, and a Homestead for Freedmen; Measures of Reconstruction: Not a Burden or Penalty," speech in the US Senate, March 7 and 11, 1867, *Charles Sumner; His Complete Works* XIV, ed. George Frisbie Hoar (Boston: Lee and Shepard, 1900), 303–304.

55 Sumner, "Further Guaranties in Reconstruction," 305.

56 Thaddeus Stevens, "Bill Relative to Damages to Loyal Men, and for Other Purposes," speech in the House of Representatives on March 19, 1867, *The Selected Papers of Thaddeus Stevens 2: April 1865–August 1868*, ed. B. W. Palmer and Holly Byers Ochoa (Pittsburgh, PA: University of Pittsburgh Press, 1998), 276–925.

57 Stevens, "Bill Relative to Damages to Loyal Men, and for Other Purposes," 284.

58 Du Bois, *Black Reconstruction*, 328.

59 For an insightful discussion of reparations as responses to rights violations, see Ellen Frankel Paul, "Set-Asides, Reparations, and Compensatory Justice," in *Compensatory Justice, NOMOS XXXII*, ed. John W. Chapman (New York: New York University Press, 1991), 97–142.

60 Contemporary arguments resting on a similar unjust enrichment claim include Bernard Boxill, "The Morality of Reparations," *Social Theory and Practice* 2 (1972): 113–123, and Howard McGary, "Justice and Reparations," *Philosophical Forum* 9 (1977–78): 250–263.

61 See Thaddeus Stevens's speech on March 11, 1867 on H.R. 29: "Reparations Bill for the African Slaves in the United States—The First Session Fortieth Congress," in *Reparations for Slavery: A Reader*, ed. Ronald P. Salzberger and Mary C. Turck (New York: Rowman & Littlefield, 2004), 63–65.

62 Judith Shklar, *American Citizenship: The Quest for Inclusion* (Cambridge, MA: Harvard University Press, 1991).

63 See, for example, Philip Pettit, *Republicanism: A Theory of Freedom and Government* (Oxford: Oxford University Press, 1997), 23 and 67; Frank Lovett, *A General Theory of Domination and Justice* (Oxford: Oxford University Press, 2010), 47.

64 Stevens, "Bill Relative to Damages to Loyal Men," 284.

65 Stevens, "Bill Relative to Damages to Loyal Men," 184.

66 Eric Foner, *Free Soil, Free Labor, Free Men: The Ideology of the Republican Party Before the Civil War* (Oxford: Oxford University Press, 1995).

67 Thaddeus Stevens, "Speech in Lancaster," Pennsylvania, September 6, 1865, in *The Selected Papers of Thaddeus Stevens*, 23. Emphasis in the original.

68 Ibid.

69 Stevens, "Speech in Lancaster," 23. Emphasis in the original.

70 Sumner, "Further Guaranties in Reconstruction," 307.

71 Du Bois, *Black Reconstruction*, 176.

72 Du Bois, *Black Reconstruction*, 176.

73 For northern opposition, see John David Smith, "'Like the Baseless Fabric of a Vision': Thaddeus Stevens and Confiscation Reconsidered," *The Worlds of James Buchanan and Thaddeus Stevens: Place, Personality, and Politics in the Civil War Era*, ed. Michael J. Birkner, Randall M. Miller, and John W. Quist (Baton Rouge: Louisiana State University Press, 2019), 185–206. Harry Haywood argues that the "ruling capitalist circles not only regarded the expropriation of the planters as a threat to capitalist property in general, but understood that it would have meant the creation of a class of independent producers essentially hostile to big capitalist domination. The path therefore was not taken." *Negro Liberation* (New York: International Publishers, 1948), 86.

74 See, for example, Desmond Jagmohan, "Peculiar Property: Harriet Jacobs on the Nature of Slavery," *Journal of Politics*, 84, no. 2 (April 2022): 669–681.

75 Margaret Jane Radin, "Property and Personhood," *Stanford Law Review* 34 (1982): 957–1015.

76 Bernard Williams, *Moral Luck* (Cambridge: Cambridge University Press, 1981), 1–20.

77 Douglass, *Life and Times of Frederick Douglass*, 612.

78 Gerald David Jaynes, *Branches Without Roots: Genesis of the Black Working Class in the American South, 1862–1882* (Oxford: Oxford University Press, 1986).

79 Richard Franklin Bensel, *The American Ballot Box in the Mid-Nineteenth Century* (Cambridge: Cambridge University Press, 2004).

80 Wilson Jeremiah Moses, *The Golden Age of Black Nationalism, 1850–1925* (Oxford: Oxford University Press, 1978).

81 Martin R. Delany, *The Condition, Elevation, Emigration, and Destiny of the Colored People of the United States*, ed. Toyin Falola (Amherst, NY: Humanity Books, 2004 [1852]), 44.

82 Martin R. Delany, "The Political Destiny of the Colored Race on the American Continent," *Martin R. Delany: A Documentary Reader*, ed. Robert S. Levine (Chapel Hill: University of North Carolina Press, 2003), 278.

83 Delany, "Political Destiny," 278.

84 Delany, *Condition*, 44.

85 Delany, *Condition*, 75.

86 Delany, "Political Destiny," 246.

87 Delany, "Political Destiny," 246.

88 Delany, "Political Destiny," 246; all emphases are in the original.
89 Delany, "Political Destiny," 246.
90 Delany, "Political Destiny," 246.
91 Delany, "Political Destiny," 247.
92 Delany, "Political Destiny," 246–247.
93 Delany, "Political Destiny," 246–247.
94 Delany, "Political Destiny," 246.
95 Delany, *Condition*, 41
96 I opt here for the male pronoun because suffrage was restricted to men at the time and Delany, despite his radicalism, did not question that restriction.
97 Delany, "Political Destiny," 248.
98 Delany, "Political Destiny," 246.
99 Delany, *Condition*, 48.
100   Delany, *Condition*, 48.
101   Delany, *Condition*, 48.
102   Delany, *Condition*, 42.
103   Delany, *Condition*, 43.
104   Delany, *Condition*, 68–69.
105   Shklar, *American Citizenship*, 63–79.
106   Delany, *Condition*, 69.
107   Delany, *Condition*, 69.
108   Delany, *Condition*, 69.
109   Delany, *Condition*, 71.
110   Delany, *Condition*, 213.
111   Stephen L. Darwall, "Two Kinds of Respect," *Ethics* 88, no. 1 (October 1977): 36–49.
112   Delany, *Condition*, 69–70.
113   Delany, *Condition*, 70.
114   Erving Goffman, *Presentation of Self in Everyday Life* (New York: Doubleday, 1963), 3.
115   Delany, *Condition*, 211.
116   Delany, *Condition*, 211.
117   King, Jr., *Where Do We Go From Here*, 33.
118   Peniel E. Joseph, *Waiting 'Til the Midnight Hour: A Narrative History of Black Power in America* (New York: Henry Holt, 2007); Brandon M. Terry, "Requiem for a Dream: The Problem Space of Black Power," in *To Shape a New World: Essays on the Political Philosophy of Martin Luther King, Jr.*, ed. Brandon M. Terry and Tommie Shalby (Cambridge, MA: Harvard University Press, 2018), 290–324.
119   King, Jr., *Where Do We Go From Here*, 49.
120   King, Jr., *Where Do We Go From Here*, 26.

121   King, Jr., *Where Do We Go From Here*, 45.

122   King, Jr., *Where Do We Go From Here*, 47.

123   King, Jr., *Where Do We Go From Here*, 48–49.

124   On the relationship between collective identity and the right to self-determination in the Black nationalist tradition, see "A Liberal Defense of Black Nationalism," *American Political Science Review* 104, no. 3 (August 2010): 467–481; Desmond Jagmohan, "Between Race and Nation: Marcus Garvey and the Politics of Self-Determination," *Political Theory* 48, no. 3 (June 2020): 271–302. For a philosophical explication and defense of racial solidarity, see Tommie Shelby, *We Who Are Dark: The Philosophical Foundations of Black Solidarity* (Cambridge, MA: Harvard University Press, 2005), 201–242.

125   *The Business of Black Power: Community Development, Capitalism, and Corporate Responsibility in Postwar America*, ed. Laura Warren Hill and Julia Rabig (Rochester, NY: University of Rochester Press, 2012); Jessica Gordon Nembhard, *Collective Courage: A History of African American Cooperative Economic Thought and Practice* (University Park: Pennsylvania State University Press, 2014).

126   Kwame Ture and Charles V. Hamilton, *Black Power: The Politics of Liberation* (New York: Vintage, 1992 [1967]).

127   Ture and Hamilton, *Black Power*, 7.

128   Ture and Hamilton, *Black Power*, 7.

129   Ture and Hamilton, *Black Power*, 44.

130   Ture and Hamilton, *Black Power*, 78.

131   Ture and Hamilton, *Black Power*, 45.

132   Ture and Hamilton, *Black Power*, 51.

133   Anna Stilz, "The Value of Self-Determination," *Oxford Studies in Political Philosophy* 2 (2016): 102.

134   Ture and Hamilton, *Black Power*, 47.

135   Ture and Hamilton, *Black Power*, 182.

136   Ture and Hamilton outlined a series of measures for attaining greater levels of self-determination, from higher levels of representation on school boards to a Black third party. It is far beyond the scope of this chapter to offer a detailed account of their democratic localism. For their plan, see Ture and Hamilton, *Black Power*, 93–145.

137   Ture and Hamilton, *Black Power*, 75.

138   Ture and Hamilton, *Black Power*, 75.

139   Ture and Hamilton, *Black Power*, 130.

140   Ture and Hamilton, *Black Power*, 133.

141   Ture and Hamilton, *Black Power*, 66.

142   Ture and Hamilton, *Black Power*, 76.

143   Ture and Hamilton, *Black Power*, 76.

144   Ture and Hamilton, *Black Power*, 72.

145   Ture and Hamilton, *Black Power*, 66–67.

146   Ture and Hamilton, *Black Power*, 68.

147   Ture and Hamilton, *Black Power*, 40.

148   Ture and Hamilton, *Black Power*, 40.

149   Ture and Hamilton, *Black Power*, 35.

150   Ture and Hamilton, *Black Power*, 41.

151   Ture and Hamilton, *Black Power*, 55.

152   Ture and Hamilton, *Black Power*, 39.

153   Brooks, *Atonement and Forgiveness*, 169. This is a real point of confusion because how can it be a necessary or constitutive part of atonement redress if it is entirely arbitrary?

154   Shelby, "Integration, Inequality, and Imperatives of Justice," 272.

155   Black Panther Party, *What We Want; What We Believe*, in *Redress for Historical Injustice in the United States*, 586.

156   James Forman, "The Black Manifesto," Speech at the National Economic Development Conference, 1969, in *Redress for Historical Injustice in the United States*, 594.

157   Republic of New Afrika, "Declaration of Independence," in *Redress for Historical Injustice in the United States*, 589.

158   They were inspired by Harry Haywood's "black belt thesis" but, in the end, offered a quite different vision. See Edward Onaci, *Free the Land: The Republic of New Afrika and the Pursuit of a Black Nation-State* (Chapel Hill: University of North Carolina Press, 2020), 43–112.

159   Republic of New Afrika, "Declaration of Independence," 590.

160   King, Jr., *Where Do We Go From Here*, 3.

161   James Baldwin, "Letter From a Region in My Mind," *The New Yorker*, November 9, 1962.

162   Christian E. Weller and Lily Roberts, "Eliminating the Black-White Wealth Gap is a Generational Challenge," March 19, 2921, *Center for American Progress*.

163   Dima Williams, "A Look at Housing Inequality and Racism in the U.S.," *Forbes*, June 3, 2020.

164   Lynne Peeples, "What the Data Say About Police Brutality and Racial Bias—And Which Reforms Might Work," *Nature*, June 19, 2002.

165   Ashley Nellis, "The Color of Justice: Racial and Ethnic Disparity in State Prisons," *The Sentencing Project*, June 14, 2016.

6

TRANSITIONAL JUSTICE AND REDRESS FOR RACIAL INJUSTICE

COLLEEN MURPHY

What should redress for atrocity look like when dealing with historic and contemporary wrongdoing whose scale and brutality in many instances outstrip our powers of comprehension? Extracting from the conversations that have occurred over redress for the Holocaust, apartheid, and Comfort Women, in "Framing Redress Discourse," Roy Brooks suggests two distinct models of repair exist: the tort and atonement models.[1] Brooks then explores the linkages between those redress models and a second set of post–civil rights models (traditionalism, reformism, critical race theory, and limited separation) developed in response to atrocities in the American context, specifically slavery and Jim Crow. Brooks's analysis is significant for bringing into the conversation two discourses that largely operate independently of one another. As Brooks demonstrates, both provide important insights for understanding how to grapple morally with the particular legacies shaping the American context.

In my comments I first argue that the set of general models of redress that Brooks offers is incomplete and propose the addition of a third model of redress, what I call the transitional justice model. Adding this third model is important, I claim, because it is the general model most relevant for dealing with the kind of wrongdoing in which atrocity like slavery consists. Furthermore, the transitional justice model offers additional theoretical tools in support of the conclusion Brooks defends, namely, that the critical race theory and limited integration models of racial progress are the most defensible models for racial progress in the United States.

Unlike traditionalism and reformism, critical race theory and limited separation are premised on a recognition of the circumstances of transitional justice that obtain in the United States. Both also specify what societal transformation, the general goal of redress from the perspective of the transitional justice model, entails in the US context. Finally, viewing racial progress from the perspective of the transitional justice model opens conceptual space to expand discussion of redress beyond the two parameters of reparations and apology to include truth seeking, institutional reform, and memorialization processes.

MODELS OF REDRESS

The first general model of redress, the *tort model*, is in Brooks's words "backward-looking, victim-focused, and compensatory (sometimes punitive)."[2] The basic model is this. Justice demands that compensation be offered by the perpetrator for wrongful losses and harms suffered by the victim. The focus of justice is backward in the sense of aiming to bring the victims to their status quo ante situation. We might add that implicit in this framework is a basic standard of care, a notion of proper conduct against which the infliction of wrongful losses may be judged. This standard explains when losses ought to be borne by the individual who suffers them and when compensation should be offered by the cause of such losses. Apology or acknowledgment of guilt is not a necessary condition for redress to have been done; redress is a function of compensation.

The second, *atonement model*, focuses on how wrongdoing can be an obstacle to ongoing interaction and on what the perpetrator can do to repair the rupture so that future interaction becomes possible. The atonement model is, in Brooks's words, "forward-looking, perpetrator-focused, and restorative."[3] For this model, apology by the perpetrator in a manner that demonstrates an acceptance of responsibility and remorse is critical. Apology in the form of words alone is often insufficient for wrongs like atrocities, and reparations are needed to demonstrate the sincerity of the apology offered. Through apology and reparations the perpetrator makes an invitation to the victim for forgiveness, and if forgiveness is offered, the perpetrator achieves redemption and the relationship is repaired.

Brooks notes that both models suffer from limits in the contexts of interest. In cases of atrocity, reparations without apology or acceptance of responsibility risk becoming "justice on the cheap," reducing a moral claim for redress to a technical legal claim that can become the site of contentious struggle impeding prospects for reconciliation. Indeed, Brooks ultimately rejects the tort model for being insufficient as a guide to responding to atrocity.

However, I want to suggest that the limits with the guidance the tort and atonement models offers for dealing with atrocities runs deeper than the problems Brooks notes. More fundamentally, both models offer a victim- or perpetrator-oriented framework appropriate for dealing with interpersonal (or interactive) wrongdoing that occurs against a background of normatively defensible relationships. However, atrocities are importantly not, or not primarily, interpersonal in nature.[4] Put differently, examining atrocities as a series of interactions between perpetrators and victims is insufficient for capturing or analyzing them. Atrocities are importantly structural, made possible by normatively indefensible terms for interaction. A model for redress must be structural to act as a response to this kind of wrongdoing. The model of redress needed in contexts where atrocities occur is a *transitional justice* model. Below, I explain why this model is needed and in what this third model consists.

Let me begin by noting what is implicitly presumed to hold in the tort and atonement models as Brooks presents them. Wrongful losses are assessed in the tort model against a baseline for conduct that is presumed to be morally defensible, and so appropriate to use when evaluating the losses for which I am entitled to compensation. Consider first the tort model, which enjoins the provision of reparations needed to bring a victim back to the status quo ante situation. Corrective justice, the kind of justice underpinning the tort model, takes as its starting point a standard of care. It is against his baseline standard of care that we judge the losses an individual experiences as *wrongful*, and, as such, not losses victims should bear themselves. Any response to the wrongful losses victims suffer must be such that they bring victims back to the situation they would have enjoyed had the wrongdoing not occurred.

But in the context of atrocity, the extant standard of care is precisely what is in need of contestation and change. In the words of Margaret Urban Walker, "Corrective justice demands 'correction' of what are presumed to be discrete lapses from that prior or standing moral baseline in particular interpersonal or institutional transactions with individuals, or unacceptable impacts of the action or omission of some individuals upon others. For this reason, corrective justice may be at least artificial and perhaps incoherent in addressing histories, acts, or forms of injustice that consist in radical *denial* of moral standing or in relentless enforcement of *degraded* moral status of individuals, especially when these are systemic conditions and persist over extended periods of time."[5] In response to atrocity, reparations are justified and to be calculated not in a way that brings victims back to the status quo ante, as the tort model prescribes, but as needed to change that status quo ante situation.

A similar presumption of background moral defensibility in the terms for interaction is at work in the atonement model as presented. To frame the process of reconciliation as predicated on atonement coupled with forgiveness, which repairs a rupture and allows a relationship to continue, is to presume the relationship in question has value. This model of reconciliation is intuitively compelling against a background of ongoing, morally defensible interaction. In such contexts, efforts at atonement and repair of a discrete wrong are possible, and the compellingness of forgiveness is evident. To refuse to forgive (which I take to entail relinquishing anger and resentment stemming from having been wronged) could demonstrate a failure to recognize one's own fallibility and reciprocal hope that you would be forgiven in cases where you wrong another.

However, precisely what is missing in the cases of historic injustice and atrocity that Brooks takes up is a morally defensible and valuable relationship. A relationship that is morally defensible and has moral value is precisely what processes of repair and redress aim in part to establish given the presumption operative in many post-atrocity contexts that political relationships must continue to exist in some form.

Importantly for my purposes, the absence of a morally defensible framework for interaction renders less compelling the steps needed to achieve reconciliation in the atonement model. Consider specifically the forgiveness it stipulates as a key aim in the context of a relationship constituted by ongoing domestic violence.[6]

To urge or risk forgiveness after an episode of abuse in such a case is morally troubling. Even if offered for a particular episode of violence, to accept amends and engage in forgiveness risk implicitly encouraging victims of domestic violence to capitulate to their own abuse by continuing relationships that are abusive in structure. Urging forgiveness risks failing to take seriously the claim that such a victim has to better treatment. And amends followed by forgiveness by itself does not address the core problem: the abusive terms structuring the relationship itself.

In contexts of atrocity, the structure of relationships is characteristically not morally defensible. Indeed, it is the basic terms for interaction themselves that enable and implicitly justify atrocity. Thus, the cases of interest to Brooks are ones in which political relationships are to some extent analogous to an interpersonal relationship of domestic abuse. In cases of state-sponsored and state-sanctioned wrongdoing, endorsing forgiveness as a goal toward which acts of amends are aimed at facilitating has the same intuitively problematic implications I just sketched. Urging or attempting to facilitate forgiveness, even if conditional on amends, risks failing to take seriously the wrongful treatment to which victims were subject, thereby wronging them a second time. This is an especially acute risk in the contexts where the initial experience of victims of atrocity is often one of disbelief and dismissal on the part of state actors. One of the central functions of atrocity is to deny the political standing and political membership of targeted groups, motivating victims and members of targeted groups to capitulate to their own subordination. This is what the forgiveness component of the atonement model risks duplicating. The atonement model moreover incorrectly locates the problem with relationships. Anger and resentment toward wrongful treatment and systemic injustice are not the problem; the sources of anger are. Those sources are wrongdoing and injustice, and the conditions that enable wrongdoing to become normalized and injustice to become entrenched. Finally, the burden of relational repair ends up being borne by victims, who hold the power to determine whether the end toward which acts of amends are aimed, forgiveness, will be fulfilled. But this means victims also then risk being the target of blame insofar as that end is not achieved, overlooking the right of victims to remain angry and not forgive.

Brooks himself acknowledges many of the points just raised. He is, for example, aware of the need for structural change given the realities of racial injustice in the United States. However, as discussed above, neither the tort nor atonement models are able to accommodate the need for structural change given the terms on which they are developed. A different general model of redress is necessary.

A THIRD ALTERNATIVE: THE TRANSITIONAL JUSTICE MODEL

Against the limits of the tort model and atonement model for dealing with atrocity, we need a third model. The third model of redress for atrocity I will call the *transitional justice* model. While the tort model is backward-looking and the amends model forward-looking, the transitional justice model is both: We look back in order to reach forward, to use the phrase prominently adopted in the case of South Africa's transition from apartheid to multiracial democracy.[7] The aim of apology and reparations in this model is the just pursuit of relational transformation. Put differently, the core subject matter for this model is the baseline for interaction that the tort model and atonement model treat as background context.[8] The goal is to fundamentally alter the structural terms for interaction among members of a political community where atrocity occurred, both horizontally among citizens and vertically between citizens and officials; that is what relational transformation entails.

This change, or transformative potential, is pursued via processes that acknowledge wrongdoing that impacted specific victims and/or hold to account particular perpetrators for specific wrongs done. The combination of an emphasis both on the structure of political interaction and on the particular claims of victims and perpetrators is unusual. Theories of distributive justice focus on what is required for a society to have a just basic structure without investigating particular interactions. The tort model of repair focuses on discrete interactional wrongs, but not the structure of interaction itself. Transitional justice brings together a concern with the structure of interaction and with the wrongness of discrete interactions.

This linkage of broader societal change with processes focused on specific victims and perpetrators is necessary for a few reasons.

From the vantage of transitional justice, failing to deal with widespread wrongdoing does not heal communities or repair relationships, nor does it mean that wrongdoing ceases to matter. Damage to relationships that is both a product and facilitator of widespread wrongdoing can be repaired only if it is first understood and acknowledged. Widespread wrongdoing must also be addressed because of how such wrongdoing, both of the distant past and of more recent periods, shapes the current structure of interaction. The thought orienting the framework of transitional justice, that repairing relationships damaged by wrongdoing requires acknowledging and dealing with such wrongdoing, is a common one in relationships; in order for relationships to improve, you have to deal with the problems and wrongs that exist. Hiding or denying problems rarely heals.

The kind of structural change required of political relationships after atrocity is capacious, encompassing the norms and rules that structure action and interaction, as well as the attitudes underpinning and supporting such rules and norms. Paul Morrow defines norms as "practical prescriptions, permissions, or prohibitions, accepted by individuals belonging to particular groups, organizations, or societies, and capable of guiding the actions of those individuals and patterning the conduct of those groups. Accepting norms entails adopting various practical commitments and normative attitudes."[9] A wide range of institutions shape the contours of interaction, defining what counts as permissible, prohibited, and required action as well as the formal and informal penalties for violating such standards. By institutions I mean any more or less formal social practice of human cooperation that exists through a coordinated, interrelated rule-governed role. The range of institutions of interest is vast, including religious, social, economic, political, and legal.[10]

Structural change requires altering the rules and norms shaping interaction, as well as the underlying ideologies justifying the form(s) interaction currently takes.[11] What is required to change norms will vary depending on the kind of norm in question.[12] Moral norms delimit conduct that is prohibited or required. In contexts of widespread wrongdoing, the prohibitions of immoral conduct against members of certain groups gets eroded often through processes of brutalization and of denial, using euphemisms to characterize immoral conduct.[13] Legal norms contribute to widespread wrongdoing by creating what Morrow calls "invidious social categories" in which members of such categories are legally marginalized and information about their marginalized conditions is restricted. In contexts where moral norms prohibiting violence or other forms of immoral conduct against a targeted group coexist with legal marginalization, Morrow writes, public debate will justify rather than challenge what law requires.

When the problem is law itself, the solution is relatively straightforward: Change the law. Unsurprisingly, in many transitional contexts legal reform is a central component of transformational efforts. Constitutions get rewritten. Policies for police and security forces get altered. Training of judges is pursued. However, widespread wrongdoing is rarely only, or simply, a function of bad law. It is also a function of flawed social norms. Social norms exist and are binding as a matter of social fact, existing as long as the norm is endorsed by members to whom the norm is taken to apply. Social norms can create peer expectations that, when at odds with legal expectations or moral norms, can serve as an impediment to social change. As Agnes Tam discusses with respect to foot binding in China, because foot binding was seen as what respectable Chinese parents did for their daughters, that social norm impeded avoidance of what was regarded by many of those same parents as an immoral practice.[14] In the context of the United States, social norms regulating racial interaction often underpinned White justifications of lynching. A Black man perceived to have violated prohibitions against sexual interactions or relationships with a White woman was seen by many White men and women as thereby eligible for extrajudicial murder. The fact that lynching violated existing legal requirements of due process and prohibitions against vigilante justice did not impede its occurrence; the ways in which law enforcement was implicated in many cases of lynching, by failing to prevent or actively contributing to its occurrence, further eroded the social understanding of to whom legal guarantees of due process applied.

I have argued above that the transitional justice model shifts the focus of attention to the broader structural context within which particular interactions occur. The "just pursuit" of transformation delimits the moral demands that must be met for victims and perpetrators to be treated in a morally fitting or appropriate manner.[15] The terms for fitness and appropriateness of responses to victims and perpetrators is a function of meeting widely recognized normative objectives. In the case of victims, appropriate responses acknowledge victims as victims, subject to treatment that was wrongful; reinforce the status of victims of rights bearers and members of the political community; and provide a measure of repair for harms suffered. For perpetrators, appropriate responses judge and hold perpetrators accountable for conduct that is condemned, ideally facilitating an acceptance of responsibility on the part of the perpetrator.[16]

But the just pursuit also focuses on categories beyond victims and perpetrators as relevant for particular instances of widespread wrongdoing that processes of transitional justice might take up. Consider torture. In cases of torture, a common form of human rights violation that occurs during periods of repression and conflict, there are specific and particular direct victims of torture. There are also specific individual perpetrators responsible for ordering and/or inflicting torture on specific victims. But when torture becomes normalized, the category of individuals implicated becomes much wider. Collaborators can provide information to authorities that leads to the arrest and subsequent torture of particular persons. Bystanders to torture witness the harm suffered without intervening. Processes of transitional justice include focus on bystanders, collaborators, and other complicit individuals as well. The opening of the Stasi archives is but one example.[17]

With historical and enduring injustices like slavery we can ask not only about victims and perpetrators but also, on Michael Rothberg's view, about who is *implicated in* temporally and spatially distant events.[18] Rothberg discusses the morally tainted legacies (where legacies are defined as the sum of money or property given to another by will or inheritance) of wealth created for White Americans, while Black Americans bear the legacies shaped by the stripping of property, privilege, and right during slavery and Jim Crow alike. Rothberg also distinguishes genealogical versus structural implication. Genealogical implication in atrocity stems from lineage and the relationship between one's family members and the atrocity in question. Descendants of slaves and of slave owners, as well as of citizens in the United States living at the time when

slavery was legal, would fall into this category. Structural implication, by contrast, does not require any genealogical connection.
It focuses on the ways in which racial privilege operates and the
experiences of those racialized as White and Black in a post-slavery
society in the United States.

From the perspective of the transitional justice model, the goal
is to change the terms that structure how citizens relate to one
another and with officials by addressing the rules and norms governing conduct and the rationales for them. Importantly, for this
model, forgiveness is neither necessary nor sufficient for relational
repair. Relational repair does not depend on the forgiveness of
victims, nor is it achieved when forgiveness is offered. The transitional justice model does not presume the terms for interaction
that exist are morally defensible. As noted earlier, forgiveness as
a demand of relational repair is intuitively plausible in contexts
where relations are broadly morally defensible. So relational repair
for the transitional justice model does not include forgiveness.[19]
Relational repair is not achieved when forgiveness is forthcoming
because such forgiveness does not alter the underlying problem
with the relationship: the abusive terms of interaction themselves.
It can implicitly encourage victims of domestic violence to capitulate to their own abuse.

Cases of widespread wrongdoing are those in which the political
relationships in question are very often structured on terms that
are abusive. The structure of interaction is one that facilitates and
in turn justifies wrongdoing against members of a targeted group.
To encourage forgiveness is often to try to repair relationships on
the cheap: It can reflect a failure on the part of a dominant group
to recognize the depth of the wrongfulness to which members of a
targeted group have been subject. It also often locates the source of
damage to relationships in the wrong place. Anger and resentment
are natural responses to being wronged and are morally defensible
as a way of protesting abusive treatment and defending the dignity one has and the treatment one deserves as a result.[20] Anger
and resentment in the face of widespread wrongdoing that occurs
against a background of terms for interaction that are abusive is
not the issue. Rather, the sources of damage are the abusive terms
and the wrongdoing they facilitate. That is what processes of relational repair must focus on.

From the perspective of the transitional justice model I defend, forgiveness is also not necessary for either the just treatment of victims or perpetrators. Refraining from including forgiveness preserves a place for respecting the right of victims to be angry in the face of injustice and abuse. It shifts the focus onto providing repair of the concrete harms victims bear, and the duties and responsibilities of direct perpetrators of abuse and wrongdoing, as well as those who are implicated in the wrongs carried out by perpetrators.

Linking Models of Redress

One reason to add the transitional justice model of redress is that it expands the conceptual space of general models for redress for atrocity in the ways discussed in the previous section. But there are two further reasons tied specifically to Brooks's project. First, the model of transitional justice provides additional resources for critical engagement with the visions of racial progress contained in the four post–civil rights models for the United States that Brooks outlines. I explain how in this section. In the next section I discuss the second additional reason: The transitional justice model expands discussion of redress and repair beyond the terms of reparations and apology to include institutional reform, memorialization, and truth telling.

Brooks articulates four models of slave redress for the United States. In presenting the four models, Brooks emphasizes two dimensions of such models: the vision of racial progress each contains and the implications of this vision for what form, if any, reparations and apology should take. I provide summaries of his four models below.

Traditionalism's starting point is that the problem to which redress is a solution no longer exists. From the perspective of this framework, race relations in the contemporary United States are not fundamentally flawed. Insofar as differentials remain in income or outcomes, the root of those differences lies in individual choices. Avoiding talk about structural causes, the source of racialized inequality that remains in the United States is viewed as the product of individual choices and specific interactions.

Past wrongdoing matters insofar as it creates backward-looking obligations of acknowledgment. Put differently, there is value in acknowledging wrongdoing that occurred for its own sake. Processes like apology can achieve the requisite form of acknowledgment. Traditionalism, like the tort and atonement models, focuses on the actions of discrete perpetrators and victims. The other obligation past wrongdoing generates is a commitment to nonrecurrence. From the lens of traditionalism, this entails an obligation of color-blindness and race-neutrality. Since the wrong of the past was race-based laws, avoiding that wrong requires avoiding race-based measures.

Reformism is predicated on recognition of the ongoing presence of racism in American society.[21] It acknowledges that race relations in the United States are not unproblematic. While it does recognize the importance of structural sources of racialized inequality and racial injustice, the underlying structure of society itself is not the focus of reformism. Rather, existing inequality is diagnosed as a product of past wrongdoing that went unaddressed, and because it went unaddressed shapes present deficiencies. A government apology is needed to atone for these wrongs, and reparations are needed to repair harm. Reparations at the institutional and individual levels can provide needed redress for the influence of the past on the present, especially when they take the form of constitutional precommitments to racially integrated schools and cash reparations to individuals as an income supplement. Such redress will facilitate racial reconciliation, which is framed as racial integration.

Critical race theory adopts a goal of racial reconciliation understood in terms of racial integration, but views the changes needed to make this possible as much deeper and more fundamental than reformism sets out. Institutions in the United States shape conduct and possibilities on the basis of terms that White Americans structure and disproportionately benefit from. Racial progress requires altering that operating presumption. The emphasis of critical race theory is on White hegemony and its role in defining and shaping power and race in our society. Reparations are conceptualized as contributing to the transformation of the social order. To play this transformative role, there must be an apology coupled with reparations. Racial quotas justified via constitutional precommitment to racial integration are necessary in schools, and cash reparations aimed at wealth creation are necessary.[22]

Finally, *limited separation* goes deeper in its challenging of White hegemony. For limited separation the normative goal is not integration. Rather, it is protecting and preserving spaces in which Black-centered institutions and interaction can flourish. Since the goal is not racial integration or repair, an apology is not prioritized or necessary. Instead, the focus from this perspective is on reparations. Reparations in support of historically Black colleges and universities, public funding of schools controlled by Blacks, and cash payments to Black-run institutions are necessary.

Brooks offers reasons to reject the underlying premises of traditionalism and reformism and in defense of the visions of racial progress outlined by critical race theory and by limited separation and reasons. Importantly, the contemporary United States, Brooks argues, continues to be shaped by legacies of slavery in ways that traditionalism and reformism insufficiently acknowledge. Traditionalism views reparations as prima facia suspicious because it is grounded on attention to race and fails to acknowledge the reality of the lingering effects of the past on the present, distorting what reparations represent as a result. Whether it is race-specific rhetoric to justify economic exploitation of Black people; the implementation of policies like redlining; or historically rooted capital deficiencies in Black communities in terms of income, wealth, formal education, and social bases of self-respect, there remain structural impediments to Black success and flourishing.[23] Only critical race theory and limited separatism recognize this reality and identify the conditions needed for true reconciliation and redress Brooks claims. Impediments and self-interest on the part of White Americans to acknowledging this may make critical race theory and limited separation less politically feasible, but they remain more defensible in principle.

Adding the transitional model of redress alongside the tort and amendment models provides additional theoretical resources in defense of Brooks's reasoning. Against the background of the three models on offer, the question becomes: Which is the appropriate model to use when thinking about racial progress and redress for racial injustice in the United States?

Philosopher David Hume provides a method of adjudication. Hume famously claimed that a set of circumstances of justice makes a particular question of justice necessary and possible for a community to address. Theories of justice then provide an articulation of the answer to that question. What Hume's methodology suggests is

that, when faced with competing models of redress, it is important
to articulate the background circumstances of justice each presupposes and the particular question of justice each takes up. This will
guide selection of a redress model to adopt in a particular case of
wrongdoing.

In my own work, I articulate the circumstances of justice assumed
by the tort and amends models as they are typically formulated,
as opposed to the circumstances underpinning the transitional
justice model.[24] Briefly stated, the tort and amends models force
communities to confront the question of "how to deal with victims
of wrongdoing" and "how to deal with perpetrators of wrongdoing" where wrongdoing is assumed to be exceptional (wrongdoing
at issue is the exception rather than the rule for what occurs in
communities) and where the background structure of interaction
is normatively defensible; there exists limited structural inequality,
as I state it in my work. In such circumstances, the rationale for
focusing on particular victims and perpetrators in isolation from
questions of the broader social context, as the tort and amendment
models do, is clear. For in cases where wrongdoing is exceptional
and the context is just to a threshold level, individuals who engage
in wrongdoing chose to violate normatively defensible rules that
resulted in harm to another, and should be held to account for
that fact. Repair to the victim should be made. Because such wrongdoing is an exceptional but unavoidable feature of any society in
which humans interact, it is important to address. But responses to
wrongdoing have little bearing on the overall trajectory of a community or its stability.

By contrast, the transitional justice model of redress is salient
when different conditions hold. Societal transformation, in addition to appropriate treatment of victims and perpetrators, is
needed when two factors are present. (1) *Wrongdoing is normalized,*
becoming a basic fact of life around which members of a targeted
group must orient their conduct. Importantly, normalized wrongdoing in contexts where transitional justice is invoked implicate
state actors. Security forces and law enforcement are either direct
perpetrators of human rights violations, or complicit in the occurrence of violations through, for example, the lack of protection of
victims from harm, absence of meaningful accountability for perpetrators, or facilitating violations by colluding with paramilitary

organizations. (2) *Pervasive structural inequality obtains.* Pervasive structural inequality is a function of norms and rules structuring interaction being such that they cumulatively impede the ability of certain groups of citizen to avoid poverty, participate in economic and political institutions, and exercise effective agency in shaping the rules and norms for conduct. Earlier in the chapter, I outlined in detail the rules and norms producing such inequality in my discussion of what societal transformation needs to tackle.

Transitional justice, the just pursuit of societal transformation, is necessary whenever normalized wrongdoing and pervasive structural inequality obtain. Transitional justice becomes possible in periods in which the status quo becomes in doubt, reflecting what I call *serious existential uncertainty* for communities. Various sources can generate such uncertainty for communities, including but not limited to the signing of a peace agreement, mass protests, or the toppling of a dictatorship. While opportunities for pursuing societal change open with such events, the achievement of transformation and a measure of justice for victims and perpetrators remains characteristically precarious. Communities pursuing transitional justice are fragile, beset by, for example, profound division, deep tensions over the pursuit of robust change, and resentment on the part of communities that benefit from the status quo. The signing of a peace agreement often does not translate into peace. Mass protests in what has become known as the Arab Spring did not lead to robust democratization. While failure is not a guarantee, neither is it a given.

Turning now to the United States, I have argued at length elsewhere that the circumstances of transitional justice are the ones that best characterize the United States in the present.[25] Structural inequality along racial lines continues to exist. Laws implementing voting restrictions after the 2020 election disproportionately target voters of color. The racial wealth gap remains largely unchanged from what it was at the end of Jim Crow.[26] The details of such inequality are precisely what Brooks lays out in his chapter.

Normalized wrongdoing is what sparked arguably the largest protests in US history, led by Black Lives Matter in summer 2020 in cities across the country in response to police violence.[27] The hashtags used to remember the names of Black men and women engaging in legal, mundane, activities and yet subject to arrest, harassment, and in some cases killing underscores the constant threat of violence confronting Black people in the United States at the hands of White private citizens or the police. The concerns of police violence and White vigilante justice echo previous forms such violence took, including, importantly, lynching.[28]

The present moment in the United States continues to be one of *serious existential uncertainty*, as the probability of ensuring widespread structural reform and accountability for perpetrators of normalized violence against Black people that protests demand remains unclear in the face of the predictable backlash against meaningful change.

Because the circumstances we confront in the United States are the circumstances of transitional justice, the salient question of justice is: What constitutes the just pursuit of societal transformation? Only two of the four models of racial redress articulate the normative goal of racial progress in terms that are transformative: critical race theory and limited separation. By contrast, traditionalism and reformism implicitly frame questions of redress in the terms the tort and atonement model lay out, and are consequently limited for dealing with atrocities past and present in the ways that those two general models of redress are. Traditionalism and reformism treat normalized wrongdoing as a product of individual failings, rather than as the product of general conditions that facilitate violence and the impunity in response to it. They fail to acknowledge the kinds of structural reform needed to achieve racial justice in the interaction among all citizens and with the state.

Transformation may entail greater racial identity and solidarity as sought by the limited separation model, as much as it may entail the challenging of White hegemony that critical race theory advocates. Insofar as critical race theory and limited separation are premised on a recognition of the circumstances of transitional justice being present in the United States, they are more adequate for dealing with our atrocities past and present and articulating a transformative path forward.

Tools of Repair: Expanding the Horizons of Possible Recompense

Beyond providing a general model of redress best suited to understanding and confronting the particular atrocities in and their legacies for the United States, the transitional justice model has one further contribution to debates about redress here: It expands the conceptual space of possibilities.

There are five widely recognized pillars of transitional justice: truth, justice, reparations, non-recurrence, and memorialization. Each pillar articulates a specific objective that must be pursued in order to achieve societal transformation in a manner that does justice to victims and perpetrators.[29]

TRUTH refers to the importance of documenting and publicly acknowledging the causes, nature, extent, consequences, victims, and perpetrators of human rights violations. Such clarification and acknowledgment of the factual record are needed in contexts where official denial of wrongdoing, its scope, or the agents responsible for it is pervasive. Given the characteristic absence of a shared, factually based understanding of how many suffered and by whom, it is important to collectively produce an accurate understanding of how and why political relationships are damaged and what is in need of repair. For individual victims, there also exists a basic right to the truth as to who is responsible for abuse and the context of abuse.[30]

JUSTICE refers to the importance of accountability for perpetrators of wrongdoing. Often accountability is equated with criminal trial and punishment, though forms of accountability can go beyond this. Accountability matters intrinsically as a demand of morality upon perpetrators. It also is necessary in order to counter a culture of impunity that facilitates normalized wrongdoing and damages broader political relationships.

REPARATION captures the need to repair the harms that victims experience, both as direct victims of normalized wrongdoing and as targets of structural inequality. Harms and losses are often of different kinds: physical, psychological, economic, and material. Reparations both respond to these losses and, in so doing, affirm the status of victims as rights bearers and full members of the political community entitled to better treatment. These latter functions are an important component of relational transformation.

NON-RECURRENCE points to the significance of reforming the rules and norms and practices structuring interaction. It can encompass constitutional reform as well as reform or even abolishment of existing security and law enforcement. MEMORIALIZATION captures the need to remember past wrongs in an enduring manner, both as a requirement of justice for victims and as a safeguard against recurrence in the future of similar violations by understanding wrongdoing and the necessity of preventing it.

All pillars are recognized as jointly necessary for transitional justice to be achieved. Truth is no substitute for justice; memorialization is no substitute for reparations. The same process of transitional justice, however, may foster and facilitate more than one pillar. Truth commissions may contribute to documenting the truth and clarifying the historical record of abuses and, at the same time, constitute a form of reparations for victims.[31]

Viewing debates of redress for racial injustice in the United States from the perspective of transitional justice expands our sense of what ought to be included in the purview. In addition to debating reparations and the form(s) they should appropriately take and the role of apology as a meaningful form of accountability, other processes are needed. Establishing the historical record of truth as to normalized forms of wrongdoing such as lynching and the factual record as to the prevalence and pervasiveness of police violence in the present moment are necessary. Pursuing institutional reform oriented around institutions, such as law enforcement, political institutions, and economic institutions, is another component. Memorializing our past to ensure we remember and thus are able to collectively prevent repetition of wrongs in the future is needed as well.

Conceptualizing demands for racial justice in this way allows us to include in the scope of debate many efforts occurring already at local and regional levels. It locates the Equal Justice Initiative's Legacy Museum as well as its Peace and Justice Memorial in the space of redress. So too is the Maryland Lynching Truth and Reconciliation Commission in this space. Calls to remove confederate statues and abolish or reform the police are calls to engage in parts of what transitional justice requires. In bringing together discussions of redress that are normally pursued separately, we are in a position to view our society and its legacies and possibilities for redress in new ways that might ultimately contribute to the achievement of some measure of transformation.

NOTES

1 Roy Brooks, "Framing Redress Discourse," in this volume.

2 Ibid.

3 Ibid.

4 I explore the limits of an interpersonal model of reconciliation and of redress for dealing with atrocities in Colleen Murphy, *A Moral Theory of Political Reconciliation* (New York: Cambridge University Press, 2010) and Colleen Murphy, *The Conceptual Foundations of Transitional Justice* (New York: Cambridge University Press, 2017). Catherine Lu discusses the limits of what she calls the interactive model in *Justice and Reconciliation in World Politics* (New York: Cambridge University Press, 2017).

5 Margaret Urban Walker, "Restorative Justice and Reparations," *Journal of Social Philosophy* 37, no. 23 (2006): 377–395.

6 I discuss this kind of case and its relevance for thinking of atrocities in both *Moral Theory* and *Conceptual Foundations*.

7 See for example Charles Villa-Vicencio and Wilhelm Verwoerd (eds.), *Looking Back, Reaching Forward: Reflections on the Truth and Reconciliation Commission of South Africa* (Zed Books, 2000).

8 Murphy, *Conceptual Foundations*.

9 Ibid., 2.

10 Arthur Applbaum, *Ethics for Adversaries. The Morality of Roles in Public and Professional Life* (Princeton, NJ: Princeton University Press, 1999).

11 On the importance of ideology, see Tommie Shelby, "Racism, Moralism, and Social Criticism," *Du Bois Review* 11, no. 1 (2014): 57–74.

12 Paul Morrow, *Unconscionable Crimes: How Norms Explain and Constrain Genocide and Mass Atrocity* (Cambridge, MA: MIT Press, 2020). For example, legal norms are valid and binding by virtue of the socially grounded procedural rules specified for creating or changing legal norms. Moral norms do not depend on social practices for their existence, and lack specific procedural mechanisms for their change or adoption. Ibid., 18–20.

13 Ibid., 18.

14 Agnes Tam, "Why Moral Reasoning Is Insufficient for Moral Progress," *Journal of Political Philosophy* (2019): doi: 10.1111/jopp.12187: 1–24, at 16.

15 Murphy, *Conceptual Foundations*.

16 On these criteria see chapter 4 of Murphy, *Conceptual Foundations*.

17 Federal Commissioner for the Records of the State Security Service of the former German Democratic Republic, www.bstu.de.

18 Michael Rothberg, *The Implicated Subject: Beyond Victims and Perpetrators* (Stanford, CA: Stanford University Press, 2019).

19 I discuss these points at length in Murphy, *Moral Theory* and Murphy, *Conceptual Foundations.*

20 Myisha Cherry, *The Case for Rage: Why Anger Is Essential to Anti-Racist Struggle* (New York: Oxford University Press, 2021).

21 Brooks, "Framing Redress Discourse."

22 Ibid.

23 Ibid.

24 Murphy, *Conceptual Foundations.*

25 Colleen Murphy, "The Movement for Black Lives and Transitional Justice," in *Philosophers on the Movement for Black Lives*, ed. Brandan Hogan, Michael Cholbi, Alex Nadva, and Bejamin Yost (New York: Oxford University Press, 2021); Colleen Murphy, "How Nations Heal," *Boston Review*, January 21, 2021, http://bostonreview.net; Colleen Murphy, "To Tell the Truth," *Sojourners*, July 21, 2021, https://sojo.net.

26 Heather Long and Andrew van Dam, "The Black-White Economic Divide Is as Wide as It Was in 1968," *Washington Post*, June 4, 2020, www.washingtonpost.com.

27 Larry Buchanan, Quoctrung Bui, and Jugal Patel, "Black Lives Matter May Be the Largest Movement in U.S. History," *New York Times*, July 3, 2020, www.nytimes.com.

28 Philip Dray, *At the Hands of Persons Unknown: The Lynching of Black America* (New York: Modern Library, 2003).

29 *Report of the Secretary-General: The Rule of Law and Transitional Justice in Conflict and Post-Conflict Societies* (2004), https://documents-dds-ny.un.org; *Guidance Note of the Secretary-General: United Nations Approach to Transitional Justice* (2010), www.un.org; The Special Rapporteur on the promotion of truth, justice, reparations, and guarantees of non-recurrence, "Memorialisation Processes: Report" (United Nations Human Rights, 2020); www.ohchr.org.

30 Eduardo Gonzalez and Howard Varney (eds.), *Truth Seeking: Elements of Creating an Effective Truth Commission* (New York: ICTJ, 2013). Available online at https://www.ictj.org.

31 Margaret Urban Walker, "Truth Telling as Reparations," *Metaphilosophy* 41, no. 4 (2020): 525–545.

PART III

PUBLIC APOLOGIES
AS MORAL REPAIR

7

THE ROLE OF THE PUBLIC
IN PUBLIC APOLOGIES

LINDA RADZIK

For years, I was a connoisseur of public apologies. As a moral philosopher, I have been decidedly pro-apology, arguing at length that wrongdoers have an obligation to make amends for their misdeeds and that apologies play a key role in the reconciliation of healthy relationships.[1] I believe in the importance of accountability for wrongdoing, and public apologies seem to involve a weightier kind of accountability than those that are kept private between wrongdoers and their victims. However, as public apologies have become more widely accessible through social media, I have become uncomfortable. I often have to force myself to watch the videos or read the texts of high-profile public apologies. Two questions are at the heart of my concern: Why is this act of apology my business, and what am I being asked to do?

One underlying fear is that, if there is not some sensible and constructive role for third parties to play, then when we listen in on public apologies, we are simply voyeurs. We are merely being nosy, indulging in schadenfreude, or basking in a sense of our own comparative virtue. Another concern is that the presence of third parties may hijack public apologies. Wrongdoers may well be more concerned with how their apologies play to the crowd than to their actual victims. Recall here the adulterous politicians who have their spouses stand next to them at press conferences like human shields.

This chapter reflects on public apologies as means of moral repair by considering the various roles the public might play in these moral dramas. Audiences to public apologies include people who are related to the transgression in different ways. This chapter focuses on those parties in front of whom public apologies are intentionally performed but who are neither victims nor wrongdoers. Do such third parties add something of value to the apology? If so, how? How might they play their role well? How might things go poorly?

The next section of this chapter briefly introduces the theoretical frame within which I am working, clarifying the use of the terms "moral repair," "forgiveness," "reconciliation," "apology," and "public apology." I then present and evaluate several different interpretations of the role the public might play in a public apology. Finally, I argue that the multiplicity of possible roles creates problems, in particular the risk of "mission creep." The purpose of this chapter is not to claim that one should never call for a public apology nor join in the audience to such an apology. Instead, it argues that these decisions are complicated in ways that theorists often overlook.

THEORETICAL FRAME

Let the term "moral repair" refer to the end-state in which the hard feelings, alienation, and mistrust, which were fitting reactions to a wrongful action, come to an end in an appropriate way. When a wrong has been fully repaired, the wrong can be safely left in the past. The labels of "victim" and "wrongdoer" no longer reasonably shape how the parties regard and relate to one another.[2] Moral repair is a matter of degree. Some wrongs, such as the minor and common mistakes of everyday life, can be completely repaired. More severe wrongs may admit of only partial repair. In addition to this *end-state* of moral repair, we can also talk about various *processes* of moral repair. Among these are forgiveness, reconciliation, atonement, and punishment.

In this chapter, "forgiveness" refers to the overcoming or forswearing of negative reactive attitudes, such as resentment, for moral reasons.[3] While this definition is often referred to as the standard account, it is far from uncontroversial. For the purposes of this chapter, however, nothing turns on whether this is the best definition of forgiveness. What matters is simply that such morally motivated changes in negative reactive attitudes reasonably count as an aspect of moral repair.

Forgiveness, on this account, is uni-directional in that it extends from the forgiver to the forgiven. Most theorists claim that only victims can forgive. But this "victims only" version of an attitude-centered conception of forgiveness is unhelpfully narrow.[4] For one thing, the victims-only view would preclude the possibility of self-forgiveness.[5] Furthermore, third parties too form negative reactive attitudes toward wrongdoers. Third parties can also forswear or overcome these attitudes for the same sorts of reasons that victims do. They acknowledge efforts at amends. They separate the "sin" from the "sinner." They take a compassionate leap of faith in the wrongdoer's favor. But if the reader insists that only victims can forgive, not much will turn on this disagreement. The more important claim is simply that, when third parties do overcome or forswear their negative reactive attitudes toward wrongdoers for moral reasons, this too contributes to moral repair.

The term "reconciliation" refers to the normalization of the various relationships that have been damaged or threatened by wrongdoing. This involves a broad range of beliefs, emotions, attitudes, and behaviors. Whereas forgiveness is uni-directional and primarily involves an internal change of heart in the forgiver, reconciliation is mutual and includes both internal and external changes. In a simple, two-person case, reconciliation involves the relationship between the victim and the wrongdoer, but also the victim's relationship to self and the wrongdoer's relationship to self. Talking about damage and threats to relationships highlights the psychological and social consequences of wrongdoing, such as resentment, distrust, loss of cooperation, loss of self-esteem, or guilt. But it also draws our attention to other forms of harm. For example, uncompensated damage to property is a material form of harm, but it also provides a continuing reason for a victim to distrust or refuse to cooperate with the wrongdoer. A physical injury is painful, but it also provides the victim with a reason to fear and resent the person who caused the injury. When parties reconcile, they reestablish—or perhaps establish for the first time—a relationship of mutual respect and a normalized degree of trust and good will for the domain of interaction in question. This means that two people who do not reconcile as friends may nevertheless reconcile as co-workers, neighbors, or simply fellow members of the moral community.

On this view, then, forgiveness and reconciliation are related but distinct forms of moral repair. Forgiveness is typically a step toward reconciliation. But it is possible to forgive without reconciling, as well as to reconcile to a significant degree without forgiving. Other processes of moral repair are punishment that is imposed on a wrongdoer by others and atonement, which refers to the wrongdoer's own efforts to make amends for the wrong. Apology is one means of atonement, as are the payment of compensation or reparations, the moral improvement of the wrongdoer, and self-punishment.[6]

For our purposes, we do not need to define "apology" in terms of necessary and sufficient conditions. Typically, the point of doing so is to identify apologies that are so inadequate that they do not deserve to be called apologies. But this chapter is interested in the contributions of audiences to both good and bad, genuine and fake apologies. Yet, while a formal definition of apology is not required, it is helpful to briefly reflect on paradigm features of apologies and why apologies are generally valuable means to moral repair.

An apology is typically an overt spoken or written communication by someone who is responsible for a wrong or harm, or by someone standing proxy for the responsible party. The communication acknowledges responsibility for the wrongful or harmful action and expresses a fitting negative reactive attitude, such as regret or remorse. Apologies might also provide explanations for how the transgression came about and promises of better behavior in the future. Apologies generally include explicit or implicit requests for forgiveness and reconciliation.

When apologies are performed well, they ameliorate the various kinds of harm the wrong may have caused to the victim and the wrongdoer, and their relations with one another. For example, the wrong may have given the victim reason to fear repeated mistreatment in the future. In apologizing, the wrongdoer gives the victim some assurance that the wrongdoer will not repeat the wrong. Ideally, the wrongdoer also listens to whatever the victim might wish to say about the wrong, its consequences, or the terms for forgiving or reconciling. This willingness to listen and respond appropriately gives the victim additional evidence of the wrongdoer's renewed respect and trustworthiness.

Sometimes, victims' relationships with themselves are damaged or threatened. Their self-respect, self-esteem, or trust in their own judgment may be affected. They may suffer from shame. By showing the victim respect and taking responsibility for the wrong, the apologizer may contribute to the restoration of the victim's sense of self. Part of the power of an apology is found in wrongdoers' willingness to place themselves in a humble position vis-à-vis victims. In apologizing, the wrongdoer puts the victim in a position to make a decision that matters to the wrongdoer—the decision to forgive and reconcile or to refuse to do so.

Additionally, apologizing can help repair wrongdoers' relationship to themselves. It can help restore their sense of self as competent and trustworthy in moral matters. It can assuage feelings of guilt. The ordeal of having to humbly approach victims might serve as a deterrent against future wrongdoing, strengthen their resolve to do better, or make it harder to backtrack.

WHAT ARE PUBLIC APOLOGIES?

With this sketch of apology in a simple two-party case in hand, we may move on to the main topic of this chapter: public apologies. Again, a formal definition is not necessary. Several types of events might sensibly be labeled "public apologies." This section introduces three different kinds of public apologies in order to focus attention on the one wherein the audience presents a distinctive puzzle.

One type of public apology is an apology in which the wrongdoer addresses a sizable group of people because everyone in the audience was victimized in some way by the wrongful action. Trudy Govier and Wilhelm Verwoerd distinguish among primary, secondary, and even tertiary victims, depending on how directly or indirectly people were wronged.[7] The previous interpretation of the value of apologies for moral repair in the two-party case extends easily to this sort of apology to a group. When the audience are all victims to one degree or another, their role is to receive a form of amends and to consider forgiving and reconciling with the wrongdoer.

A second kind of public apology is one where the audience is made up of a group of both victims and fellow wrongdoers. Imagine a spokesperson for a bank who addresses a written apology to customers who have been harmed by the bank's corrupt practices, but who also sends the text of the apology to the employees who were complicit in those corrupt practices. When a wrongdoing group is large, they are unlikely to coordinate on the content of the apology. They are also less likely to share all the relevant beliefs, attitudes, and intentions. So, the one delivering the apology often plays the role of recruiting fellow wrongdoers into the project of atonement. This is an important aspect of political apologies, such as apologies delivered by political leaders for historical injustices. Here, the members of the wrongdoing group are being asked to confront their group's shared responsibility for the past, to join their own remorse to that of the spokesperson, and to commit themselves to a more just future. Cases of collective or group responsibility raise a number of familiar and difficult metaphysical and moral questions.[8] Yet, insofar as responsibility for wrongdoing is shared by a group, apologies such as these, where the audience is composed of both victims and fellow wrongdoers, are not particularly puzzling. It is still fairly clear how to adapt the standard story about the value of apologies to the project of moral repair. Victims in the audience are offered amends and asked to consider forgiveness and reconciliation. Fellow wrongdoers are represented as also apologizing or enjoined to participate in offering amends.

The sorts of public apologies that are the main focus of this chapter are a third kind: where the apology appears to be, not just knowingly, but *intentionally* performed in front of third parties. In these cases, the apology is addressed to the victims. Fellow wrongdoers may or may not be part of the intended audience. But the apology is performed before people who do not fit in either of those categories. They are onlookers or spectators. Sometimes the audience is still limited to a particular community, as when a boss apologizes to a specific employee in an email to all (but only) the employees of the firm. But other apologies are performed in front of more general audiences, such as when apologies are sent out as press releases or posted on public Twitter feeds. Those audiences purposefully include thousands of onlookers.[9]

Here, third parties are simply people who are neither victims nor wrongdoers—or, at least, the apology does not represent them as being either victims or fellow wrongdoers. This clause about how the apology "represents" various members of the audience acknowledges how ambiguous and morally fraught the category of third parties is. Consider a case where a police chief apologizes for patterns of police violence committed against Black citizens. The apology is addressed both to the direct victims of specific violent actions (or their survivors) and the Black citizenry, who were indirect victims. The apology is intentionally performed in front of the entire community, however, including the White citizenry. Arguably, these audience members should instead be classified as fellow wrongdoers, insofar as these particular abuses by police are manifestations of a systematically racist political system in which they participate and from which they benefit. But suppose that the text of the apology and the apparent intentions of the police chief only attribute responsibility for the abuses to the police force. Perhaps members of the broader White community will be moved to consider the extent to which they are complicit in the violence and what they need to do in response. But the apology itself does not ask them to do this. In this case, the White citizens in the audience may in fact be fellow wrongdoers, but they are addressed as third parties.[10]

POSSIBLE ROLES FOR THIRD PARTIES

The question this chapter asks is: What is being requested of audience members qua third parties in public apologies? This section proposes and evaluates several possible interpretations of the role spectators might play. The goal here is not to identify one interpretation that will fit all cases. The role any particular spectator plays is highly context-dependent. Instead, the aim of this section is to survey the possibilities and to ask how each role might contribute to the goal of moral repair, but also to note how the third parties' involvement might create additional problems.

Proxy for Victims

One possible role for third parties to public apologies is to serve as proxies for the victim or victims. We might see this, for example, in a case where the victims are dead, incapacitated, or otherwise beyond reach. If the third parties are proxies, then this means that they may decide to forgive or reconcile, or to refuse to do so, on behalf of the actual victims.

Depending on how we theorize forgiveness, it may not be possible to forgive on another person's behalf. A mother cannot literally overcome her son's resentment for him. Yet, perhaps it is possible for her to forswear it for him—that is, to renounce his entitlement to resent the wrong. The mother would thereby give the person who mistreated her son a kind of permission to treat the past as resolved or to let go of the person's own guilt.

It is easy to see how this kind of practice could go wrong. Earlier I rejected the view that only victims can forgive, but victims do have a special sort of standing or authority. The wrongs in question were wrong because of how *the victim* was treated. The victim is the one who was disrespected. The victim is the one who was harmed most directly and probably most severely. To take away the decision about forgiveness from the victim risks a second wrong.

Proxy forgiveness requires a transfer of authority. The proxy must be entitled to make this particular decision on behalf of this victim. Third parties certainly do not gain the authority to act as proxy forgivers simply by being addressed as such by the wrongdoer. There must be some very good reason for taking proxy powers in the first place. In order to play their role properly, proxies also need some sort of substantive connection to the victims and understanding of the victims' values. Ideally, the proxy's decision should be guided by whether the victims would have forgiven, were they able to do so.

Independent Party to the Project of Moral Repair

The second possible role for third party audience members asks them to make their own decisions about their own relationships with the wrongdoer. That is, they are not being asked to forgive or reconcile *on behalf of victims*, but instead to decide about whether to forgive or reconcile with the wrongdoer themselves.

Wrongs committed against a victim sometimes damage or threaten the relationship between the wrongdoer and other members of a community. These third parties may experience negative reactive attitudes like anger, indignation, disappointment, or grief.

The transgression may provide them with reasons to fear or distrust wrongdoers and so to avoid them. We need not imagine here that the wrong was an indirect wrong against the community as a whole. We can continue to see these audience members as third parties rather than as secondary or tertiary victims if they are indignant over what the wrongdoer did *to the victim* rather than to themselves. Yet even though the victim remains the focus of their concern in this way, third parties' own relationships to the wrongdoer have been negatively affected, perhaps seriously so.

The fact that community members stand in relation to wrongdoers is brought to the fore these days in calls to "cancel" public figures who have been caught doing something wrong. Canceling involves widespread social withdrawal. Members of the community work together to deny such figures a public platform—they will no longer listen to wrongdoers' music, watch their TV shows, or follow them on Twitter. It is a refusal by the community to continue their previous relationship with the wrongdoer in light of the wrong.

A public apology may help to repair the relationship between the wrongdoer and the community even though the apology is addressed to the victim. The apology provides some evidence that the wrongdoer is once again willing to respect the victim and conform to moral rules. It provides at least some reason to let go of anger and to believe that the wrongdoer can be trusted once more. Interestingly, calls to "cancel" someone frequently occur when the wrongdoer's public apology has been deemed inadequate by the audience.

A public apology is also a moment in which the third parties might be invited to repair their relationship *with the victim*. The wrong may have damaged the community's attitudes toward or interactions with the victim. Cases of bullying provide helpful examples here, because most bullying itself takes place in front of an audience.[11] The bully publicly humiliates the victim. Too often, the witnesses walk away viewing the victim as a lower sort of person who deserved abuse. At other times, they avoid the victim out fear of attracting the bully's attention to themselves or in shame over their own passivity.[12] In publicly apologizing, the bully acknowledges that abuse of the victim was wrong. Third parties are thereby encouraged also to see the victim as deserving respect and good will and to act accordingly.

In interpreting the third parties as independent parties to the project of moral repair, we see their task as one of coming to their own conclusions about the wrong, the wrongdoer, and the victim. They are not deciding whether to forgive on the victim's behalf, as in the proxy case. Instead, they pay attention to public apologies in order to make decisions about their own relationships. Should I let go of my indignation? Can I vote for this politician again? Should I reach out to the victim?

This role for third parties can be not just coherent but also a valuable part of the project of moral repair. Yet it too can go wrong. Sometimes, the spectator's relationship with the wrongdoer and victim are simply too thin. For example, I frequently see stories in mainstream news outlets about celebrities getting into some sort of trouble and then issuing public apologies. I often have no idea who these people are. I was never likely to interact with them in any way in the first place (not even by watching their YouTube videos, or what have you). I would not say that I have *no relationship* with these people. We are all part of a shared moral community. But there is no significant sense in which I need to come to my own conclusion about how I will interact with these people in the aftermath of the transgression and apology. I was not going to interact with them before and I have no reason to now.

Another source of concern is that wrongdoers might be far more interested in repairing their relationship with the community than with victims. The apology may be more closely tailored to addressing their interests than the victims'. One can well understand why the wrongdoer might play to the crowd. Celebrities, politicians, or CEOs may have far more to lose if the general public retains a bad view of them than if their particular victims do. Such apologies risk denying victims the respect they deserve.

Similarly, victims may have good reason to be concerned about how the community responds to the apology and whether the community members reconcile with the wrongdoer. If the community is conciliatory, victims may well feel pressured to reconcile as well. This might interfere with the victims' ability to evaluate the apology on their own terms. Yet, on the other hand, if victims and the community agree that the apology is inadequate, this can strengthen the victims' demands for more substantive forms of atonement.

In response to these worries, one might recommend that the community's responses simply be guided by the victims, out of respect for their special standing in the case. Perhaps they should only forgive or reconcile when the victims do. Yet this recommendation may be overly idealistic. For one thing, victims do not always make good choices. They may be either too quick to forgive and reconcile or too slow. But another issue is that there is a cost to the community in allowing their relationship with the wrongdoer to remain impaired. Perhaps it would be best for me to avoid doing business with every wrongdoing corporation that has not made things right with its victims. But, given the costs of such avoidance, we are probably now in the realm of supererogatory action rather than duty.

Interesting and difficult issues arise here about how third parties should come to their own conclusions about whether to forgive or reconcile in response to public apologies. The most important point for this chapter, though, is simply this: By entering into the dynamic of public apologies as independent parties who are entitled to make their own decisions, third parties tend to affect how both wrongdoers and victims play their own roles. So, here too, we might think that third parties would need some form of authority or standing. To see oneself as an independent party to reconciliation is to see the original transgression as, somehow, *one's business*. But surely not all wrongs *are* our business.

Advisors or Referees

Other possible roles for third parties are to serve as advisors or referees. Here, their work is largely epistemic. They would form judgments about whether the apology was an appropriate response to the victim—whether it correctly identified the nature and severity of the wrong, whether it is sincere, whether it expresses fitting emotions, etc. The spectators' position here is more modest than in the first two categories, and so, intuitively, would require a weaker form of authority or standing. They are not making decisions about forgiveness and reconciliation; they are instead forming judgments about the quality of the apology.

When third parties voice these judgments they may thereby provide advice to victims, who must then make their own decisions about how to respond to the apology. The third parties may also advise the wrongdoers, for example, by recommending that they rephrase their apology or offer some additional form of amends (such as restitution). In addition to thinking of the third parties as serving as advisors (which sounds like a rather friendly, helpful sort of role), we might also think of them as referees. They might cry foul when an apology is insincere or misidentifies the wrong, or when a victim is either too quick or too slow to forgive. In other words, they might cross the line from advising to something more like criticizing or subtly pressuring the main parties to the interaction.

Theorists often speak favorably about the role third parties can play in strengthening the victim's position. For example, Margaret Urban Walker describes the community as providing the "social scaffolding" that makes forgiveness a reasonable option.[13] Victims need their community to clarify and maintain norms of behavior— the norms that identify both what counts as a wrong and what moral repair requires. It is only in such a context that victims can choose to forgive or reconcile in a way that is consistent with their safety and self-respect.

Moral theorists are often notably less enthusiastic about the possibility of communities criticizing victims. Some view forgiveness and reconciliation as things that can never be earned by a wrongdoer. They are instead gifts that victims give to wrongdoers—or that they choose not to give. On this model, any pressure from third parties appears inappropriate. In my view, the "free gift" view is over-stated. While victims of significant wrongs typically should be given a wide degree of latitude, they do make mistakes. They can be too hard-hearted or too lax. They can be hypocritical or lacking in self-respect. If victims can make mistakes, then the advice and even the criticism of third parties could be constructive.

How might things go wrong when third parties act as advisors or referees? The third parties might have poor judgment. They may not have enough information about the situation as a whole, or they may have corrupt values. The advisors' voices might drown out or intimidate the victims in the ways mentioned above. We might also worry about the wrongdoer who apologizes in public *so that* the spectators will have his back. This might be a way of perpetuating the conflict with the victim rather than of making a good faith effort to repair the relationship.

Witnesses or Publicizers

Thinking of third parties to public apologies as advisors or referees suggests that the importance of their role is to be found in their actively responding to the apology by voicing opinions about it. But perhaps some value can be found in their simply serving as passive witnesses. This might provide a way of getting around some of the worries about spectators hijacking public apologies.

Apologizing in front of witnesses creates an external memory or official record. In cases of political apologies for the state's transgressions this will be particularly important, since so often those wrongs are initially compounded by official denials of wrongdoing. When there is a public record and memory of the apology, it is more difficult for wrongdoers to backtrack. Victims' self-esteem may receive support simply from knowing that they are being shown respect in public and that their decision to forgive or reconcile is the one that matters. Victims may feel safer when the wrongdoer publicly acknowledges that victims have been telling the truth about the past and that they deserved better. Apologizing in front of witnesses, even silent witnesses, also likely intensifies the experience of apologizing for the wrongdoer. The wrongdoer may feel more humbled simply by being seen taking a humble position by more people. This might be an aid to the wrongdoer's efforts at reform.

It is also possible that the third parties themselves gain something simply by acting as silent witnesses to a public apology. For example, public apologies provide moral lessons about what actions are permissible and who deserves respect. This can be particularly valuable when the spectators are at risk of committing similar sorts of wrongs. When I read the apology of Amy Cooper (the White woman who called the police on a Black birdwatcher in Central Park and falsely accused him of threatening her life[14]), I am led to reflect on my own forms of privilege and the moral hazards they present.

This contribution to the moral education of the public can even be considered a means by which a wrongdoer makes amends. This is a plausible interpretation of some of the #MeToo apologies. The wrongdoers partially atone for their past insofar as they help create a greater recognition of the wrongfulness of sexual harassment and assault.[15] Insofar as simply witnessing a public apology supports moral education, perhaps third parties also make a contribution when, rather than remaining silent, they publicize news of an apology that was already performed in public to a still wider group of witnesses—say, by reporting on or reposting the apologies on social media.[16]

Passively witnessing a public apology can be valuable, then, and perhaps publicizing can be as well. Intuitively, merely witnessing would require a lesser degree of authority or standing than the other roles we have considered. The bar for something counting as "my business" is lower when I am merely watching than when I respond in some way, such as publicizing or advising.

How might the roles of passive witness or publicizer go wrong? Expecting third parties to stay silent may be unrealistic, and, as mentioned above, they do not always respond in constructive ways. But, on the other hand, the audience's silence might also convey a lack of caring about the victim or the fact that that individual was wronged. Finally, we should acknowledge issues of privacy. The victim might experience the wrongdoer speaking about the transgression in public as an intrusion, and joining in the audience might make the intrusion worse. Although an apology may have been appropriately viewed in one community, publicizing it to other communities may violate either the victim's or the wrongdoer's privacy.

Punishers and Implements of Punishment

This chapter has frequently discussed apology qua communication—as sending messages about norms of behavior, comparative trustworthiness, and respect among wrongdoers, victims, and third parties. But apologies—and especially public apologies—may also be viewed through the lens of punishment. Apologizing in public is an unpleasant, humiliating experience. This very unpleasantness might serve the purposes of retribution or deterrence, both the specific deterrence of the wrongdoer and the general deterrence of the community. The more extensive the audience, the more intense their gaze, the greater the suffering for the one apologizing. The interpretation here is not that the wrongdoer apologizes in public view and that the public then decides whether and how much to punish the wrongdoer. That might happen, of course. But my suggestion here is that the exposure to the gaze of the public *is* the punishment. The voluntary acceptance of suffering is an ancient and familiar form of atonement for wrongdoing. A wrongdoer taking a humble posture under the gaze of the audience can be the means through which this suffering is incurred.

This punitive aspect of public apologies is one of the larger sources of my growing discomfort with public apologies. In joining an audience, one is recruited into the task of social punishment. One's very attention is turned into a tool for imposing suffering. This should be disconcerting, even for people who are not generally skeptical about the value of punishment.

One reason for concern has to do with questions of desert. People often wander into the audiences of public apologies rather uninformed. Was this person really in the wrong? Was he really responsible? One is already part of a punitive scheme before knowing if it is deserved. One might object that guilt can be assumed in these cases. After all, the person is apologizing, thereby admitting guilt. Yet, public apologies are sometimes coerced and apologizers are sometimes mistaken about the moral valence of their own actions.

A second set of concerns has to do with the proportionality of punishment. Again, many third parties may join the audience without knowing the scope of culpability and so without being in a position to judge whether a public apology is an excessive punishment or not. Furthermore, when apologies are recorded in electronic media, the scope of the audience and so the intensity of the punishment are literally uncontrollable. No one is in a position to limit how many times texts and videos will be shared or how other viewers will respond. In the Central Park birdwatching case, the victim, Christian Cooper, voiced concern over the public's reaction to the wrongdoer, Amy Cooper (no relation). He worried that the intensity of the response, and particularly her being fired from her job, may have been excessive. "I'm not excusing the racism," he said. "But I don't know if her life needed to be torn apart."[17]

Interestingly, the way that audiences might attempt to tailor the amount of suffering imposed on the wrongdoer is by actively responding to the apology. If they voice their recriminations or further publicize the apologies, they increase the punishment for the wrongdoer. But if instead they praise the apology, saying that the wrongdoer has learned a lesson or has been punished enough, or if they show a willingness to forgive or reconcile with the wrongdoer themselves, then they reduce the wrongdoer's suffering.

In addition to these concerns about desert and proportionality, we might also add questions about the authority or standing to punish. Third-party witnesses to the apology might ask themselves: Why is this wrongdoer answerable *to us?* In virtue of what is it appropriate for me to participate in punishing the wrongdoer? The philosophical literature gives us almost no guidance on how to answer this question: Which wrongs are accountable to whom?[18]

But posing the problem as one of the authority or standing to hold the wrongdoer accountable may well misrepresent the dynamic in these cases. When I am not the victim of the wrong, but merely a third-party spectator to a public apology, is the wrongdoer answering *to me?* Am I one to whom that individual is held accountable? Or am I merely the means of holding that person accountable? Am I just the hammer being brought down upon the person's head?

MISSION CREEP

At the beginning of this chapter, I noted two questions that bother me when I watch or read public apologies: Why is this my business, and what am I being asked to do? This chapter presents several possible roles that third parties might play when they listen to apologies. They may be proxies for victims, independent parties to the project of moral repair, advisors, referees, passive witnesses, publicizers, punishers, or implements of punishment. This is a long list, and it is not exhaustive. The point in going through these possible interpretations is not just to show that the context is ambiguous— that it is unclear exactly what audience members are being asked to do. The situation is worse than that. These roles are unstable in a problematic way.

In asking whether a particular apology is "my business" as a third party, I am asking whether it is permissible for me to take up one of these roles. I am asking whether my connection to this wrong, this wrongdoer, or this victim is robust enough to legitimate this level of involvement by me. Otherwise, in viewing the apology, I am simply being nosy or worse. As emphasized above, some of these roles appear to require a higher form of standing or authority than others. The standards for granting me the entitlement to act as a proxy should be much more demanding than the standards for permitting me to passively witness an apology.

But even simply acting as passive witnesses makes us complicit in a kind of social punishment of the wrongdoer. Our gaze is the means by which wrongdoers are made to suffer for their misdeeds. The witnessing role transforms into the punitive role. Surely, if we are going to allow ourselves to become the implements for imposing harm on wrongdoers, then we need to take responsibility for what we are doing to them. We need to be attentive to questions of desert and the proportionality of punishment. We should also be attentive to what else the wrongdoer has done, in addition to apologizing, to make amends. The degree of deserved punishment should reflect not just wrongdoers' original degree of culpability, but also their efforts to put things right.

But the way to take responsibility for what we are doing to wrongdoers qua punishers (or implements of punishment) is to take a more active role. We must take care to form proper judgments about the case, perhaps by collecting more information and consulting with others. We must decide when enough is enough and speak out when we believe things have gone awry. Notice, at this point, we have become something more like referees or independent parties to reconciliation, roles that presumably require stronger forms of standing or authority than mere witnesses do.

This instability in third-party roles now presents a problem of mission creep. The term "mission creep" comes from military contexts, where armed forces enter a situation in a relatively modest role (say, military advisor or peacekeeper), but then, given the exigencies of the situation, are drawn into more and more active roles (e.g., combatant). Similarly, being involved at all in these moral dramas of public apology seems to provide reasons for getting more and more involved, taking on more active roles that, considered initially, would not have been appropriate.

CONCLUSION

What should we do in light of the ambiguity of the role of the public in public apologies and the risk of mission creep? My goal in this chapter has been to draw attention to a set of moral concerns rather than to solve them. When I turn to the question of how to respond to these worries, I find myself drawn in two opposite directions. Part of me says that, when given access to a public apology, I should first ask myself whether there is a sensible role for me to play. If there is not, I should avert my gaze. If there is, then I should be mindful of the limitations of that role and be careful not to overstep. A similar sort of caution should also guide our behavior in calling for public apologies in the first place.

But the other part of me is inclined to embrace the messiness of these moments. Christian Cooper, the birdwatcher from the earlier example, apparently feels this same tension. In the interview where he worries that the public response to his abuser has been too harsh, he also says, "If this painful process . . . helps to correct, or takes us a step further toward addressing the underlying racial, horrible assumptions that we African-Americans have to deal with, and have dealt with for centuries, that this woman tapped into, then it's worth it."[19]

Public apologies inspire public debates. These are moments when the communities in which we live wrestle over what our values should be. What is acceptable behavior? What isn't? Who deserves respect? Who is answerable to whom? It is not surprising that public apologies are most controversial on precisely those issues where either there has not been a clear consensus on appropriate norms (e.g., Aziz Ansari's #MeToo moment[20]) or where the norms to which we give lip service are repeatedly violated (e.g., racial harassment and police brutality). Constructing and regulating a moral community is messy, but we cannot simply avert our eyes from it.

NOTES

1 Linda Radzik, *Making Amends: Atonement in Morality, Law and Politics* (New York: Oxford University Press, 2009).

2 This image is due to Jean Hampton, who uses it to characterize forgiveness rather than moral repair. See "Forgiveness, Resentment, and Ha-

tred," in *Forgiveness and Mercy*, ed. Jeffrie G. Murphy and Jean Hampton (New York: Cambridge University Press, 1988), 35–87.

3 See Jeffrie Murphy's chapters in Murphy and Hampton, *Forgiveness and Mercy*.

4 See Glen Pettigrove, "The Standing to Forgive," *The Monist* 92, no. 4 (2009): 583–603.

5 Per-Erik Milam, "How Is Self-Forgiveness Possible?," *Pacific Philosophical Quarterly* 98, no. 1 (2017): 49–69.

6 Radzik, *Making Amends*, ch. 4.

7 Trudy Govier and Wilhelm Verwoerd, "Forgiveness: The Victim's Prerogative," *South African Journal of Philosophy* 21 (2002): 97–111.

8 See, for example, Deborah Tollefsen and Saba Bazargan-Forward, eds., *Routledge Handbook of Collective Responsibility* (New York: Routledge, 2020).

9 Public apologies might also have unintended spectators, of course, and sometimes these parties are known to be present. For example, a mayor who intends to televise an apology to their spouse in view of their electorate knows that people in other cities will have access to the footage. For the sake of simplicity, I leave unintended spectators out of the rest of the discussion. It is complicated enough to figure out the role of third parties when they are meant to be part of the audience.

10 Other cases that present ambiguities are those in which the apologizer explicitly addresses the apology "to anyone who may have been offended by my actions." Are the people who took offense best categorized as indirect victims or as third parties?

11 Paul D. Flaspohler, Jennifer L. Elfstrom, Karin L. Vanderzee, Holli E. Sink, and Zachary Birchmeier, "Stand by Me: The Effects of Peer and Teacher Support in Mitigating the Impact of Bullying on Quality of Life," *Psychology in the Schools* 46, no. 7 (2009): 636–649.

12 In these cases, the witnesses to bullying may cross the line from being third parties to being complicit in the wrong itself.

13 Margaret Urban Walker, "Third Parties and the Social Scaffolding of Forgiveness," *Journal of Religious Ethics* 41, no. 3 (2013): 495–512. See also Alice MacLachlan, "In Defense of Third Party Forgiveness," in *The Moral Psychology of Forgiveness*, ed. K. Norlock (Lanham, MD: Rowman & Littlefield, 2017), 135–160.

14 Sarah Maslin Nir, "White Woman Is Fired after Calling Police on Black Man in Central Park," *New York Times*, online edition, May 29, 2020, www.nytimes.com.

15 For a powerful example, listen to Nancy Updike, "Finally," in "Get a Spine!," *This American Life* (podcast), Episode 674, Act One, May 10, 2019, www.thisamericanlife.org/674/get-a-spine.

16 This point was made by an audience member at the Kulturwissen-schaftliches Institut in Essen. I have forgotten who made this point, but offer my thanks.

17 Sarah Maslin Nir, "The Bird Watcher, That Incident and His Feel-ings on the Woman's Fate," *New York Times*, online edition, May 29, 2020, www.nytimes.com.

18 For some discussion, see Linda Radzik, "On Minding Your Own Business: Differentiating Accountability Relations within the Moral Com-munity," *Social Theory and Practice* 37, no. 4 (2011): 574–598; Garrath Wil-liams, "Sharing Responsibility and Holding Responsible," *Journal of Applied Philosophy* 30, no. 4 (2013): 351–364; and Thomas Wilk, "Trust, Commu-nities, and the Standing to Hold Accountable," *Kennedy Institute of Ethics Journal* 27, no. 2 Supplement (2017): 1–22.

19 Nir, "The Bird Watcher, That Incident and His Feelings on the Woman's Fate."

20 In 2018, comedian Aziz Ansari was accused of pressuring a date to have sex with him. The debate raised the question of when persuasion becomes coercive.

8

THE PUBLIC CHORUS AND PUBLIC APOLOGIES

MARTHA MINOW

Despite some notable exceptions among top political leaders, we live in an era of public apologies.[1] Former USA Gymnastics physician Larry Nassar for sexually abusing more than 150 women patients.[2] Equifax apologized—thought not well—for breaching the data privacy of 145 million people.[3] Then-Vice President Joe Biden apologized during his presidential campaign for supporting tough-on-crime legislation in the 1970s and 1980s.[4] Pope Francis apologized for slapping the hand of a woman who had grabbed him.[5] Discussing and evaluating public apologies is a subject debated in classrooms, at dinner tables, and online.[6] But these discussions generally focus on what is a good or a poor apology.

Linda Radzik asks, instead, why is any of this business for her, and what is she supposed to do about it?[7] And then she turns to speak to and for us all with this great question: What role do and should members of the public play when individuals make public apologies—for their own wrongdoing or on behalf of their communities or institutions? I thank Radzik for turning our attention this way, and for her illuminating exploration. Along the way, Radzik's chapter offers many pearls of insight, such as: it cannot be that forgiveness is only something that victims can give, because that would make self-forgiveness impossible; and such as: the wrongdoer may often be as or more interested in repairing relationships with a broad public than solely with direct victims.

Radzik also usefully maps within the larger frame of moral repair several potential roles for the public audience for public apologies—and identifies as worries roles as mere voyeurs. Public audiences may be candidates to forgive by proxy, or may seek themselves to repair their own relationships with victims, because members of the public perpetrate the same or similar wrongs. She is especially interested in the situation where "third parties are simply people who are neither victims nor wrongdoers—or, at least, the apology *does not represent them as being* either victims or fellow wrongdoers."[8]

Or members of the public could act as advisors; as independent parties to the public expressions of contrition and potential responses of forgiveness; as passive witnesses or publicizing agents; or as punishers or instruments of punishment. She notes the danger that even if the public audience acts passively, it could have a kind of complicity as tools of punishment, especially by treating the issue at hand—or public accounts of it—as judgment of the underlying wrong. Instead, she calls for a more active role, through which we strangers of the public could

> take care to form proper judgments about the case, perhaps by collecting more information and consulting with others. We must decide when enough is enough and speak out when we think things have gone awry. Notice, at this point, we have become something more like referees or independent parties to reconciliation, roles that presumably require stronger forms of standing or authority than mere witnesses do.[9]

Radzik's analysis brings to my mind three additional possibilities—or points of reference: the Greek chorus; the current, halting steps toward national and international reckonings with racial injustice; and the developing practices of restorative justice in the United States.

GREEK CHORUS

These days, if any of us can obtain access to an apology from someone we don't know to others we don't know, it is likely through media, and often, social media. We become an audience or observers of what is inevitably, at least in part, a performance. In this light, perhaps the public given access to an apology serves as the chorus in ancient Greek drama. I am hardly an expert on the subject, but I have seen performances and read about the practice that puts a group of people in a spectator role, often of tragic tales. A nineteenth-century expert on the topic described the Greek chorus as "the ideal spectator," whose presence and voice on stage convey to the actual spectator "a lyrical and musical expression of his own emotions, and elevates him to the region of contemplation."[10] Later critics point out that the chorus on stage actually often knows less about the facts and context than the actual audience would.[11] In addition, often the chorus would be composed of women, while the actual audience would be men. Perhaps the women in a chorus created a more intimate, private, and communicative setting while the male audience would be more distant and political in character. In any case, the Chorus would tap into traditional cultural values and memories.[12] In keeping with Radzik's call for active roles for current public viewers of public apologies, the Greek chorus would often actively question main characters and comment on the action.

The classic Greek chorus typically expresses and comments on the moral issued raised by the dramatic action, or conveys emotion matched to each stage of the unfolding drama.[13] According to long-established understanding, the Greek chorus "expresses the fears, hopes, and judgment of the polity," and provides a judgment as "the verdict of history."[14] American film director Woody Allen (who some might say probably should be offering some public apologies) cast a Greek chorus in his film, *Mighty Aphrodite.* There, the chorus gave advice to the main character. In sum, the Greek chorus offers advice and consolation, urges restraint, comments on the action, and reflects on its meaning not only for the victim, but for the broader collective of people.[15]

This comparison suggests (1) public audiences for contemporary public apologies could provide sources of connection with moral intuitions as well as sources of emotion and responses that include advice, consolation, and judgment; and (2) the public offerings of apologies represent contemporary performances serving a function with parallels to the role of theater. Greek theater also gives us the idea of "spectacle." From ancient Greek theater, spectacle means all aspects that contribute to sensory experiences of the theater: costumes, scenery, the gestures of the actors, the sound of the music, and the resonance of the actors' voices.[16] Perhaps it is time to reclaim this earlier meaning, invoking sensory experiences and memorable resonance, providing touchstones in daily life, despite the contemporary negative connotations.[17]

HALTING STEPS TOWARD SOCIETAL RECKONING WITH RACIAL INJUSTICES

Many of us spent time during the summer of 2020 asking, will this moment of acknowledgment of systemic racism endure? Or: "Will This Be the Moment Of Reckoning On Race That Lasts?"[18] In the wake of George Floyd's murder by police in Minneapolis, waves of protests, and statements of concern by nonprofit organizations, colleges, and corporations, some small steps of actual change are taking place. Washington's football team finally retired an offensive racially demeaning name. The government leadership of Ashland, North Carolina, has committed to reparations. So has Evanston, Illinois. Leaders in other cities and the governor of California say they are looking into similar possibilities.

Yet nothing thus far has begun to meet the scale of the need and the challenge. Racial disparities structured by local, state, and national policies and practices permeate housing, education, employment, wealth, law, policing and punishment systems, elections, and positions of power and authority. One of the great warriors for civil rights, Supreme Court Justice Thurgood Marshall, warned shortly before his death in 1992 that we "play ostrich"—complacently keeping our heads in the sand, ignoring ongoing injustices, and he urged Americans to recall the ambition of what can be.[19] Missing for now is that scape of ambition in meeting this moment, and in recognizing that the rectifications to come will require efforts, large and small, in every community, every home, and institution.

Radzik notes that some wrongdoers making a public apology might be far more interested in repairing their relationship with the community than with the particular wrongdoer. When it comes to racial and class divides in this country, the question is whether the public, with all our differences, divisions, and diversities, will be interested in building relationships—often for the first time—and creating the predicates of fairness and respect required to do so. Also promising, and closely linked to my final suggestion, is the possibility of apologizers using the public forum to recruit others to apologize and engage in repair.

RESTORATIVE JUSTICE LENS: WE ARE EACH IMPLICATED

Perhaps more dramatically revealed by our nation's racial relations, gender relations, and other matters involving different groups, the public dimension of public apologies very often is not just about third-party observers to the exchange of contrition and possible forgiveness by two or a few individuals. Repeated acts of sexual abuse and assaults involve countless bystanders and widespread cultural attitudes even if commonly perceived as a single, violent individual attacking individual victims. The title and details of Amos Guiora's 2020 book, *Armies of Enablers*, paint a horrible but convincing picture of this pattern of conduct. When we speak of "implicit bias" around race, gender, and class, we are capturing the nearly invisible imprint of the patterns of wrongdoing implicating concentric circles and systems all made by human beings.

Our conventional justice system converts systemic issues into dyadic disputes between plaintiff or prosecutor and defendant because it was set up to address disputes between individuals. Some public apologies may be addressing wrongs between just an individual perpetrator and an individual victim, but most do not, because most implicate attitudes, patterns, and structures that implicate many, many others. In some sense, then, I am questioning how large is the number of public apologies that meet Radzik's description of a public made of strangers, not involved as wrongdoers of victims.

Efforts gathered under the name "restorative justice" represent a recognition that even conflicts that seem to be between two individuals implicate larger communities—in both the origin of the problem and its resolution.[20] These efforts in the United States and elsewhere focus more on accountability and service rather than punishment and as much on what those in the concentric circles surrounding individuals most directly affected can and should do.

Many schools in the United States now use restorative justice methods to resolve and even prevent conflicts, curb delinquency, and disrupt the school-to-prison pipeline. Some American high schools replace "zero tolerance" discipline policies and automatic suspensions with opportunities for victims to narrate their experiences and for offenders to take responsibility for their actions. As they describe their experiences and feelings about the theft, hateful graffiti, a physical or verbal assault, victims and offenders often express strong emotions, and other members of the community describe the impact of the offense on them.

The leader—often a student peer—de-escalates the conflicts, and orchestrates a conversation about what the offender could do that would help the victim. Together they come to an agreement about how to move forward, what the wrongdoer can do to repair injury and what everyone can do better to avoid future conflicts.

Consider this reported example: Mercedes M. enrolled in a California high school after she was suspended for having too many fights at another school.[21] As two classmates one day called her a liar, and the "b"-word, a facilitator talked with her for a while, and earned enough trust to discover that Mercedes had in fact stolen another girl's shoes, but also that she and the two other students had been fighting for years and did not know any other way to communicate. The three young women agreed to attend a "circle," a confidential conversation facilitated by a trained leader. There, they each initially expressed anger. Then, Mercedes apologized and explained that she'd stolen the shoes to sell them to help her mom pay for a drug test. If her mom could prove to the court that she was clean, she might be able to get Mercedes's younger siblings returned to her from protective custody. When the other girls saw Mercedes crying, they empathized and gave her a hug. They didn't ask her to replace what she'd stolen, but they wanted a restart—an assurance that, going forward, they could trust her.

Mercedes later said that without this process, the conflict would have escalated and she probably would have been suspended or expelled. Her school, with the help of such restorative justice circles, has reduced suspensions by more than half. Restorative justice alternatives involve offenders and victims in discussion, in learning more truths than are revealed when people are defensive and adversarial. The participation by broader groups than those immediately involved does not introduce a punitive gaze but instead involves those who may contribute to changes going forward. Restorative justice focuses on reparations and other constructive steps. This model is now the go-to legal tool for prosecutors in the District of Columbia and initiatives including one track within the Teen Court in Los Angeles. Restorative justice does not excuse those directly committing wrongs, but locates responsibility—whether with a past or current ability to respond—also in other individuals, groups, institutions, and structures. Attributing blame to individuals for circumstances largely outside their own control is a mistake. Restorative approaches widen the lens to enable glimpses of these larger patterns and to work for new choices that can be enabled, not only through the exchange of apology of forgiveness between individuals, but within communities and through public involvement.

Radzik describes the remarkable grace of Christian Cooper, the victim of the racialized threat by Amy Cooper in the Central Park birdwatching case.[22] Christian Cooper, a birdwatcher, had asked Amy Cooper to comply with the requirement to leash her dog only to have her warn that she would and then actually did call the police to report that a Black man was threatening her. The story spread when his sister shared the video on social media. The Manhattan district attorney charged Amy Cooper with making a false report.[23] She publicly apologized. A graduate of Harvard College and a writer, Christian Cooper accepted the apology. Her asset manager employer fired Amy Cooper and she became the face of mass media discussions of White privilege.[24] As Radzik reports, Christian Cooper expressed concerns about public reaction to the wrongdoer—not to excuse the racism but to question the proportionality of the response. Citing restorative justice, the prosecutor dropped the charges of false report after Amy Cooper participated in five therapy sessions that included some racial bias education.[25] Christian Cooper also indicated his greater concern was to fix the underlying racism in a world where Amy Cooper could imagine it appropriate, acceptable, and beneficial to herself to assert weaponizing Christian Cooper's racial identity as a threat to him and as an invocation of government assistance. In a way, Christian Cooper's stance invited a kind of restorative justice process, although the public media spectacle did not follow through on that promise.

CLOSING REFLECTION

Individual, visible public apologies can be moments of drama, gossip, shame, or awkwardness for those who are witnesses. Besides being judges of the quality of a particular apology, proxy forgivers, or simply audiences unable to avert their gaze, public witnesses to apologies can also educate themselves and others about the larger patterns in which the wrongs, the apologies, and the responses arise and persist. It is not an excuse for those who most directly commit wrongs to locate those wrongs in larger structures of social attitudes, practices, and institutions, connected with power and sexual entitlement, power and race, or the ethical lapses or deeper corruption of a given society. Ultimately, as Radzik suggests, public audiences can be more than passive witnesses. Instead, we and others who become public audiences for apologies can be pivotal players who question central actors about their conduct and engage with a broader community in searching out the concentric circles of proximate and more distant contributing factors behind the harms at issue. Public audiences can take up the deeper issues, for example, of structural racism or contribute to expanding roles of community members in restorative justice efforts. We can allay concerns about what Linda Radzik describes as the risk of "mission creep" for public audiences when members of the public audience turn the attention back to ourselves and our roles, past and future. Perhaps, public audiences can turn media spectacles into transformative moments of public meaning-making and actions.

NOTES

1 Barbara Kellerman, "When Should a Leader Apologize—and When Not?," *Harvard Business Review* 84:4 (2004), https://pubmed.ncbi.nlm.nih.gov.

2 Ashraf Rushdy, "The Art of the Public Apology," *The Conversation* (Jan. 30, 2018), https://theconversation.com.

3 Bill Murphy, Jr., "17 Worst Apologies of 2017 Ranked in Increasing Order of Despicableness," *Inc.*, inc.com.

4 Astead W. Herndon and Sydney Ember, "2020 Democrats Agree: They're Very, Very Sorry," *New York Times* (Feb. 3, 2019), www.nytimes.com.

5 Gwendolyn Smith, "The Pope's Apology Could Teach Other Public Figures About Being Contrite," *The Guardian* (Jan. 4, 2020), www.theguardian.com.

6 See Devan Delfino, "The State of Public Apologies in 2019," (Dec. 2, 2019), www.grammarly.com/blog/public-apologies/; Murphy, Jr., "17 Worst Apologies of 2017."

7 Linda Radzik, "The Role of the Public in Public Apologies?," in this volume.

8 Ibid., in "Punishers and Implementers of Punishment" section.

9 Ibid., in "Mission Creep" section.

10 August Wilhem Schlegel, *Vorlesungen über dramatische Kunst und Literatur I.* Vol. 5 of *Sämtliche Werke,* ed. E. Böcking. Leipzig. Trans. John Black under the title *Course of Lectures on Dramatic Art and Literature* (London, 1846; reprint, New York, 1973).

11 See Helen Foley, "Choral Identity in Greek Tragedy," *Classical Philology* 98:1 (January 2003): 1–30, www.jstor.org (discussing scholarly literature).

12 Ibid., at 21.

13 Merriam-Webster Dictionary, www.merriam-webster.com.

14 Encyclopedia Britannica, "Chorus," www.britannica.com.

15 See George Clinton Densmore Ordell, "Introduction," in George Clinton Densmore Ordell, ed., *William Shakespeare, Henry the Fifth* (New York, NY: Charles Scribner's, 1905).

16 Bettina Bermann, "The Art of Ancient Spectacle," in *The Art of Ancient Spectacle,* ed. Bettina Bermann and Christine Kondoleon, 9–35 (New Haven, CT: Yale University Press, 1999).

17 See Dana Milbank, "The Democratic Apology Tour Is a Sorry Spectacle," *Washington Post* (Feb. 6, 2019), www.washingtonpost.com.

18 Ron Elving, "Will This Be the Moment of Reckoning on Race that Lasts?," NPR (June 13, 2020), www.npr.org.

19 Justice Thurgood Marshall, Acceptance Speech, Liberty Medal, July 4, 1992, https://constitutioncenter.org. See Christina Coleburn, "The Ostrich Rears Its Head: America's 2020 Racial Reckoning Is a Victory and Opportunity," *Harvard Civil Rights-Civil Liberties Law Review* (June 29, 2020), https://harvardcrcl.org (Amicus Blog).

20 For a thorough and thoughtful review and assessment of recent developments in restorative justice in the United States, see Adriaan Lanni, "Taking Restorative Justice Seriously," 69 *Buffalo Law Review* 635 (2021), https://digitalcommons.law.buffalo.edu.

21 Stacey Teicher Khadaroo, "One High School's Path to Reducing Suspensions by Half," *Christian Science Monitor* (March 13, 2013), www.csmonitor.com

22 See also David Bentacourt, "Christian Cooper Hopes America Can Change. Because He's Not Going To," *Washington Post* (June 23, 2020), www.washingtonpost.com.

23 Ivan Pereira and Aaron Katersky, "Amy Cooper Charged in Central Park False Report Against Black Bird Watcher," ABC News (July 6, 2020), https://abcnews.go.com.

24 Annie Massa, "Franklin Templeton Fires Amy Cooper After Christian Cooper Park Video Goes Viral," *Financial Planning* (May 28, 2020), www.financial-planning.com.

25 Aparna Polavarapu, "Amy Cooper's Charges Were Dismissed. But White Privilege Isn't Restorative Justice," *Think* (Feb. 20, 2021), www.nbcnews.com/.

9

APOLOGY, ACCUSATION, AND PUNISHMENT/HARM

AUDIENCES AS MULTIPLIERS

BURKE A. HENDRIX

In her extremely interesting chapter, Linda Radzik has mapped out a number of roles that audiences might play in relation to public apologies. There is much that is worth responding to in her arguments, but I would like to take up the final role that Radzik addresses: the participation of audiences in punishment. I will be especially interested in the possibility that such participation creates excessive punishment.[1] My primary goal, following Radzik's method of analysis, will be to map out a field of options for thinking about these issues. The chapter's target is thus largely typological and analytic rather than recommendatory, though I will close with some tentative recommendations for social practice going forward.

In what follows, I want to call attention to some broad similarities between the ways that audiences might over-punish in relation to the apparently dissimilar cases of *apologies* and *accusations*, showing that there are multiple distinctive ways in which the apologizer/accused might experience psychological suffering as a result of what bystanders do. Sometimes this suffering seems normatively justified, while other times it does not. I want to consider especially whether there are reasons to expect that larger audiences will lead to increased suffering in some conditions, with a focus on those bystanders who seek to ensure that the apologizer/accused suffers *humiliation* rather than more productive forms of psychological suffering. It is here, I will argue, that worries about disproportionate suffering become most acute.

In the latter sections of the chapter, I will turn to the ways in which attempts by bystanders to create humiliation—even when they may be normatively justified in relation to specific targets—can lead to longer-term cycles of attempted retaliation by other bystanders who come to regard the first set as wrongdoers in their own right. In this way, it is possible to build deep and ongoing cycles of mutual recrimination of the kind that we witness in much of our current political practice. Determining how to escape them is a much more difficult task. I will make some tentative suggestions in this regard, but these social patterns of mutual recriminations fit within a broader pattern of persistently reinforcing social divisions. How precisely these might be overcome is unclear, if indeed there are ways in which they might be overcome at all.

PUNISHMENT AND FORMS OF HARM

In her chapter, Radzik raises a number of concerns about public participation in apologies, with particular worries about the ways in which public witnessing of the apology might be understood as participation in a process of punishment. Radzik states that the "punitive aspect of public apologies is one of the bigger sources of [her] growing discomfort with public apologies."[2] She expresses the worry from the perspective of a bystander that "In joining an audience, one is recruited into the task of social punishment. One's very attention is turned into a tool for imposing suffering."[3] One need not do much for this additional suffering to occur: "Even simply acting as passive witnesses makes us complicit in a kind of social punishment of the wrongdoer. Our gaze is the means by which the wrongdoers are made to suffer for their misdeeds."[4]

Radzik's discomfort reflects multiple normative worries. Some of these worries are about the harms to audience members themselves. While Radzik calls attention to the inappropriateness of participation in matters that are, in some basic sense, not one's business,[5] she does not strongly chart out the more precise kinds of harms that might come to audience members from such participation.[6] To me it seems that bystanders might be made worse off by such participation in at least three quite different ways: (a) they might be harmed emotionally by their horror after learning about the wrongs for which the apology occurred, particularly if they hear about them in great detail; (b) they might be harmed by being drawn away from their own projects as they are conscripted into projects of punishments in which they mistakenly feel a duty to participate; or (c) they might be made morally worse by coming to enjoy the experience of administering public punishment itself, such that they become less fit judges of the world around them in general. It seems to me that Radzik is most concerned about something like (c). I think there is a great deal to say in this regard, and I will return to the problem of damaged judgment in the later sections of the chapter, since I believe it is even more troubling than Radzik's brief discussion suggests.

In addition to concerns about the harms to audience members, Radzik expresses deep concerns about the proportionality or disproportionality of the punishments received by the apologizer.[7] It is on harms to the apologizer, and the question of proportionality and disproportionality, that I want to focus my initial attention. I will be especially interested in *multiplicative harms*, in which a larger number of bystanders leads to increased suffering for the person subject to their gaze—and, usually, to their public feedback. I will presume in the initial discussion that the person offering the apology did in fact commit the relevant wrong: They are not "apologizing" for something they did not do. Instances in which this presumption is relaxed going forward will be indicated clearly. Insofar as harms are multiplicative in the sense I will outline, the dangers of disproportionate punishment increase. At the same time, the processes that result in multiplicative harms seem to me especially likely to lead audience members to become normatively tainted judges as noted above.

To think clearly about proportionality and disproportionality, we must not only ask questions about normative balancing, but also prior questions about the kinds of suffering the audiences might be *able* to create. If we are worried about audiences imposing undue suffering on those whose apologies they witness, exactly how might that occur? Until we know what kinds of harms audiences are capable of creating in such cases, we are not able to begin any sort of proportionality or disproportionality calculation. Some ways of conceptualizing what audience participation entails suggest few reasons to worry about disproportionate punishments, while others give us more substantial reasons. Insofar as bystanders are silent witnesses, there may be fewer reasons to worry about multiplicative harms. But I believe we should not imagine most audiences this way. Because we live in an age of social media, we should imagine not only that bystanders are witnesses, but that they will act in more participatory ways as well. We should presume that they bring not only their gaze to bear on the target of their attention, but at least some of their emotional and normative responses as well, including their retributive responses. These responses are likely to be diverse and often contentious, even if they include many reiterated ways of reacting. To think about them vividly, we might refer to those involved as *clamorous audiences.*

In the remainder of this section, I want to consider the kinds of psychological suffering that apologizers might in principle be put through by such clamorous audiences, to see both how these might operate and which might be most prone to multiplicative effects. I will consider three kinds of psychological discomfort that may occur for those who recognize their culpability for the original wrongdoing, and one additional form for those who do not recognize it. These categories are guilt, shame, humiliation, and persecution. Although they run together in many actual cases, they have sufficient analytical distinctness for investigation to be fruitful. I will thus write as if the separation between them is clear, even if things are more complex both in actual cases and in some of our uses of the concepts themselves.[8]

Guilt

What kinds of psychological states might those who undertake public apologies experience as they find themselves before an audience and begin to receive some of its feedback? Perhaps most obviously, those who engage in public apologies might feel a deep sense of guilt for their wrongdoing. Presumably it will be the guilt that has led them to apologize in the first place, if they are doing so in a sincere and voluntary way. This is fully appropriate: We should want those who wrong others in substantial ways to feel a deep sense of regret about their actions and to wish that they had not occurred. This represents both a ground for hope that they will not behave this way again and, plausibly, an appropriate acknowledgment of their own moral agency and responsibility for their choices.

Would it be possible for a wrongdoer to feel *too much* of a sense of guilt for their actions, such that we should worry about multiplicative effects and thus disproportion as the number of bystanders increases? It is not obvious to me that we should have this worry, so long as the feelings of guilt remain properly correlated to the wrongdoing committed. To choose one possible example of wrongdoing among a vast variety, if I have intentionally injured a child out of anger or impatience, I should feel badly about what I have done and take full responsibility. It will no doubt be psychologically painful to be aware of my moral failure and of the harm done to another person. Once I have taken responsibility, however, it is not obvious that I will or should feel *more* guilty as the audience for my apology becomes larger, since the wrongdoing itself will remain unchanged. The scale of the wrongdoing is generally fixed by the act itself, so what matters is whether my guilt is correctly correlated to the original harm. If I do continue to feel increasing guilt in the face of a larger audience, it will probably be because I have not fully absorbed the nature of my wrong in the first place. Breaking a child's arm does not become more or less wrong because other people know about it. At least from the perspective of guilt as an experience, it is not obvious that bystanders can create additional harms, and it seems possible that they could play a public role in leading the apologist to even more fully absorb the nature of their wrongdoing.

Even if bystanders actively set out to over-punish through the clamorous means available to them, the fixed nature of the wrongdoing itself seems to make this difficult. The inability to over-punish seems clearly the case if they are simply passive observers, but it also seems to be the case if they seek to become participants in a broader social discussion about the original wrong, whether via Twitter, Facebook, or other kinds of reactive social media. So long as bystanders focus on the nature of the wrong itself, and so long as the apologizer is thinking in those terms, multiplicative effects seem unlikely.

Shame

Engaging in a public apology is likely to bring with it other feelings of psychological suffering as well. If guilt focuses on what individuals have done, shame focuses more strongly on the kind of person that they are.[9] As I will use the term throughout the chapter, "shame" denotes suffering caused by a sense of one's failures to meet normatively appropriate standards of human character.[10] I will presume for the purposes of discussion that the term best picks out what might be described as *productive shame*, which is calibrated to desirable and actually achievable qualities for creatures such as ourselves.[11] If an alcoholic has committed grievous wrongdoing while drunk, for example, we would want the wrongdoer to feel shame at their alcoholism and to get sober. Because we are currently presuming that the apologizer has a sense of guilt at what they have done, they presumably fall into the category of those who know that they had the appropriate human capacities to live up to an appropriate standard of behavior. They are thus potentially subject to the experience of productive shame.[12]

It seems plausible to want wrongdoers to feel productive shame of this sort. Even if we set aside retributive goals—the suffering of the wrongdoer for the sake of their suffering itself—it seems important for wrongdoers to experience such feelings of insufficiency so that they are motivated to become better people. This experience is often psychologically agonizing, in ways that can be more intense than guilt itself, but suffering is usually unavoidable for those who must learn to rethink and re-engineer basic traits of their character. Can it be made more intense in potentially disproportionate ways by the observation of bystanders, however, whether they are silent bystanders or clamorous bystanders?

Presuming that we are focusing on productive shame, it is not obvious to me that audiences can make the suffering of the wrongdoer a great deal worse, nor that an increasingly large audience will make those feelings even more severe, so long as that audience clearly targets the personal failing that needs to be overcome.[13] If I have broken a child's arm while drunk, and admit to doing so while apologizing, it is not obvious why anything about my psychological suffering will increase as additional audience members come to know of this serious insufficiency in my character (drunkenness), or as they try to remind me of it through the clamorous means available to them. The most serious source of pain is my awareness of my own insufficiency, and my sense of the difficult work to be done in becoming a person who is more capable of abstaining from harm or otherwise behaving morally. As with guilt, if bystanders do succeed in leading me to feel more productive shame in this way, it will probably be because I have not fully absorbed the nature of my original failure itself. If anything, larger numbers might help me to more accurately gauge what is needed in the future.

Or at least, this is the case so long as audiences target my failure to meet a standard that is plausibly achievable for human beings and normatively appropriate to pursue. What happens if people instead try to diminish my self-regard by focusing on failures to meet criteria that are either unattainable or normatively inappropriate? Here I think we enter the realm of cases that should especially concern Radzik, because in these cases the suffering of the apologizer can quickly become multiplicative, particularly in the presence of clamorous bystanders who are eager to contribute to the suffering of the wrongdoer.

Humiliation

As humans, we are creatures that are deeply responsive to the social esteem of others. We are, moreover, often *over*-responsive to it, so that we can be made to feel badly about ourselves even when we should not. This means that we can often be made to feel badly about our own limited capacities even when there is nothing that we could do to change them or to bring them up to the standard that others tell us to meet. We can also be made to feel badly about characteristics that are normatively no one else's business, even if we might in principle be able to change them. These are cases of unproductively diminished self-regard, and they frequently lead to feelings of helplessness and profoundly diminished self-worth.[14] I will refer to such unproductive harms to self-regard as examples of *humiliation*.[15]

The nature of attempts to foster humiliation is easy to grasp because they are so common. Consider a schoolyard bully who taunts children in wheelchairs for being unable to walk. There is fundamentally nothing that targeted children can do to change their circumstances, but they may nonetheless feel extreme levels of personal insufficiency relative to their peers, particularly if their self-esteem has not been repeatedly buttressed before this time. Such exercises in humiliation, especially when carried out repeatedly, can profoundly hamper individuals' capacity to lead flourishing lives, if they come to feel that fundamental aspects of their own lives are mistakes or failures. Such feelings are not able to guide fruitful action to change oneself, but this does not mean that they do not drive other forms of action. In some cases, they can lead to dire outcomes like physical self-harm or suicide. Even when they do not, they can lead to profoundly foreshortened capacities for personal flourishing.

The relation between individuals' wrongdoing and the kinds of psychological pain they may be made to suffer is likely to come apart in deep ways where audience responses to public apologies are concerned, with strong possibilities of multiplicatively harmful effects and therefore disproportionate punishment. Consider the politician who offers a public apology for embezzling public funds to support an illicit lover. It seems entirely appropriate for audiences to hold the politician to account for this failure, and to spotlight personal failings of lechery, greed, spousal betrayal, and so on. At the same time, it would not be appropriate to satirize the politician's appearance, or advanced age, or speech impediment, or physical infirmities. These are matters entirely beyond the politician's control. Nor would it be appropriate to satirize the politician's involvement in a same-sex relationship or aesthetic tastes, since these are matters that, even if changeable, no one can appropriately be called upon to change. Forms of productive shaming should focus on the personal characteristics that are connected to the relevant wrongdoing, rather than seeking to make the apologizer feel badly about elements of themselves unrelated to their wrongful acts.

Unfortunately, large audiences seem unlikely to limit themselves to attempts at creating productive shame rather than painful humiliation. All things being equal, the broader the audience for a particular apology, the more likely it is that some bystanders will seek to humiliate the apologizer for features of themselves unrelated to the wrongdoing involved.[16] Whatever its evolutionary roots, this kind of mockery seems to represent a deep thread of human behavior, such that those who are disliked are often caricatured for precisely those things that are beyond their control, in hopes that this will hurt them most deeply. Humans make fun of one another's appearance, manner of speech, ways of moving, physical impairments, age, and all sorts of other things all the time, and social media in particular provides a forum to multiply this kind of attempted humiliation.[17] Many will do this simply because they find such trolling or recreational nastiness enjoyable in its own right.[18] Precisely which features will lead to humiliation when highlighted and mocked will not always be clear in advance, but we all doubtless have such areas of vulnerability. With enough attempts, at least some of these forms of mockery are likely to psychologically hit home. The larger the audience and the larger their capacity to communicate their feelings through the clamorous means available to them, the greater the chance becomes that they will succeed, both because they are larger in number and because there are greater chances of finding the specific and often multiple weak spots of the apologizer. Here we seem to be in the presence of multiplicative effects, with more chances for humiliation the larger the audience becomes.

It might seem that it is never normatively defensible for bystanders to attempt to create humiliation of the kind described here. By definition such unproductive shaming cannot make the apologizer a better person, and those who attempt to humiliate through sheer malice or for their own entertainment are clearly on bad moral ground. However, there may be conditions when such attempts are, on balance, normatively permissible and even appealing. If the erstwhile apologizer has largely gotten away with their wrongdoing, for example, such attempts at humiliation offer some chance to right the scales of justice, albeit in an indirect way: The wrongdoer will be made to suffer, even if not in a way that reflects directly on the nature of their wrongdoing.[19] If someone apologizes for sexual harassment when there are reasons to believe that they committed rape, for example, it is not obvious that it would be inappropriate to seek to humiliate them for, say, their unusual or dysfunctional genitals.[20] The psychological suffering they might experience is in any case unlikely to be worse than the suffering that they actively created in another. Arguably, multiplicative audience effects may be normatively desirable in cases of this punitive kind.

At the same time, there is much that can go wrong here. For sincere apologies that appropriately describe the wrongs done, attempts at humiliation would clearly be inappropriate, and increasing audience efforts would be multiplicatively inappropriate. Are audience members well-placed to evaluate whether this is the case or not? It seems likely that they often are not well-placed. Even when they are well-placed, can they reliably know that they are? There are many reasons for normative concern here.

All things considered so far, it seems to me that humiliation is where our moral attention should be turned, so that we are watching closely what it is that clamorous bystanders do after hearing about an apology, and thinking about how we might develop appropriate metrics for measuring the proportionality or disproportionality of punishment. As I will argue below, it is likely not the case that anything we can do will control the ways that crowds respond overall, but there may be things that we can do as individuals or as institutions to lessen the chances of inappropriate humiliation for those who have appropriately apologized.

Persecution

So far I have generally presumed that the person offering a public apology really believes that they have committed the kind of action for which they are apologizing. But there can be other reasons for public apologies as well. It is not unprecedented for corporations to demand that one of their employees apologize for actions that they did not in fact commit, or for government agencies to do the same. Under some kinds of political regimes, "apologies" of the latter sort are all too common. Indeed, the more that we come to expect public apologies, the more cases of such apologies by the innocent we should also come to expect.

In circumstances of this kind, the experience of the apologizer is likely to be one of persecution. They will understand themselves to be wrongly under attack by others, even if they understand how this has come about, and they are likely to feel increasingly under attack as the number of witnesses to the apology increases. This is especially so if the bystanders are clamorous rather than silent. While attempts at humiliation of the kind discussed above are likely to impact the apologizer at certain points of weakness, where they feel themselves to be insufficient in some way (even if unavoidably so), for persecution the primary experience is likely to be of large numbers of people who are allied against one in their animus. Because we are social animals for whom being outnumbered can be dangerous, this can lead to a great deal of fear for the apologizer, in ways that diminish their capacity for personal flourishing. It may also lead to anger that is renewed over and over again, with similar impacts. More broadly, there are reasons to expect that a sense of being persecuted will lead to feelings of distance from large parts of the human community. Persecution can thus create real harms, even if it does not lead those involved to doubt their own capacities in the way that humiliation can.

Similar feelings of persecution seem likely to occur to some of those who commit and apologize for one kind of wrongdoing, and then receive attempts to humiliate them for reasons unrelated to the original action. Even when such attempts at humiliation fail to find their target, so that the person to whom they are directed does not feel that they themselves have failed to live up to an appropriate standard in relation to them, they are likely to be felt as raw animus and thereby to create suffering through that route. The harms involved can easily become disproportionate here as well. Such an experience of persecution can also be straightforwardly counterproductive, as any contrition associated with the original apology becomes weakened to at least some degree. Failed attempts at humiliation can thus make people worse than they would otherwise be, in deepening a sense of alienation between the apologizer and the broader human community. When they go wrong, then, they can go wrong in particularly acute ways.

Summing Up

This discussion has covered quite a bit of territory, but the key claim is that an increasing audience is unlikely to have multiplicative effects on experiences of guilt or productive shame. On the other hand, increasing audience size is likely to go along with an increasing sense of humiliation or persecution. From a retributive perspective, as noted above, humiliation may sometimes be appropriate for the guilty when other means of punishment are not available. The fear-based elements associated with persecution may have similar punitive appropriateness in some conditions. But things can easily become disproportionate as well.

Although there is doubtless much more that could be said about these issues, this discussion gives us some tools to work with going forward. In the next section, I want to change track somewhat and to consider the kinds of punishments and harms that are possible when what is involved is not an apology, but an *accusation* of wrongdoing by others. It may turn out that there is less that is distinctive of apologies than it might seem, particularly where concerns about harmful audience effects are involved. There are, moreover, troubling audience dynamics that are easiest to recognize where accusations rather than apologies are concerned, which I believe should increase our discomfort with audiences as agents of well-calibrated punishment.

ACCUSATIONS

Public accusations are often a step toward a public apology. They are not always a step toward apologies, however, nor is it obvious that they should be. Human nature and capacities being what they are, some accusations will be wrong, either intentionally or accidentally. As bystanders, we are often ill-placed to know whether guilt or innocence actually obtains. At the same time, we are often not very good at recognizing our weak informational position, especially when others seem to agree with our evaluation of specific cases. In this section, I want to consider the degree to which accusations on their own can lead to excessive punishments or excessive harms as the size of the audience increases. I will, once again, presume that bystanders have a variety of clamorous means by which they might become participants in larger public debates that will be known about by the accused in at least some form. I will consider both those who are guilty and those who are innocent of the accusations, and will try to make clear the stakes for each.

As the discussion progresses, I will turn my focus to the broader social impacts of retributive attempts by clamorous audiences toward accused wrongdoers. The urge to punish those who deserve it is essential to human moral life, since the threat of such punishment is essential to preventing many forms of wrongdoing. Yet attempts to punish can often backfire. This is especially the case, I suggest, where attempts to humiliate those that audiences judge to be guilty are involved.

Guilt

Consider the potential audience effects for someone accused of wrongdoing where guilt is concerned. Here, matters seem fairly straightforward. If you have been correctly accused of seriously wronging another, you should feel guilt for the act that you have committed. If you have not, then you should not. An audience should not change this basic relation.

As outlined above, it seems that an increased audience size should not increase the sense of guilt that someone who actually engaged in wrongdoing feels. If a continually larger audience leads the wrongdoer to continually feel worse about what they have done, this is arguably because they have not grappled with the real scope of their wrong in the first place. Since increased audience size seems unlikely to be harmful along this axis of evaluation, as argued above, and since it might be helpful for example in leading the wrongdoer to eventually apologize, there seems to be little downside to an increasing audience in this regard. For someone wrongly accused, on the other hand, an increasingly large audience may well lead to feelings of persecution (see below), but it should not lead to increased feelings of guilt.

Shame

Matters seem similar in most ways where shame is concerned. If one has engaged in wrongdoing because of failures to live up to appropriate standards of human character, one should make amends to those who have been wronged, and work to develop the relevant capacities to avoid such wrongdoing in the future. As noted, this can be difficult and agonizing work, but it seems normatively essential. If one is guilty, then an increasing audience that uses productive forms of shaming seems likely to bring about a stronger recognition of the character changes that are necessary, with a relatively limited potentiality for harm. Eventually, it might play a role in helping to bring about an apology by the wrongdoer, and thus the commencement of a process of appropriate atonement.

One might be tempted to conclude that nothing at all can occur in relation to those who are innocent of the wrongdoing for which they are accused. However, this need not be correct. Because shame in the sense discussed here focuses on one's failures to live up to appropriate standards of human character, it is possible to feel shame for being the kind of person who *might* have engaged in such wrongdoing, even if one did not actually do so. Consider a movie producer who did not actually coerce a sexual relationship from an aspiring actress, but who would have done so if not for fears about being caught. Insofar as being mistakenly accused of wrongdoing of this nature might lead to greater introspection, even a false accusation might lead to efforts at normative improvement. What seems to matter here is if the accusation is at least in the ballpark of the kind of wrong that one might have engaged in had circumstances been somewhat different. If it is, and one takes this to heart, an increasing audience once again seems unlikely to do harm, though beyond a certain threshold it seems unlikely to provide additional benefits either. At a minimum, seeking as a bystander to make an accused person feel shame for having a certain kind of failing seems to hold no threat of over-punishment if the person does in fact have that kind of failing.

There are of course reasons to be wary of easy predictions here, and to exercise caution in our normative recommendations. Personal failings are complicated things that are often difficult to calibrate. We all have personal failings, and it is often not clear exactly which ones we should seek to overcome with the greatest priority. Committing a serious wrong against another can be a powerful marker in that way, since the nature of the action itself is so unambiguous. In the absence of a specific marker of this kind, the accused may continue to have a sense of a personal failing but regard it as relatively limited compared to other areas in which they should seek to improve themselves. (The producer suggested above did not actually engage in the wrongdoing of which he is accused, so perhaps his insufficient charity to the badly off should have priority instead where moral self-improvement is concerned. More worrisomely, he might also try to overcome the character flaw of cowardice.) So the feedback of bystanders may well be ignored, even if it is substantially on point about character if not specific actions. In these cases, accusations may well be interpreted as persecution.

If these character-based charges are interpreted as persecution by the person receiving them, does this by necessity constitute over-punishment for the accused? Remember, they did not commit the particular crime at issue, but they share failings of character with those who commit such crimes. I confess that I am unsure if feelings of persecution should always lead to worries about over-punishing in cases of this kind, where a person really does have a ballpark-area failing about which they should feel shame. In general, we do not punish people for their human failings, but only for their actions. But this is perhaps only a matter of what we can manage effectively, rather than something at the core of retributive justice. Perhaps it is thus not inappropriate for someone who is prevented from sexual exploitation only by their cowardice to be held up for public shaming about their failures of character, even if they interpret this as persecution. But perhaps it is inappropriate after all; I am not sure precisely how one should react to a case of this kind. This uncertainty is nonetheless relevant to the current discussion. It points to hard issues that audience members must decide for themselves, with many possibilities for deciding wrongly in the face of uncertainty.

For someone who is falsely accused of wrongdoing and who also does not have the relevant flaw of character, it seems that we have obvious reasons to worry about increased multiplicative effects of audience size, but the relevant axis here is uncomplicatedly that of persecution.

Humiliation

As outlined above, I understand humiliation as resulting when one is attacked for things that one cannot or need not change, as when a clamorous crowd seeks to non-productively mock a political leader for a physical handicap or other features that are beyond their control, or for features that are within the normatively appropriate realm of individual variation and choice (e.g., sexual preference or aesthetics). Because attempts at humiliation are unrelated to instances of culpability or failings of personal character, they are likely to have similar psychological impacts on the accused whether or not they are guilty of the actions they are said to have performed. Innocence is no psychological shield against such attempts.

In general, we have strong moral reasons to seek to avoid such humiliation. Yet, as noted above, there may often be normative

grounds for audiences to seek to bring about retributive humiliation for those who are accused, particularly when there are reasons
to expect that judicial or other processes will not clearly address the
wrongdoing at stake. If an individual has in fact engaged in wrongdoing and refuses to feel any sense of guilt for it, while also rejecting any feelings of productive shame for their normatively relevant
insufficiencies, it arguably constitutes a kind of retributive justice
if they are made to suffer unhappiness and discomfort in a way
not directly tied to their understanding of the wrongdoing itself.
To give a pointed example from recent politics, it would surely be
inappropriate in ordinary circumstances to seek to humiliate Donald Trump because of the size of his hands, or to seek to humiliate
Mitch McConnell because his face purportedly resembles that of a
turtle.[21] There is an argument from retributive justice that suggests
that they deserve to suffer for various forms of political wrongdoing, however, and that the only way to bring about the suffering
that they deserve is through means like this.[22]

My sense is that something like this retributive argument lies
behind the bulk of attempts made to caricature public figures
in painful ways when they are believed to have behaved wrongly.
When public figures are accused of wrongdoing, it is common for
bystanders to reiterate calls for them to be investigated or to apologize for what they have done, often through amplifying the spe-
cifics of the accusations made against them.[23] This seems straightforwardly to fit within the realm of attempts to create guilt and
productive shame. At the same time, the normative presumption
of many bystanders seems to be that public figures will be able to
avoid legal forms of punishment, and that they will feel neither
guilt nor shame for what they have done, such that they are morally liable to being mocked for most any aspect of their personality or personal traits that seem to cause them pain.[24] Our current
social life is strongly marked by such clamorous audiences because
they have several convenient modalities for promulgating precisely this kind of mockery.[25] Twitter posts, Facebook memes, and
many related modalities of political communication can be used
to engage in nuanced discussion by those who choose to use them
this way, but they lend themselves more readily to the circulation
of caricatured descriptions, unflattering photos with insulting text
attached, brief assertions of a public figure's stupidity, and so on.[26]

For the authentic wrongdoers who are unlikely to be punished by legal means and who seem unable to feel guilt or shame, this kind of treatment is arguably appropriate. If so, the primary goal of audience members should be to *find the form of humiliation that works best,* so that retributive justice is carried out as well as it can be.[27]

There are unfortunately two deep problems with such responses to accusations of wrongdoing, however. Though they are distinct, they are also interlinked in their social effects. The first is that such attempts to humiliate may well be deployed wrongly. An accusation of wrongdoing might well be mistaken.[28] With an apology or a judicial conviction, bystanders have good reasons to believe that the accused did in fact carry out the relevant wrongdoing, even if they cannot always be fully certain that this is the case. (As noted above, people can apologize when they have done no wrong, and of course courts make mistakes with some frequency.) With accusations, the grounds for confidence are likely to be highly variable depending on the kinds of evidence that are publicly available both about the specific actions of the wrongdoer and about their basic character. While in some cases bystanders will be able to judge more reliably than courts do, with their focus on demonstrating guilt beyond a reasonable doubt,[29] in other cases the evidence will be much more difficult to evaluate.

In the face of uncertain evidence, there is an understandable and perhaps unavoidable tendency for many bystanders to revert to rougher methods of evaluation, including particularly those that evaluate whether "people of this kind" are likely to commit wrongdoing, with this presumption likely to vary in its character depending on who is doing the evaluating.[30] This sort of heuristic can be problematic in obvious ways, as it lumps together individuals based on presumptions about their shared characteristics, and then makes presumptions about their likelihood of having committed wrongdoing after they have been accused (or even, in some cases, before). It will thus often be wrong about specific individuals. Consider an evaluatory chain of this kind: "Harvey Weinstein is a White male movie producer who was guilty of sexual brutalities, so this other White male movie producer who has been accused of a similar crime is likely to be similarly guilty." Or: "Bill Cosby is a Black male comedian who was accused of sexual brutalities, so this other Black male comedian is likely to be similarly guilty." This is not a plausible basis for ensuring accuracy in a system of public evaluations of wrongdoing.[31]

At the same time, the results of flawed heuristics are easy to convey in quick form, such that they can easily cascade throughout the judgments of clamorous audiences.[32] Memes can easily tie people together visually,[33] and short Twitter declarations can easily do the same: "Another one of X accused of crime Y; are we surprised anymore?" Analogies of this kind may be especially central where documentable evidence is relatively low, such that there is little to be said about it to really make the case for specific wrongdoing. Once the apparent case for guilt has been made, the case for attempts at humiliation seems likely to follow afterward. In these cases, for the same reason, there is likely to be little that the accused can say or evidence that they can present to demonstrate their innocence of the specific charge, at least to those who rely primarily on heuristics of this kind rather than on (the often thin) evidence itself. There are strong chances of multiplicative audience effects here, with attempts at punitive humiliation coming thick and fast.

The difficulties of audience judgment lead to the second problem with attempts to humiliate: the creation of cycles of attempts to counter-punish by further humiliation.[34] Cases of apparent over-generalization or other flawed heuristics can reasonably lead to anger and distress by those who judge the evidence against the accused public figure differently, and this can lead to attempts to counter-punish "the mob" or specific figures within it (e.g., particular journalists or commentators) via humiliations of one's own.[35] Moreover, and perhaps most troublingly, such consequences can occur even if the accusations against specific individuals turn out to be true. Insofar as heuristics of comparison are explicitly made clear, many of them can reasonably be interpreted by others as an attack on all members of a social category in general—all of those who are "people like that."[36] This can be experienced as deeply distressing both because it will be perceived as persecution (see below) and because it seems to portray individuals as guilty of serious failings as human beings based simply on their membership in a general category that is likely to be substantially beyond their control.[37] So some of those who have apparently made categorizations of this kind are charged with wrongdoing themselves, and away the cycle goes.[38]

My sense is that we should be especially concerned with out-comes of this kind, in which bystanders seek to participate in a process of bringing about justice through humiliation, which then leads to cycles of similar attempts. Social media allows for a kind of experimentation with caricatures that increase the chances of hurting those one wishes to hurt. While many of these attempts will not stick, that is all the more reason for those involved to try harder, and all the more reason for those who see such attempts as unfair to seek to humiliate the perceived wrongful attackers in turn. It does not take long for cycles of this kind to lead to the emergence of clear patterns of friends and enemies among those involved, with a further deepening of animosity and a redoubling of effort to balance the scales of justice as they are understood. This is particularly so insofar as cycles of attempted punishment and counter-punishment become interwoven with political party differences, where similar kinds of "people like them" claims are often made.[39] It is too strong to say that contemporary American debates about wrongdoing have become an arena in which attempts at humiliation are the dominant strain, but we arguably live in conditions where such attempts are increasing in frequency given the capacity of social media to sustain them. However normatively defensible the use of clamorous means against particular culpable individuals may be, the broad social results can be deeply dissatisfying and even psychologically harmful to many of those who take part in them.[40]

Exactly what one should do about this is hard to say, if I have characterized it with something approximating accuracy. It is not obvious how societies can extricate themselves from such deeply felt conflicts once they are underway, though I will try to make some suggestions after discussing the final form of harm that the accused may suffer, persecution.

Persecution

What can be said about persecution in relation to accusations is, I believe, fairly straightforward. The difference between humiliation and persecution as I use it here hangs in part on whether attempts to portray a person as insufficient hit home in any meaningful way or not. Most attempts to humiliate are not likely to hit home in this way, even if some do. Those that do not hit home are likely to be interpreted as persecution by those who are their targets. Persecution can also come, of course, not from attempts to humiliate, but from straightforward attempts to terrify or intimidate—something that social media also makes strikingly easy. The sense of having one's character attacked can cause substantial psychological harm to those who experience it even in the absence of literal threats, because we are creatures who can be endangered by one another in a variety of ways, and larger audiences are likely to increase the sense of ourselves as profoundly outnumbered. Even if there are no direct signs of imminent physical harm in being outnumbered by what seem to be hostile others, we are creatures who can respond to this situation in ways that prepare us for worse to come, with many negative psychological implications from such expectations. The situation is obviously worse where straightforwardly direct threats are involved. We are again in the realm of multiplicative effects.

Are attempts at humiliation likely to be taken differently by those who are innocent of particular accusations, compared to those who are guilty of them? The innocent accused may of course experience humiliation given many of the things that bystanders say about them, since as outlined above many of the insufficiencies with which they are charged may bite at their self-respect. The attacks that misfire, on the other hand, are likely to be felt as straightforward persecution. The innocent, at least, can thus experience both persecution and humiliation in multiplicative ways, with their innocence as no protection. Perhaps ironically, the guilty may feel somewhat less persecuted, since they are likely to have an awareness of the kinds of action that originally brought them into the public crosshairs. Though it seems they can also face multiplicative consequences from persecution, they may somewhat troublingly be less likely to experience its full intensity compared to the innocent.

As with humiliation, it may sometimes be normatively appropriate to seek to cause psychological suffering to those who have engaged in serious wrongdoing but who might otherwise get away without punishment or soul-searching. Even if all attempts to humiliate fail to find traction, the sense of being vastly outnumbered by a hostile and potentially threatening audience is likely to diminish capacities for personal flourishing, perhaps in ways that are in some rough normative balance with the original wrong. There are thus plausible reasons for audience members to see attempts to humiliate those they judge to be guilty as a no-lose proposition, since even failed attempts may have some role in diminishing their well-being. The social consequences of such choices unfortunately are less positive, particularly given the deep pain that persecution is likely to create among those who are innocent of the accusations against them. Much of what I have said about the social effects of even normatively appropriate attempts to humiliate seems likely to carry over to punitive persecution. Where there is not yet any sort of formal decision about wrongdoing, bystanders are likely to fall into divided judgments about whether the wrongdoing at issue has been committed, and to disagree about the heuristics that are appropriate in as-yet-uncertain cases. They are then likely to regard attempts at humiliation or expressions of outright animus by those on the other side as instances of wrongdoing in their own right, which deserve some form of answer to restore the moral balance. They may also feel directly threatened themselves, insofar as they see themselves as similarly placed to a wrongly accused person who seems to be experiencing the threats of a large crowd, and therefore seek alliance partners to achieve an upper hand in any direct conflicts that may occur, and to engage in coordinated actions against their perceived and anticipated enemies.[41] And so the cycle continues.

Summing Up

Taken together, it seems to me that the deepest problem with bystanders is not that the simple number of silent observers might increase punishments to excessive proportions, but that the actions of an ever-increasing number of clamorous bystanders are likely to do so. The problem seems to lie specifically with attempts to humiliate, which are not likely to track the subject matter of actual acts of wrongdoing in any direct way. These attempts are instead likely to involve broader claims about human insufficiencies, often put forward on the basis of limited evidence to see what potential areas of humiliation stick, and often seen (sometimes appropriately) as efforts to do justice by other means. Similar acts of direct persecution (e.g., physical threats) are likely to proceed in roughly the same way. Insofar as such attempts to pick out likely perpetrators before they have been formally tried are likely to invoke generalized social categories of people rather than simply given individuals, such efforts seem likely to be perceived as sources of humiliation or animus by those who are not the direct targets of such efforts. This seems likely to encourage further incidents of attempted retribution, and so the cycle of animosity begins or continues.

THINKING ABOUT ALTERNATIVES

What should be done in conditions of deep social division of the kind described here? Although current patterns of acrimony and recriminations are doubtless not primarily the product of audience reactions to apologies or accusations, I have suggested that there are grounds to see clamorous audience reactions to perceived wrongdoing as one causal force contributing to them.[42] Is there useful guidance that normative theorists can offer about how audiences should respond more appropriately to apologies and accusations, such that they perform their role in a way that is maximally productive and minimally destructive?

Radzik suggests that she is tempted to just let social processes go forward as they will, on the expectation that new and better standards emerge from social practice on their own.[43] I am tempted by this non-interventionist position as well. After all, philosophers and political theorists are not terribly skilled predictors of which solutions will work in what conditions, whereas large groups of people can often find solutions to their own challenges through various forms of experimentation. Depending on precisely how serious of a problem one believes that cycles of attempted humiliation and persecution are, the relative need for such a fix will vary, but there are unquestionably a vast number of serious concerns in the world to which normative analysis might contribute in more confident and fruitful ways.

Yet the obligations of normative investigators do not end with typological categorization and analysis. As scholars, we have been placed by our societies specifically in the role of experimental thinkers, who are supposed to offer suggestions on how particular social projects might be better carried out. We are thus called upon to take the intellectual risk of being wrong. If audiences are an unavoidable part of public apologies and accusations, are there ways in which they can be helped to play their role more effectively? In instances of this kind, we should look not only for hopes of what might happen in a better world, but for what might be achievable in our own. With this in mind, we must distinguish between infeasible and potentially feasible social options, and think of the costs and benefits of the latter kind. In this final section of the chapter, I will outline what seems to me the most plausible sort of option, taken broadly, and try to sketch the basic approach that it would require for our future work as political and normative thinkers.

Exhorting Others to Abjure Humiliation

Unfeasible ideal points are those that would be desirable if they could come about, but that cannot in fact do so given fixed features of human character or institutional impossibility.[44] One appealing but infeasible solution to the cycles of attempted humiliation and persecution outlined above is simply to tell our fellow human beings to limit their feedback as bystanders to the realm of guilt and productive shame, where it seems difficult for them to engage in excessive punishment. Because these are realms where the primary topics of debate are informational and specific, they seem less likely to create vicious cycles. If what bystanders must debate is "what is the evidence of wrongdoing?" and "What does this person need to improve about their character?" we would still have many quite heated conversations, but we would be operating much more clearly in a realm of reasons.

Exactly how far attempts to exhort bystanders to limit themselves in this way might shape the choices of some members of clamorous audiences is hard to say with certainty, but in my judgment, changing the basic patterns of bystander feedback via such limitations is permanently unfeasible. Even leaving aside the potential normative case in favor of humiliation as an alternate mechanism of justice when more formal mechanisms fail, we just seem to be the kinds of creatures who *like* trying to humiliate and intimidate one another.[45] Humans are, in short, often jerks, and there does not seem to be much that we can do about that. On my evaluation, while we could try to create a culture in which humans do not try to mock or bully one another—as we are in fact trying to do—this is not likely to prevent at least a substantial subset of individuals from trying to do precisely this. It seems especially unlikely to stick where accusations of wrongdoing are involved, given basic human tendencies to pursue retributive harms even where evidence is ambiguous or, often, entirely missing. And once we start a cycle, it is hard to bring to a close. It seems to me that persuading people to limit their speech only to discussions of guilt and productive shame is not a feasible ideal point to be pursued. Audiences are made of humans, and humans are more recalcitrant than such options are likely to make available.

Intensifying Mediation in Social Media

It may seem that the best response is to ask or require social media companies to do the relevant work for us. How effective we are at spreading attempts at humiliation in a public way depends upon our broader communicative environment. Historically, the "media" were strongly *mediating*, given the logistical difficulties, costs, and time delays of trying to spread one's opinion widely. In such circumstances, bystanders largely were confined to bystanding, without many ways to be effectively clamorous. The vastly more open-ended social media of the present day allow for a much greater circulation of specific kinds of information, particularly about the misdeeds of the powerful that would otherwise have been ignored.

Is there a potentially feasible ideal point in which social media companies, perhaps prodded by legislation or lawsuits, can return to this sort of mediating role, and do so in the right way? Might they, perhaps, clean up information flows through content filtering to ensure that claims about guilt and productive shame get through, while attempts at non-productive humiliation and persecution do not? Because I have insufficient expertise in the technological possibilities involved, it seems possible that information filtering of this kind might be feasible, and that there might be social routes by which companies could be led to undertake it.[46] Even if they could so, however, there seem to be strong reasons to hesitate in asking them to try especially hard. We should be generally skeptical that such censorship can be put in place without at the same time blocking a great deal of communication that is more fruitful in character. Earlier periods of strong mediation were far from ideal, because they allowed powerful curators to largely control what information was spread into the public sphere and how it was interpreted. A situation in which accusations of wrongdoing are easier to bring forward seems to work toward flattening many patterns of social hierarchy in salutary ways. The broader circulation of substantive political positions that social media makes possible also seems quite valuable. The benefits of increasingly free information flows are thus high, and arguably greater than the costs, even when those costs involve a great deal of psychological suffering and deep polarization. Perhaps most acutely, we should exercise skepticism about the imagined mediating forces themselves: Are there reasons to expect public policies on information circulation for social media corporations to be done well, given the recurrent failures of governments to calibrate policies appropriately and the likelihood that such capacities will be intentionally misused by profit-seeking social media corporations?[47] There are familiar reasons for doubt.

Naming and Marking Humiliation

What, then, might be a plausible direction to pursue in seeking to keep the beneficial aspects of actions by clamorous audiences while blunting the excess harms, both individual and social, that they may create? There is a good chance that any such proposal will be mistaken, but it nonetheless seems worth hazarding one here, so that this chapter might play a role in working jointly toward more well-targeted audience performances.

My primary recommendation is that we should encourage people to clearly mark the difference between productive shame and attempts to humiliate, so that they can more effectively recognize what they are seeing, and encourage them to name what they see as precisely as they can, while developing ways of marking this quickly and clearly on social media. As outlined above, the problem with attempts to humiliate is that they can easily become disproportionate even in relation to those who are culpable, and, where accusations rather than apologies are involved, they often entail overbroad heuristics that reach conclusions on the basis of thin evidence while at the same time extending the force of attempts to humiliate against entire classes of people. These attempts to humiliate are then themselves seen as forms of wrongdoing that deserve humiliation in turn. It seems likely that we can at least blunt these cycles by helping audiences to recognize how and why they are forming, and to clearly name instances of attempted humiliation when they see them. We already try to teach children to recognize both physical and intellectual bullying, and we already have terms for those who try to humiliate others through non-productive "shaming" about features of themselves that they cannot change or have no good reasons to change (e.g., fat shaming, gay shaming, Muslim shaming, and so on). These distinctions are useful, and they already rest on a distinction between that which people can control and that which they cannot or need not, even if standards of this kind are generally applied in inconsistent ways even by those who most publicly endorse them. Here the goal would be to mark all attempts to involve features of a person that are not directly related to whatever specific wrongdoings they are believed to have committed, along with attempts to deploy caricatured traits as a substitute for missing evidence. Those who seek to mark such attempts could be said to engage in a morally praiseworthy act of *humiliation shaming*. This would not, of course, make a difference against the trolls who seek only to do damage. But it might make a difference for the vast majority who understand themselves to be engaged in something better motivated and more calibrated to bringing about a better world.

On its own, additional clarity in the distinction between productive shame and humiliation might not make much difference until there were effective ways to mark it clearly and quickly. These might be done by audience members themselves, utilizing the familiar toolkit of hashtags, emojis, and other tools that can be used to quickly convey an immense range of textured meanings. One might imagine, for example, the widespread use of markers like #AttemptedHumilation or #HumiliationFail. Although it is unlikely, one might also push for social media companies to be brought on board directly, either by inducements or requirements. As an alternative to censorship, the range of tools for audience members to mark what they see could be increased in a variety of ways. Why is there no "this is an attempt to humiliate" button on Facebook, for example, which does not report a post for removal, but simply notes what it is? Other social media platforms could create analogous options. The idea would not be to *remove* such content, but to clearly mark it for what it is. Those who are trying to humiliate, whether with what they consider good cause or not, would then frequently have the character of their efforts noted by those who disagreed with them. This strategy of reducing the force of attempts at humiliation by recurrently marking them would, one expects, have its own normative costs. A general practice of calling attempts to humiliate for what they are would seem to make it harder for attempts at humiliation to succeed, since swift categorization of such attempts by others should have at least some neutralizing effects. This would make it more difficult to use humiliation as an alternate form of punitive sanction even for those who deserve it. Those who are guilty and able to avoid legal punishment might be comforted by seeing multiple clicks of the "this is an attempt to humiliate" button whenever something otherwise-acute is said about them. Presuming that most of those who are accused of wrongdoing in serious ways in the public sphere are guilty, and that many of those who are powerful would get away with what they have done, this would rob bystanders of some of their appropriately used retributive powers. Would the loss of this option be a cost worth paying, to reduce some of the agony of those who are wrongly accused, and to cool down some of the cycles of attempted humiliation and counter-humiliation outlined above? It seems to me that it would. Protecting the innocent and improving the texture of our political discourse would be a great good, perhaps even a sufficiently important one to allow a larger number of wrongdoers to avoid the frequently legitimate attempts at humiliation that clamorous bystanders may ferociously aim their way.

Notes

1 Radzik, "The Role of the Public in Public Apologies," in this volume.

2 Ibid.

3 Ibid.

4 Ibid.

5 Ibid.

6 Radzik focuses more strongly on how the role of audience member can go wrong than on the ways in which members themselves might be made worse off. See, e.g., "The Role of the Public in Public Apologies."

7　Radzik, "The Role of the Public in Public Apologies."

8　The chapter is in part an exercise in conceptual ethics, in outlining the uses of these concepts that seem to me most fruitful, rather than cataloging the variety of ways in which they are currently used. See, e.g., Alexis Burgess and David Plunkett, "Conceptual Ethics I," and "Conceptual Ethics II," *Philosophy Compass* 8 (2013): 1091–1101, https://doi.org/10.1111/phc3.12086 and 1102–1110, https://doi.org/10.1111/phc3.12086.

9　This basic distinction is drawn from Bernard Williams, *Shame and Necessity* (Berkeley: University of California Press, 2993), 92–93. Williams focuses heavily on the productive possibilities of appropriate shame.

10　My use of this term is akin to what Rawls describes as "moral shame," in its focus on failures to live up to appropriate standards of human behavior (though Rawls gives more centrality to associative feelings than I do here). See John Rawls, *A Theory of Justice (Revised Edition)* (Cambridge, MA: Harvard University Press, 1999), 391. See also Richard J. Arneson, "Shame, Stigma, and Disgust in the Decent Society," *Journal of Ethics* 11 (2007): 31–63, https://doi.org/10.1007/s10892-006-9007-y at 37–38, and Jennifer C. Manion, "The Moral Relevance of Shame," *American Philosophical Quarterly* 39 (2002): 73–90, https://www.jstor.org/stable/20010058, at 81–85.

11　For the use of this phrasing, see, e.g., Arneson, "Shame, Stigma, and Disgust in the Decent Society," 49. See also Manion, "Moral Relevance of Shame," 81–85.

12　There is substantial variation in the ways that the terminology of "shame" is used in psychological research. While it always refers to psychological experiences of personal insufficiency, this research often combines what I refer to as productive shame with what I refer to as humiliation. Thus, feelings of insufficiency in relation to moral aspects of one's character are often not studied in separation from feelings of insufficiency in relation to non-normative aspects such as body shape. See, e.g., June Price Tangney, Jeff Stuewig, and Debra J. Mashek, "Moral Emotions and Moral Behavior," *Annual Review of Psychology* 58 (2007): 345–372 at 355, https://doi.org/10.1146/annurev.psych.56.091103.070145.

13　For evidence that properly calibrated social feedback can have positive effects, see, e.g., David J. Y. Combs, Gordon Campbell, Mark Jackson, and Richard H. Smith, "Exploring the Consequences of Humiliating a Moral Transgressor," *Basic and Applied Psychology* 32 (2010): 128–143, https://doi.org/10.1080/01973530003738379 at 142.

14　Feelings of humiliation can also lead to feelings of anger and a desire to strike back, but I set these feelings aside here, to be considered in relation to the category I describe as persecution. See Combs et al., "Exploring the Consequences of Humiliating a Moral Transgressor," including discussion of the term "humiliation" at p. 140 as I used it here.

15 Lucy McDonald, "Shaming, Blaming, and Responsibility," *Journal of Moral Philosophy* 18 (2020): 1–25, https://doi.org/10.1163/17455243-BJA10064, distinguishes between agential shaming and non-agential shaming. The category of humiliation that I discuss here is generally non-agential, but not exclusively so, because it also includes attempts to humiliate individuals for features of themselves that there is no normative warrant for them to change (e.g., their sexual activities or their aesthetics).

16 It seems helpful to separate attempts at humiliation that arise because of perceived culpability from those that occur to people simply for being well-known. Human nature being what it is, those who put themselves in front of the public in fields like athletics, music, and acting seem to be inevitably subject to attempts at humiliation. (This is particularly so of actors who play heroic roles that attribute illusory capacities to them.) Whether this is sufficient to render attempts to humiliate them substantially less troubling is a separate question.

17 Some areas might seem to be connected to productive shaming, but to ultimately fall outside of its ambit. Would it be legitimate to mock the corrupt politician's bad hairpiece, or his excessive weight? Perhaps the first could be subsumed within his lechery and bad judgment, while the second might fall within his broader lack of self-control. But it is hard to be comfortable with this degree of permission.

18 I draw the language of "recreational nastiness" from Emma A. Jane, "'Your a Ugly, Whorish, Slut': Understanding E-bile," *Feminist Media Studies* 14 (2014): 531–546, https://doi.org/10.1080/14680777.2012.741073.

19 For an argument that a great deal of rancor on Twitter is driven by a sense of helplessness about real-world political and social outcomes, see, e.g., Roxanne Gay, "Why People Are So Awful Online," *The New York Times*, July 17, 2021, www.nytimes.com.

20 See, e.g., Christina Cauterucci, "The Weinstein Trial Isn't the First High-Profile Case to Feature a Graphic Description of the Defendant's Genitals," *Slate*, January 31, 2020, https://slate.com.

21 For Trump's hands, see, e.g., Nate Hopper, "Why You Shouldn't Laugh at Donald Trump's Hands," *Time*, October 20, 2016, https://time.com. For McConnell's appearance, see, e.g., Morgan Watkins, "New Animated Political Ad from Amy McGrath Refers to Sen. Mitch McConnell as 'Swamp Turtle,'" *Louisville Courier Journal*, August 27, 2020, www.courier-journal.com.

22 Members of the press are clearly interested in participating in efforts at humiliation as well. See, e.g., Martin Longman, "Trump's Tulsa Rally Was a Humiliating Debacle," *Washington Monthly*, June 22, 2020, https://washingtonmonthly.com.

23 Sometimes these can be fairly clever in their execution, such as a Reddit meme mocking both Joe Biden and those who support him despite allegations of sexual assault, including the text "Biden: The Rapist With Better Policies"; https://preview.redd.it/4m87r5z7mup41.jpg?width =960&crop=smart&auto=webp&s=4c45096309f8b8c10135d3b5940234141 b92bcae.

24 Often those who take the lead in doing so are public figures themselves. Much of the rhetoric of Fox News hosts, Breitbart writers, and others traffic in such treatment of those who are regarded as political enemies, while the left has much of Twitter, much of Hollywood, and Stephen Colbert to engage in the same treatment. Caricatures of this kind are likely to be amplified by others, while these public figures are likely to amplify in their turn attacks that seem to them especially effective. For a discussion of tropes used by media figures seeking to stoke anger or mock those they disagree with politically, see, e.g., Jeffrey M. Berry and Sarah Sobieraj, *The Outrage Industry: Political Opinion Media and the New Incivility* (Oxford: Oxford University Press, 2014), ch. 2. The *New York Times* columnists are not immune. See, e.g., Frank Bruni, "Ted Cruz, I'm Sorry," *New York Times,* June 17, 2021, www.nytimes.com.

25 They can also sometimes play a role in bringing people to justice or something closer to it. See, for example, "#CosbyMeme. Bill Cosby Is Getting the R. Kelly Treatment. But, This Isn't What Justice Looks Like," *Superselected,* November 11, 2014, https://superselected.com.

26 As one example among too many, consider a meme with a photo of Hillary Clinton and the text "I'm not saying Hillary is ugly, but all of her male friends are rapist [sic] and she's never been raped": https://i. redd.it/frnehxktrko11.jpg. Most charitably, this meme might be taken to represent attempted retributive justice for Hillary Clinton's treatment of Bill Clinton's accusers. But it is hard to grant anything like such charity to memes of this kind.

27 See, for example, Daniel Kurzman, "Funniest Memes Reacting to Trump's Groping Scandal," *liveabout.com,* January 13, 2020, www.liveabout. com.

28 Joe Biden either is or is not guilty of sexual assault. My own judgment is that he is not guilty, such that he falls into the category of the wrongly accused. Those who believe otherwise have sought to link this to broader failings, particularly his current age and mental abilities. Consider, e.g., a Reddit meme with a photo of Biden and the text "I don't recall sexually assaulting that woman. I don't actually recall much of anything anymore": https://i.redd.it/95ebz6g3jsv41.jpg.

29 See, e.g., Kate Shaw, "How Strong Does the Evidence Against Kavanaugh Need to Be?" *New York Times,* September 18, 2018, www.nytimes.

com. For examinations of how strong the evidentiary standards against Joe Biden should be relative to those for Brett Kavanaugh, see, e.g., Nicholas Grossman, "The Crucial Difference Between Joe Biden and Brett Kavanaugh," *Medium*, April 28, 2020, https://medium.com, and Cathy Young, "A Tale of Two Scandals," *Medium*, April 21, 2020, https://medium.com/.

30 See, e.g., Chauncey DeVega, "The Brett Kavanaugh Case: This Is How White Male Privilege Is Destroying America," *Salon*, October 4, 2018, www.salon.com.

31 Consider potential comparators to Harvey Weinstein: movie producers; Jewish people; males in positions of power; men in their sixties; men who are not judged to be physically attractive; White men; men with erectile dysfunction. Using any of these categories of comparison as a heuristic seems likely to generate high levels of false positives, even if some of them are demonstrably more plausible than others.

32 For a discussion of such cascades, see, e.g., Cass R. Sunstein, *#Republic: Divided Democracy in an Age of Social Media* (Princeton, NJ: Princeton University Press, 2017), ch. 4.

33 Consider for example meme combinations of Joe Biden and Harvey Weinstein (https://i.kym-cdn.com), or those linking Bill Clinton to Weinstein and others (www.snopes.com).

34 For concerns of this nature about the effects of satire in general, see Sophia A. McClennan, "The Joke's on You: Satire and Blowback," in *Political Humor in a Changing Media Landscape*, ed. Jody C. Baumgartner and Amy B. Becker (Lanham, MA: Lexington Books, 2018).

35 See, e.g., Jordan Carpenter, William Brady, Molly Crockett, Rene Weber, and Walter Sinnott-Armstrong, "Political Polarization and Moral Outrage on Social Media," *Connecticut Law Review* 52 (2021): 1107–1120, https://opencommons.uconn.edu.

36 For concerns about overgeneralization, see, e.g., Conor Friedersdorf, "Does White Male Rage Exist?" *The Atlantic*, October 10, 2018, www.theatlantic.com. Feelings of anger at over-generalization can occur even after convictions for wrongdoing. For concerns about how Bill Cosby's conviction was seen by some African Americans as the result of long-standing racist patterns, see, e.g., Hannah Giorgis, "Bill Cosby Is Not a Political Prisoner," *The Atlantic*, September 26, 2018, www.theatlantic.com.

37 This is an example of a broader process of *metadehumanization*, which is "the perception that another group dehumanizes your own group." Alexander P. Landry, Elliott Ihm, Spencer Kwit, and Jonathan W. Schooler, "Metadehumanization Erodes Democratic Norms During the 2020 Presidential Election," *Analysis of Social Issues and Public Policy* 2021 (electronic early view): 1–13, https://doi.org/10.1111/asap.12253 at 1. The authors draw on Nour S. Kteily, Gordon Hodson, and Emile G. Bru-

neau, "They See Us as Less Than Human: Metadehumanization Predicts Intergroup Conflict via Reciprocal Dehumanization," *Journal of Personality and Social Psychology* 110 (2016): 343–370, https://doi.org/10.1037/pspa0000044.

38 See, e.g., Karol Marcowitz, "No, 'Not All Men' Are Like Harvey Weinstein—but Apparently the Left Wants You to Think So," *Fox News*, October 18, 2017, www.foxnews.com.

39 Hillary Clinton described her remarks that half of Trump supporters were a "basket of deplorables" as "grossly generalistic" right before making them, and the remarks were often taken so by many Republicans who opposed her candidacy. See "Read Hillary Clinton's 'Basket of Deplorables' Remarks About Donald Trump Supporters," *Time*, September 10, 2016, https://time.com.

40 For an account of the painfulness of such interactions, see, e.g., Gay, "Why People Are So Awful Online."

41 See, e.g., Kteily et al., "They See Us as Less Than Human," 364–366.

42 For evidence on other kinds of causes, see, e.g., Shanto Iyengar, Yphtach Lelkes, Matthew Levendusky, Neil Malhotra, and Sean J. Westwood, "The Origins and Consequences of Affective Polarization in the United States," *Annual Review of Political Science* 22 (2019): 129–146, https://doi.org/10.1146/annurev-polisci-051117-073034; Mathias Osmundsen, Alexander Bor, Peter Bjerregaard Vahlstrup, Anja Bechmann, and Michael Bang Petersen, "Partisan Polarization Is the Primary Psychological Motivation behind Political Fake News Sharing on Twitter," *American Political Science Review* 115 (2021): 999–1015, https://doi.org/10.1017/S0003055421000290.

43 Radzik, "The Role of the Public in Public Apologies."

44 For an investigation of feasibility, particularly relative to social progress, see, e.g., Holly Lawford-Smith, "Understanding Political Feasibility," *Journal of Political Philosophy* 21 (2013): 243–259, https://doi.org/10.1111/j.1467-9760.2012.00422.x.

45 See, e.g., Jane, "'Your a Ugly, Whorish, Slut'."

46 Social media companies already do a great deal of content moderation of this kind. See, e.g., Richard Ashby Wilson and Molly K. Land, "Hate Speech on Social Media: Content Moderation in Context," *Connecticut Law Review* 52 (2021): 1029–1076, https://opencommons.uconn.edu.

47 See concerns about patterns of both under- and over-broadness in Wilson and Land, "Hate Speech on Social Media." See also Jack M. Balkin, "How to Regulate (and Not Regulate) Social Media," *Journal of Free Speech Law* 1 (2021): 71–96, www.journaloffreespeechlaw.org.

INDEX

Abu Ghraib, 48

affirmative action, 94, 96, 139n115; Black opposition to, 146

alienation: from historical narratives, 18; and justice, 10–12, 24, 30, 35n23, 66; of military service members, 44, 51, 52, 54

Allen, Woody, 225

Amnesty International, response to police violence, 7

apologies, 108, 206; inadequate, 212; insincere, 214; and persecution, 242; and punishment, 216, 217, 224, 233; and remorse, 121, 182; role of the public, 203, 207, 208, 211, 216, 220, 254; for slavery and Jim Crow, 80, 81, 88, 89, 102; as spectacle or theatre, 225

Bagram Air Force Base, 48

Balbus, Ike, on the psychological barrier to support for reparations, 107

Baldwin, James, 2, 168; on the Nation of Islam, 70; the role of love in overcoming racial domination, 73–75; on white racial identity, 68

Bass, Gary, 46

Baudet, Thierry, on *oikophobia*, 25

Bell, Derrick, 94; on diversity in college admissions, 96; interest convergence theory, 149

Bell, Duncan, 20

Biden, Joe: apology for tough-on-crime legislation, 223; response to January 6th, 10

Black Lives Matter Movement: 8, 195; founding, 33n5

Black nationalism, 155–157, 161, 162, 165, 169

Black News Channel, 116

Black Panther Party, 70, 167

Black Power, 161–166

Blight, David, 105, 109

Brooks, Risa, on the norm of an apolitical military, 45

Brown, Elaine, 70

Brown, Kevin, 99

Brown v. Board of Education, 87, 99; interpretation by current justices, 101, 121; reception among Black Americans, 98

Bureau of Refugees, Freedmen, and Abandoned Land, 149

Buzan, Barry, 14

Carter, Robert, on concerns over *Brown v. Board*, 98

Césaire, Aimé, 29

charter schools, 137n95

Chauvin, Derek: convictions for murder and manslaughter, 32n1

Cold War, 13

colonialism: acknowledgment in Canada, 9, 29; Dutch, 25; legacies and reproduction of, 15–17, 31

convict leasing, 83

Cooper, Amy, and apology, 215, 229. *See also* Cooper, Christian

Cooper, Christian, 220; concern over public reaction, 217, 229

265